The First Mrs Thomas Hardy

The First
Mrs Thomas Hardy

Denys Kay-Robinson

Sweet passion and the long long pain
Of souls that love but cannot meet again;
Soft longings through sad weary years forlorn –
Oh! tell me that at last
There will be dawn.

M

ISBN 0 333 22007 2

First published 1979 by
MACMILLAN LONDON LIMITED
*4 Little Essex Street London WC2R 3LF
and Basingstoke
Associated Companies in Delhi, Dublin,
Hong Kong, Johannesburg, Lagos, Melbourne,
New York, Singapore and Tokyo*

Printed in Great Britain by
REDWOOD BURN LIMITED
Trowbridge & Esher

Contents

List of Illustrations

Between pages 128 and 129

Acknowledgements

IT HAS BEEN SAID, it has been suggested in print even by members of the Hardy Society, that too many books have been written about Thomas Hardy, in particular those that pry into his private life. But, although the most important feature of that private life was his long courtship and far longer deteriorating first marriage, no one has made the marriage, with all its implications for Hardy's work, the subject of a full study, still less attempted to view it through Emma Hardy's eyes. I therefore make no apology for this book, only for my inadequacies in its composition. Such inadequacies are certainly not due to lack of encouragement and help. From the most eminent members of the 'Hardy Industry' down to people for whom Thomas Hardy was just a name, but who possessed some relevant item of information, I have received unhesitating assistance; and if, in the following list of those to whom I am sincerely grateful I have left anyone out, I offer him or her my contrition as well as my acknowledgements, and my publisher will be happy to make the appropriate arrangement with the copyright-owners it has not been possible to trace.

Foremost I should like to thank the one man who inevitably caters for *all* the writers about Hardy, yet who continues the task with apparently undiminishing enthusiasm: Mr Roger Peers, Secretary of the Dorset Natural History and Archaeological Society and Curator of the Dorset County Museum in which the overwhelmingly greater part of the Thomas Hardy records, correspondence and relics are kept. Next I must name

Dr Robert Gittings, who kindly lent me a typescript of *The Older Hardy* before it was available in print and also pooled many of his later research findings with mine. After him I list my other helpers in no deliberate order; they include Mr J. Fraser Cocks III, of Colby College, Maine; Professor Henry Gifford, of the University of Bristol; Mrs Ethel Skinner, Emma Hardy's great-niece; Mr and Mrs William Jesty, of Max Gate; Mr Kenneth Phelps, of Boscastle; Mrs Pat Munn, of Bodmin; Mr L. E. Long, also of Bodmin; Mr David L. Masson, of the Brotherton Library, University of Leeds; Reverend Prebendary Gordon Lawes, Rector of Lanivet; Mr John Holder, great-great-grandson of the Reverend Caddell Holder; Professor Michael Millgate, of the University of Toronto; Professor Tom Moser, of Stanford University, California; Professor J. O. Bailey, lately of the University of North Carolina; Messrs James and Gregory Stevens Cox, of the Toucan Press; Mr A. D. Martin, for the Trustees of the Hardy Estate; Reverend and Mrs John Hodgins, of Grantham; Mrs Anne Lee Michell, granddaughter of Dr Richard Garnett, and other members of the Garnett family; Mrs Rosella Voremberg, daughter of Reverend Richard Grosvenor Bartelot; Mr Arthur B. Venning, editor, *Launceston Weekly News;* the staff of the Reference Room, Dorset County Library; the staff of the public libraries at Bedford, Greenwich and Plymouth; Miss Olive Knott, of Sturminster Newton; Mr Vivian Warry, of Holwell; Dr Richard H. Taylor; Mr Geoffrey E. Worssam, of Swanage; Mr Steven Hobbs, of the County Record Office, Truro; Mr R. McD. Winder, Curator, C. H. Hoare & Co.; Mr Alan Clodd; Miss Caroline Hobhouse, of Macmillan London Ltd, for her patience and helpful criticism; and, last but not least, my wife, who once again chauffeured me to innumerable places on innumerable occasions and provided much help with the taking of notes.

Burbage, Wiltshire,   DENYS KAY-ROBINSON
December 1978

CHAPTER ONE

Emma Lavinia Gifford before March 1870

ON 24 NOVEMBER 1840, in her husband's house at 10 York Street, Plymouth, Emma Gifford, *née* Farman, wife of John Attersoll Gifford, sometime solicitor, gave birth to her second daughter, destined to be christened Emma Lavinia. There were two sons, with a third to come, making an eventual total of five children: a typical middle-class family in a large town (not yet a city[1]) in which, partly because it was a garrison town and naval base with many officers, that class was well represented. In 1840 the middle class was everywhere still developing. Before the Industrial Revolution it had hardly existed, at least as a conscious entity. Its formation and growth had been a direct outcome of the rise of the new industrialists. Before the constantly increasing power of men, many of whom had risen from nothing, all of whom seemed to have materialised from nowhere, the dismayed minor landed gentry (those who did not belong to the aristocracy), members of the professions and persons of leisure, found both their influence and their affluence becoming submerged by a tide that, unlike marine tides, did not stop rising. Faced by this crisis, the threatened group fell back on what seemed the only defence available – emphasis on its pure lineage and culture. The mill-owner or the railway-promoter might have five times the income of the squire or the magistrate, but the squire could show that only a couple of generations back the railway magnate's grandfather had been sweeping the squire's grandfather's chimneys.

1

Along with this stress on 'good birth' went assiduous cultivation of the qualities supposed to stem from it: delicate manners, refined tastes, respectability in all forms. Several more or
less fortuitous factors helped the trend. It chanced that after a
century and three-quarters of great sexual licence throughout
society the long-delayed swing of the pendulum (greatly
helped in its motion by the accession of Queen Victoria)
brought a sudden change-over to much zeal for sexual mor-
ality. Men were encouraged to give up seducing one another's
wives. An unmarried girl was not only a virgin, but more likely
than not remained in total ignorance of the procedure by
which that state was customarily ended. If brothels and ladies
of the town continued to flourish, largely for the delectation of
middle-class men, their existence must no longer be acknowledged in the domestic circle: piano-legs were not the only
things to be hidden behind the drapes of decency. Another aid
to the new cult of gentility was the reawakening of the Church.
Fired partly by the example – and the inroads – of Wesley,
partly, a little later, by the threat from the evolutionists and
other sceptics, the Church of England also found a new respectability, if not quite the Nonconformists' fervour. Along
with the rebuilding of the churches, and indeed the erection of
many new ones, went the rebuilding of their incumbents'
morale. Regular church attendance became an essential part
of middle-class behaviour, if only to show the social
superiority of the worshippers over the chapel-goers, who were
largely working-class.

Above the middle class, in social terms, was the aristocracy.
Its members were prepared to admit selected middle-class
representatives to their communal functions – one need look
no farther than Hardy's autobiography to be made aware of
that – but they, too, had very clear notions of status, and were
not disposed to pull down the barriers merely to rescue the
middle class from submergence. So the gentry waged an uphill
fight, and it is not surprising that in the course of it they
learned a great deal of snobbishness, which may be defined as
the ostentatious parade of social standing before those suspected of being unaware of it or, worse, of harbouring an
unjustifiable belief that they shared it. Naturally there were
exceptions; demonstrating a well-known principle of human

nature, those with the best claims were often the least vocal in proclaiming them. But for most, as the pressure from 'below' increased and later generations grew up in the atmosphere established by their parents, snobbishness became a natural feature of life, part and parcel of refined conduct.

Next in importance to birth and connections came occupation, which at least was easier to control. Ideally the middle-class subject should have no occupation at all, but live a life of graceful leisure, financed by an inherited income. Where, however, there was no such income and it was necessary to earn one, the work must never be associated with 'trade' – that was the dark preserve of the enemy. It must lie in one of the professions – the Law, medicine, the Church, the armed services, and a few more. Thus it was as natural for Emma Lavinia to write in her memoir, many years later, that 'trading was not adopted by the family – the scholastic line was always taken at times of declining fortunes'[2] as it was for her to recall with neither embarrassment nor disapproval that her grandmother, on finding her father disliked being a solicitor, made provision for him to retire and 'live a life of quiet cultivated leisure'[3] instead.

Gentility was at an especially high premium in the Gifford family because, truth to tell, the record on neither the father's nor the mother's side was particularly impressive. John Attersoll Gifford was the son of a Bristol schoolmaster, an occupation only just on the right side of respectability, and though he could point to several relatives who were doctors or clergymen he also had a brother who was a bank manager, an activity even nearer the borderline than schoolmastering. Furthermore, he himself was subject to heavy bouts of drinking. His wife Emma, also Bristol-born, was the daughter of a prosperous accountant, but not many generations back her ancestors had been in 'trade' as merchants. The basic facts of births, marriages and occupations we can ascertain from the public records; for the rest we are largely dependent on the account by Hardy's Emma already mentioned, the memoir, which she entitled *Some Recollections*, completed in strict secrecy less than two years before her death in 1912.[4] It is a remarkable essay, and, as we shall see much later in this book, the circumstances surrounding its creation were even more remarkable.

3

After John Gifford had moved his wife and older children from Bristol to Plymouth, then back to Bristol, and finally to Plymouth again, the household was augmented, at his invitation, by his recently widowed mother, who immediately took charge. Here is Emma's description of her grandmother:

All the time we lived in Plymouth – till I was about eighteen – Grandmamma lived with us; she had an income of £700 a year from the New River Company which was considered a good income in those days. She was a remarkably beautiful person as I remember her even when aged. Her portrait in oils shows too the diamond brooch given her by her husband on her wedding-day which I have had and worn many years. She was dressed all day long in black silk, summer and winter, with pocket-holes at the two sides of her gown and a black velvet cross-over (fichu) or a white lace one according to season. She never sat in front of the fire or in any easy chair, or lay on a sofa or couch, but sat upright in an arm chair at the side of the fire, her velvet slippered feet on a footstool. Her eyes were bright yet softly brown, her complexion delicate with colour and but few wrinkles, her expression cheerful and patient, her front of wavy hair, her own. She had a good quantity of back hair – worn under a lace cap with satin ribbons and she made a most charming picture and dearly we loved her; her hands and feet were small and beautiful, and her voice sweet; her deportment and stately manners were of the style of English gentlefolk of her time. She used occasionally some obsolete words and pronunciations. . . .[5]

Very much the *grande dame*. From her £700-a-year income she financed the home, encouraging her son to relinquish his practice on the strength of her help.

She preferred to live with my father, whom she loved the best of all her children in spite of his occasional outbursts of drink. He was her first-born and she sympathised with him in the great sorrow of his life. He married my mother after the death of her sister – a lovely golden-haired girl of eighteen to whom he was engaged shortly to be married; both had been ill of scarlet fever at the same time – immediately after her death he drank heavily, and in after life never a wedding, removal, or death occurred in the family but he broke out again. . . .[6]

Gittings doubts the story of the flaxen-haired sister, dying so

romantically on the eve of her wedding.[7] There is no official
record of such a death, and the tale may have been an invention of his mother's to explain his drinking. His partiality for
the bottle may also have influenced her advice to give up his
practice. Although, by her own standards, she could have justified her action by pointing to the enhanced social standing
that a father who could live a life of leisure would bestow on his
family, she perhaps reflected that if he should happen to
indulge in one of his drinking sessions just before he was due to
handle a case in court the results could undo the family's
position at a stroke. For all her emphasis on genteel dignity,
Grandmamma Gifford was probably no fool.

Emma's portrait of her parents reveals them as an odd mix-
ture of quintessential middle-class outlook and marked indi-
viduality. She makes no bones about her father's drinking,
apparently accepting it in her old age as she had in her youth,
on the same terms that she would have applied to tuberculosis
or a tendency to gout.

My father was bred to the profession of the law and practised as a
Solicitor for some years, keeping a pledge of temperance both before
and after my birth for many years, so that I was almost a born tee-
totaller. In his youth he went to wine parties and he also gave them –
which wine-parties were a curse in those days. He went a great deal
into society, he was liked and he had a handsome presence, resembling his mother, with the deportment and stately manners of his
time, being polished and courtly even at home; his conversation
good, his intellect keen and even brilliant; in politics a Conservative,
or Tory as then denominated. . . . Whenever we changed our residence in Plymouth we had to find a good garden as he was an amateur gardener and he adored flowers, and so did I. . . .
    My father was a splendid narrator of history – was altogether a
well-read man with a good memory for literary anecdotes and a good
classical scholar; he was fond particularly of writing and speaking
Latin; his love of Shakespeare was great which he constantly quoted.
On one occasion when he was in drink, he took possession of the
dining-room in the afternoon, laid out a fine volume – a folio – he
prided himself upon, lighted the candles, though the sun was shining
outside – (the candlesticks I have now) – drew the curtains behind
him and declaimed Shakespeare to great effect. I, a girl of thirteen
opened the door at a venture, peeped in, took a seat bravely, but near

the door and listened quietly; he gave a quick fiery glance at me but proceeded. I was delighted with the performance. . . .[8]

Whether Emma's mother ever went to the length of being actually delighted by her husband's antics when in liquor is open to doubt, but she seems to have regarded them with the same equanimity as the rest of the family. The picture we get of her is more shadowy than that of John or his mother, but one derives an impression that this is by no means because she was insipid.

My mother however was not a reader of books or papers except East Lynne, read many times. Her Bible, kept near her, she knew well. . . . My mother read the Bible with exceeding diligence and results wonderful beyond the devotional ones. She was a deeply religious woman she was imbued with scripture and talked its phraseology in ordinary conversation as a balance I suppose to my Father's secular quotations and remarks. She had a large vocabulary besides, of old Bristol words, some obscure words closely resembling those in Shakespeare, some doubtless picked up from my Father, but many quite her own of early days. . . . She was remarkable in the healthy management of her children – hygienic – though not knowing it, or the word either.[9]

There is a foreshadowing of Emma's disputes with Hardy in Mrs Gifford's habit of countering John's secular quotations with Biblical ripostes. Yet the exact nature of her religion, although it was clearly the foundation of Emma's own, is not easy to deduce. One feels that when the Plymouth Brethren were founded in 1830 she might well have joined them, but in fact her only 'conversion' was by the incumbent of St Andrew's Chapel, George Hadow, whose eloquent preaching overmastered the adverse impression inspired in his proselyte by his rather ostentatious diamond ring. Otherwise she accompanied the rest of the family either to St Andrew's Church (the 'cathedral of Plymouth', not to be confused with St Andrew's Chapel) or to the Charles Church where some of her husband's forebears lay buried. Though both churches were Anglican, both offered Low Church services. Towards the end of her life Emma wrote to her then parish vicar, the Reverend Richard Bartelot, 'I have been attached to *Low*

6

Church Protestantism by my saintly mother.'[10]

As the foregoing excerpt shows, her saintly mother also attached her, with the other children, to an exemplary belief in the juxtaposition of godliness and hygiene, insisting that they have frequent baths, dips in the sea, and, after the Royal Baths in Union Street had opened in 1850, dips in them also. At one of the Gifford homes there was actually a primitive form of shower in the wash-house, even the servants using it. That this early training in the virtues of ablution remained with Emma throughout her life is evidenced by a letter she wrote to a friend in 1900, in which, after deploring the new medical encyclopedias with their 'illustrations and explanations of the insides of us all', she observed that 'cleanliness and carefulness for ourselves and others are the chief remedies'.[11]

Of her three brothers and a sister, only the youngest brother, Walter, and the sister, Helen Catherine, figure at all prominently in her adult life. During their upbringing the family evidently possessed the customary Victorian sense of unity, but it was not due to the security of a settled home. Until Hardy installed her at Max Gate at the age of forty-four, Emma had never lived longer than eight years at one address, and the average period was less than three years. Her two decades in Plymouth were spent in five houses.[12]

Dances, parties, invitations to tea, coach expeditions to visit much-loved relatives at Launceston, walks to Stonehouse and Devonport, sketching expeditions by ferry to Cremyll and Mount Edgcumbe on the Cornish side of the Sound, regattas and military displays, and of course regular appearances at church with its opportunities for making as well as hearing music, render Emma's first twenty years, as depicted in *Some Recollections*, an ideal existence for a middle-class girl. The 'occasional lameness, suffered from early childhood',[13] which was later to keep her from the dance-floor to her disadvantage in more ways than one, appears to have been no handicap as yet, just as in still earlier years it had not prevented her from flitting over the slippery rocks of the Hoe, which in the 1840s was only just having its ruggedness blasted into suitable shape for the present terraces and promenades.

The Hoe is greatly altered now from what it was then. The rocks were being daily blasted where now stands a little townlet. The fine flight of steps leading to the Queen's beach had been put newly for Victoria but never used by her. I often dream of the dangerous pathways over cliffs and rocks leading to spots almost inaccessible. Once I hung over the 'devil's hole' by a tuft of grass while my schoolfellow shouted to a mussel-seeking man far below, who rushed up the steep ascent and rescued me and who was never rewarded, as we had slipped away from our homes hoping not to be missed nor were we, fortunately. 'Lightly then I flashed along', over those lovely slippery rocks with sure feet – a very usual thing for children to do, thus for ever giving an easy balance and exemption from giddiness through the years.[14]

Her upbringing coincided with a national mania for dancing. A steady stream of new dances, many as ephemeral as the music that accompanied them, appeared in the ballrooms until about 1860, when, almost as though the Giffords' departure from Plymouth were the signal for this particular Terpsichorean boom to depart as well, it abruptly died out.[15]

But there were other aspects of these early years that her memoir ignores. At home, her father's drinking bouts must have often occasioned behaviour a good deal more distressing than the declaiming of Shakespeare in a darkened dining-room. When he was sober, his treatment of Emma as his favourite child no doubt originated the jealousy that she tells us she later experienced from her sister. It would be surprising if there were never quarrels among the five children. The very multiplicity of social excitements must have entailed periods of boredom. The many changes of abode can hardly have been effected without heartaches.

Nor was Plymouth quite the Paradise she paints. When she was nine a cholera epidemic killed more than 800 people in four months. There was constant fear of a mass-escape of Dartmoor prisoners. In 1856, aboard a ship waiting to take convicts sentenced to transportation, a sergeant-major was murdered in full view of the crowds ashore. Eleven years earlier, readers of the local press had learned of toasts being drunk in the blood of men flogged aboard a slave-ship that had just been brought into the Sound after its crew had slaughtered a boarding-party. By the time of Emma's birth body-snatching had been suppressed in the Plymouth area, but relatives still mounted a rota of guards over the graves of their loved ones. Even the Hoe, that happy playground, was being improved by the Corporation only in the teeth of repeated claims to exclusive use by the Army and violent denunciations by what would now be called conservationists.

Yet the town must by the standards of the day have been an agreeable place to live in, particularly for people with intellectual tastes. Whereas most young ladies had to be content with a governess, Emma went to school and, although it was only that much-disparaged class of establishment a dame school, at least its curriculum included languages, and it was therefore fairly certainly responsible for grounding her in the French that she learned to speak and read fluently. The drawing and dancing classes that she attended were not part of the school, but it probably shared with her father the inculcation of an early taste for literature. Long afterwards she told a friend that she had been 'an avid reader from the age of ten'.[16]

To help her there was a public library, founded in 1811, which she tells us she used, and to which was added in 1853 a second library, the Coltonian. Two theatres flourished, the Dock and the Royal, attracting performers of the calibre of Kean, Macready and Taglioni. She does not list theatre attendance among her recreations, but since the pastime was in favour with good society Mrs Gifford senior is likely to have encouraged the young people to be seen sometimes in such company, and Emma's later taste for theatre-going probably began in Plymouth.

Nor do we know for certain whether, despite the large part played in her early life by music, she ever went to the opera; but she does mention going to concerts and 'entertainments' at the Mechanics' Institute, and no doubt there were others. Subscription concerts had been available at the Royal Hotel since 1821; philharmonic and choral societies came and went, but there was generally one in existence; recitals were held in St George's Hall, and for sixty years by a Mr Weekes in his own home, despite the fact that it held so few people that every performance had to be given three times.

Liszt visited Plymouth in the year of Emma's birth, but at the age of nine she may have been taken to hear Jenny Lind, whose success was so great that on the following Sunday, when

9

it was rumoured that she would be attending service at St Andrew's Church, a record congregation listened rapturously to, and afterwards mobbed, a lady who turned out to be someone else. The Giffords must also have been aware of a remarkable phenomenon in the town, the Crouch family, consisting of Mr and Mrs Crouch and their sixteen children, all highly musical. Frederick Crouch composed songs, including that well-known 'Irish' piece 'Kathleen Mavourneen', and Mrs Crouch sang, very movingly, an assortment of English ballads and Swiss peasant numbers. What the children did we are not told, save for one, whose subsequent fame as the courtesan Cora Pearl was due to talents other than musical.

But it was music in the home that really counted in a musically minded Victorian household, if only because Queen Victoria and Prince Albert both liked it, which made it not merely respectable but patriotic. In homes where the enthusiasm, or at least the anxiety to do the right thing, outran the talent, the musical evenings must have been somewhat trying to the nerves. The Giffords, however, were exceptionally well equipped to follow the fashion:

. . . we were all except one musical, and singers. My father played the violin and my mother could play beautifully on the piano and sing like a professional. Her musical abilities were much enjoyed by us all as we stood round her piano to hear the Battle of Prague – Mary Queen of My Soul, and pieces and songs then in vogue. They taught us to sing harmony and our four voices went well together. . . . We sang rounds, such as 'See our Oars with feathered Spray' and 'Wisdom is better than silver or gold' etc. A brother's alto was particularly melodious. Sometimes my Mother and my Father sang their old songs together as in their youth. Our regular church music at Charles Church were Jackson's and Macdonald's for the canticles, and very beautiful we considered them to be, and regularly did we all attend church and sing them – all four children and our Mother, in a row on a long seat. . . .[17]

In view of the part music was to play in attracting Hardy to Emma, in holding them together, and in her attempts to break through the barriers of estrangement, it is not without interest to consider what those old songs and airs she remembered to the day of her death included in addition to those she mentions. She herself names very few, but there was a wealth to choose from. For the pianist there were, in addition to the more popular works by the great masters of earlier centuries, the comparatively recent compositions of Weber, Chopin, Liszt, Schumann, and of course Her Majesty's dear Mr Mendelssohn, who died so inconsiderately in 1847. Field had not long since devised the nocturne, Weber's 'Invitation to the Dance' for solo piano had appeared in the 1820s, Mendelssohn's 'Spring Song' in 1844, Liszt's 'Hungarian Rhapsody No. 2' in 1851, and Rubinstein's 'Melody in F' arrived to delight the family pianist in 1855.

As for songs, Emma's Plymouth years saw the publication of an astonishing number the names of which are still household words: 'Kathleen Mavourneen' aforesaid, 'The Two Grenadiers', 'Come into the Garden, Maud', 'What Are the Wild Waves Saying?' 'Jingle Bells', 'Simon the Cellarer', 'Il Bacio', 'Santa Lucia', nearly all the best work of Stephen Foster, 'Excelsior', 'Long, Long Ago', 'I Dreamt That I Dwelt in Marble Halls', 'Scenes That Are Brightest', 'Roll On, Silver Moon', Gounod's 'Ave Maria', and many more. Other arias from the operas of Balfe, Wallace, Bishop and Benedict were still very much in fashion, and certainly the Giffords would not have ignored the new hymns and carols, especially those which were the work of Devon writers: 'Rock of Ages' being the favourite, to be rivalled in 1861 by 'Abide with Me'. The two girls must have included among their piano duets one that the organist at St Peter's Church, Tiverton, not so very far from Plymouth, was soon to have the idea of arranging for organ and playing for the first time at a marriage ceremony: Mendelssohn's 'Wedding March' from his incidental music for *A Midsummer Night's Dream*. But it would be helpful to know whether the family shared the objection of many strict Protestants to having anything to do with religious works by Roman Catholics. In some homes even Schubert's or Gounod's 'Ave Maria' was prohibited fare.

The supposition that Emma's repertoire was, like that of most young people in all epochs, based largely on the *derniers cris* of the day is strengthened by the information that even her mother would sing and play 'the pieces and songs then in vogue'. As late as 1881, in her old age, she asked Emma to lend

her a copy of 'The Blue Danube', apparently to replace an earlier one, because her son Walter liked to hear her play it.[18] The
railway reached Plymouth in 1849; and although it was a long
time before, by facilitating communication with London, it
rang the death-knell of the old country songs, as lamented by
Hardy, knowledge of the latest metropolitan 'hits' soon became part of the status-symbol embodied in the possession of a
piano and the holding of musical evenings.

The euphoric if sometimes overclouded life in Plymouth
came to an end with great suddenness. In February 1860
Grandmother Gifford died, and it was found that, far from
having financed the household out of income and being in a
position to leave enough for the process to continue, she had
been spending the capital, of which less than a thousand
pounds now remained, even this having by the terms of the will
to be divided. It was clearly impossible to continue living
where they were; and rather, one must assume, than demean
themselves in the eyes of their friends by moving to a much
humbler house in the same town, the Giffords betook themselves to Cornwall.

It was the first serious blow in Emma's life. She adored Plymouth, to the point that at no time during the half-century
remaining to her was she to live anywhere that contented her
so well, if indeed any of her later environments contented her
at all. Even the two years of early married life spent at Sturminster Newton, the 'Sturminster Idyll' as Hardy called it, 'our
happiest time',[19] may have been the happiest for him, but is revealed on inspection, which we shall make later, to have been
less than idyllic for Emma. Her 'happiest time' was her first
twenty years in Plymouth, rivalled only by the brief phase
during which Hardy was paying his first visits to St Juliot. Well
may he have lamented in 'The West-of-Wessex Girl', a poem
composed shortly after her death, that he had never complied
with her wish for him to visit Plymouth with her: his failure to
do so suggests that during her lifetime he shrank from evoking
a comparison between Plymouth and Max Gate.

The family might have moved to Launceston, where the
children's adored uncle, aunt and cousins lived.[20] But either
the exiles were averse to displaying their new penury here, too,
or Uncle George, who as a bank manager had a position to

keep up, discouraged his alcoholic and ne'er-do-well brother from coming. In fact the household went to Bodmin, leaving Plymouth on a day of symbolically pouring rain and making a poor start in the new home-town, the brother sent on ahead to find a house having chosen one far too small for the furniture. With great difficulty his mother, who now proved herself less of a cipher than she is generally held to have been, cancelled the purchase and took the only other house available. This, in Tower Hill near St Petroc's Church,[21] was large enough and central enough, but shocked the hygiene-conscious Emma by having a semi-basement larder overlooking the graveyard and 'therefore quite unfit for food'.[22] The house is still there – appropriately near a board bearing the name 'Emma Place' – and the window of the former larder still looks out on the former churchyard; but the gravestones are nowadays ranged by the wall, and the grass could be simply that of a meadow.

The Giffords had not been in residence long when they were visited by John Cole Grose, who had twice been Mayor of Bodmin and lived in Great Kirland Manor House, about a mile south of the town between the St Austell and Lostwithiel roads. Emma does not mention Grose's name, nor that of Kirland (except in an unrelated diary), nor the reason for his call; but suddenly after his visit the family find themselves installed in the manor house. Grose must have heard, probably from the Bodmin house agent, of the Giffords' difficulties, and wishing to let the manor he scented likely tenants. That Kirland was let, not sold, is evident from his will, in which he left it to a descendant;[23] but John Gifford and his wife continued to occupy it for many years after Grose died in 1866. The transfer from the Tower Hill house must have been speedy, for the family were already living at Kirland before the end of 1860.

The contrast between the life there and in Plymouth could hardly have been greater. Suddenly, in place of busy streets, the nearby houses of friends, a crowded programme of social events and entertainments, and the atmosphere of a large, lively, and culturally advanced town, here was this ancient manor house in the depths of the country, shut in by rook-abounding trees, 'and "where no air or anything else" could come to us, as the people said'. True, there were compensations: comfortable if old-fashioned rooms, an orchard and an excellent garden, a bathing-pool and a stream in which one of the brothers and the cat shared the fishing. But Bodmin, out of the way and 'a town that never enlarged itself', was no substitute for Plymouth, and the rooks were a poor exchange for human friends. Emma, despite some half-hearted denials in later life, did not take to a country existence now or ever. Not for her the dictum of Sir William de Stancy in *A Laodicean*: 'With a disposition to be happy, it is neither this place nor the other that can render us the reverse'; on the contrary, when she was sixty she wrote to a friend of her agreement with the Chinese maxim that places do affect one's happiness.[24]

But, if she did not take to the country, neither, when later on she had experience of it, did she take to London, which was too big, too complex, too socially cruel. The only milieu for her was a big provincial centre, and after her twentieth year she never had the satisfaction of living in one again. This factor was not the least to cast its shadow across the prospect of a happy marriage with Thomas Hardy.

What was she like, in 1860? No portrait or photograph survives older than the well-known painting of 1870, from which one must deduce her appearance as a young woman. 'We were very noticeable,' she says of herself and Helen, 'she dark and I fair, wearing our hair curling over our shoulders.' Her friends called her The Peony.[25] The heavy jaw seen in the portrait would already be conspicuous, as would the high colouring and narrow eyes. It was by no means a beautiful face, nor did her contemporaries think it so: 'They mostly considered themselves to have more brains and beauty than I, allowing me to be "attractive," however, with a very sentimental kind of mind. . . .' The attractiveness sprang from the squirrel-like vivacity of movement and inconsequential chatter that were to captivate Hardy. The 'sentimental kind of mind' would have been most conspicuous in her passionate love of animals, the kindness (except towards her husband) that, as so many were to testify, never forsook her, and possibly a taste for the more sugary type of song. No comments are available on the quality, then or later, of her singing or playing. Her watercolour sketches include some that are far above the normal amateur quality, and her flower-paintings are of professional standard.[26] Later in life she learned to paint in oils, including

14

portrait work, but no examples survive.

It must have been their training in gentility that rendered the whole family so incapable of mending their fortunes. John Attersoll made no attempt to resume his profession. Richard Ireland, the eldest son, having failed as a civil engineer, went on to fail as a schoolmaster. It took 'some years' – probably two or three – before Helen found a post as a governess, and six months later she was back home, persuading Emma (who had meanwhile done nothing) to take her place. This Emma did, but after a further six months she, too, was back home, not of her own volition but because her charges were being sent to school. More months passed, the dull routine of Kirland dragging on until, spurred apparently by further evidence of Richard Ireland's incapacity (Emma's curious description runs: 'His heart was wretched for many years, and his getting-on frustrated'), Helen 'started off again', this time as companion to an old lady at Tintagel, thought to have been a Miss Robartes. Fortunately the experiment succeeded; Helen and her employer 'thoroughly enjoyed each other's society full of gossip as they both were', and Helen 'enjoyed her life immensely'. Sometimes they drove over to Plymouth, no doubt to Emma's envy, and once Helen fetched Emma over to Tintagel to recuperate from an illness. But the family must have felt themselves to be marked down by Fate, or by the wrath of God. For one day, while driving her elderly friend into Launceston in a dogcart with a dangerously high and narrow seat, Helen was thrown out on to her head and knocked unconscious. She was taken to the White Hart Hotel at Launceston, whither Emma was summoned to nurse her until she could be moved to their uncle's house. Here, too, she continued to be nursed by Emma, despite the presence of their beloved aunt and girl cousins; and by the time Helen had recovered Emma was so exhausted that she herself needed a period of recuperation, the latter part of which she spent with friends at Lanivet.[27]

Such is Emma's account of this important event. She does not tell us when it happened, whether the unnamed old lady was also injured, or why Helen was carried to the White Hart when the Gifford house was only a few hundred yards along the street. Probably we shall never learn more. The White Hart still flourishes, but during its many changes of ownership all the early records have been lost. The files of the *Launceston Weekly News*, though filled with reports of much lesser road accidents, say nothing of this one. There are living descendants of the Launceston Giffords, but family papers and traditions are alike silent. All we can do is arrive at the approximate date of the mishap. The Lanivet friends with whom Emma recuperated were Captain and Mrs Serjeant, Charles and Jane respectively, of St Benet's Abbey. She records that while she was there china clay was discovered on the estate; and it is known that this occurred during prospecting in 1865 and 1866.[28]

The extent of Emma's friendship with the Serjeants has an important bearing on events in her life and Hardy's in 1872, and it is consequently of value to note that her stay at St Benet's in 1865 or 1866 was not her first, although she writes as if it were. Her description of the house includes the passage:

An invalid with a spinal complaint, the actual owner, lived in his bed, boarded upon three sides. He had much wealth and cultivation, was a Rector, had the advowson of the living, and a county ancestry, had quarrelled with all his relatives, but possessed a remarkable power of winning in any lottery. Packages and parcels arrived without fail of value whenever he ventured and the house had many handsome possessions thus acquired. He lived to a great age, and was read and sung to, nursed and cooked for, and amused to the end of his days by these chosen friends. I stayed with them some months of the autumn and winter and never saw him.[29]

This bizarre individual was the Reverend William Phillipps Flamank, Rector and patron of Lanivet until his death there at the age of seventy-five, when by his will he devised the Manor of Bodwannick 'and other lands' – including St Benet's – to Jane, wife of Charles Serjeant.[30] Flamank spent much money on alterations to the Abbey, 'in which', according to one historian, 'taste and architectural consistency were set at nought'.[31] Another chronicler says he 'mutilated and spoilt' the building.[32] But he died in 1861,[33] so to be in the house during his lifetime Emma probably visited the Serjeants from Plymouth; she is most unlikely to have absented herself for several months immediately after the move to Cornwall.

When reminiscing so many years afterwards she must have either forgotten this or telescoped two visits into one. An indication that she had stayed at St Benet's before her recuperation from nursing her sister is that she describes the house as 'dark, gloomy and not very healthy' – scarcely a place in which to recuperate unless under the stimulus of old friends.

Emma's description of Helen's own fight back to health is that she 'recovered, but though practically well was never after the same at all times'.[34] Hardy, who edited his wife's manuscript after her death, entered no note of disagreement at this point, yet there is nothing in the *Life* or among other sources to suggest that Helen remained either physically or mentally impaired. At all events, some time after her return to Tintagel little can have seemed amiss to the Reverend Caddell Holder, one of the few callers at the old lady's home, for he made a proposal of marriage, which Helen accepted.

There is a hint of desperation on both sides. Holder, a frail man of sixty-five with a married son and several grandchildren, had been a widower for more than a quarter of a century, but had recently moved to a new parish, St Juliot in darkest north Cornwall, which he found more difficult than its predecessors to run without help.[35] Helen, now aged thirty and by the standards of the time not only on the shelf but near the back of it, and leading a life into which hardly any strangers entered, must have found a proposal even from a grandfather more than twice her age little short of a gesture from Heaven. The Holders had been sugar-plantation owners in Barbados, one of them, Caddell's grandfather, having also written books on French syntax, an essay on slavery, and a polemic entitled 'A Tract Against the Pernicious Doctrine of Masons'.[36] Caddell had been a gentleman commoner of Trinity College, Oxford, and had held several previous livings. A fellow-clergyman Richard Rawle, Vicar of Turnworth and shortly to become Bishop of Trinidad, was the patron of St Juliot and had appointed him to the living.

The couple were married from Kirland Manor House in 1867, in Bodmin; and when Holder took his bride to St Juliot he took his sister-in-law as well. To the parents and brothers left at Kirland he must have appeared to have married both. The parish was small and meagrely populated, but scattered

over the steep hills east of the little port of Boscastle, the whole
area being so isolated that until well past the end of the nineteenth century coal and most of the supplies for the Boscastle
shops were brought in by sea because of the poorness of the
roads. But Emma was largely independent of poor roads, for
at the end of her stay at Tintagel her elderly hostess had given
her a mare, Fanny, which by the time of her arrival at St Juliot
she could ride as though trained from infancy. All the more
distant parish work was immediately undertaken by her, undoubtedly with great enjoyment. Except for some Sunday
School teaching in Plymouth and her six months as a governess, it was the first time she had tasted work.

But having something useful to do can only partly have mitigated the monotony, the lack of company, the sense of frustration for this woman brought up to enjoy urban life. If
Bodmin was no Plymouth, Boscastle was not even a Bodmin.
The newcomer found the local inhabitants, with a few exceptions, 'primitive', evil-speaking, believers in witchcraft, 'a cold
mostly ill-natured working class'. The nearest neighbours of
any interest were nine and more miles away, the nearest railway station sixteen. Holder himself was driven to complain
that he had no social equals in his parish, and from outside it
the only visitors, according to Emma, were the occasional
brother-clergyman, missionary, or school inspector, and one
regular caller, the Camelford dentist.

However, we know from letters written by Caddell's grandchildren to their father, his son Cecil, that the Rector sometimes travelled the nine miles to their home at Lanteglos-by-
Camelford to see them, and it seems improbable that the visits
were never returned. Why the very existence of these close relatives of her brother-in-law is unmentioned by Emma, and later
by Hardy, is a mystery still awaiting explanation.[37] The sole
mention of Cecil in connection with St Juliot is in the 'Statement of Receipts and Expenditure on the Restoration of St
Juliot Church' discovered by the late Howard Bliss and quoted
by Phelps, in which the list of donors to the Restoration Fund
includes the entry 'Captain Holder £1–1–0'.[38] (He had been in
the Army but, although only in his thirties, had already
retired.)[39]

Emma's silence is the more surprising because throughout

her life she loved children, and here were some with whom she could actually claim a tenuous link. Nor was she likely to hear the Rectory resound to the cries of others linked more closely. The Reverend Caddell, despite his age and frailty, was not necessarily incapable yet of mounting a female, but his handicaps, added to Helen's maturity, made their production of a child improbable. Yet her sister's new status as a wife must have sharply reminded the twenty-seven-year-old Emma that if she herself was ever to have children, or even a husband, time was slipping by and St Juliot offered minimal opportunities. These did, however, include one admirer:

One stands out among them [the Cornish 'working orders'] with worth of character and deep devotion, though rather dumb of expression, a man gentle of nature, musical, Christlike in guilelessness, handsome of face and figure, David-like farming his own land: he never married, and told after I left of his disappointment, and attraction on first seeing me on the stairs.[40]

Phelps associates this with Emma's previous description of the welcome given to the Holders on Caddell's return with his new bride:[41]

Then the welcomers (all men, and nearly all young) came into the hall to drink the healths of the bridegroom and bride, and a speech was made by the foremost young farmer. . . . Whether they could have expected me I do not know. I remained on the stairs, looking on, much entertained with it all.'[42]

Phelps suggests that the farmer may have been Henry Jose, aged twenty-three at the time, and that Jose may have been the earlier suitor of Emma implied by Hardy in his poem 'The Young Churchwarden', the manuscript of which bears the note, deleted, 'At an Evening Service/August 14. 1870'. On that day, a Sunday, Hardy attended evening service with Emma at the church of Lesnewth, a short distance across the valley from St Juliot. Phelps's only source, however, is Henry Jose's great-nephew, Walter Henry Jose, who shortly before his death at eighty-seven, in 1975, said his father had told him 'Uncle Henry had a great fancy for Emma Gifford'. Like the many family traditions about Tryphena Sparks, it may be true

– in the days before widespread literacy oral tradition was often remarkably accurate – but it is unsupported by other evidence. As to 'The Young Churchwarden', if the subject is Henry Jose, Hardy either did not know he was still alive when the poem was composed, or falsified the truth to hinder identification, for the last stanza represents the warden as already dead.

It used to be suggested that the poem 'The Face at the Casement' refers to an early aspirant to Emma's hand. But now that the poem has been shown[43] to be about William Serjeant,[44] son of the curate at St Clether, a village just near enough to St Juliot for their respective clergy to exchange visits, the likelihood has greatly diminished. William Serjeant died of tuberculosis in 1872 at the age of twenty-three, so that to have courted Emma before Hardy's first appearance in Cornwall he would have had to be a youth of at most twenty, wooing a woman eight years his senior. No doubt he admired the vivacious Emma, who must have entered his sickroom in his last year like a shaft of sunlight, but that he ever had any serious aspirations is difficult to believe. Probably as Hardy drove away with Emma after this 1871 visit he glanced back in time to see the hapless young man drawing away from his window, and poetic imagination did the rest.

Much prominence is given by Emma in *Some Recollections* to her belief that Hardy was her Man of Destiny, for whom God had intended her and to whom He had guided her from the day of her birth. But it seems clear that this was something she realised only after she had met Thomas, albeit in the very first moment. Hardy himself, evidently informed in due course of his status as a fulfilment of the Divine Will, bears this out in his poem 'A Man Was Drawing Near to Me', which depicts her entirely unsuspecting what his first approach to St Juliot portends. It is impossible to guess to what extent this sense of destiny at work was influenced by a disposition, due to temperament, advancing years, and the longing to recover her Plymouth life-style, to fall in love with the first man who seemed to promise fulfilment of even a part of her romantic needs. It can be argued that her identification of Hardy as the appointed of God was the first of the illusions that beset them both for forty-two years, bringing so much sorrow and misunderstanding. Yet it can also be argued, as in this book it will be, that in the end Emma was shown to have been, in the context of her religious beliefs, perhaps not very far wrong.

CHAPTER TWO

Thomas Hardy before March 1870

LESS THAN SIX MONTHS before Emma's birth in her father's elegant town house in Plymouth, Thomas Hardy was born in a thatched cottage in the hamlet of Higher Bockhampton near Dorchester in Dorset. The date was 2 June 1840. Like most of his information about his family and early years, Hardy's portrait of his parents is misleading. His father, also named Thomas, was not, as the son implies, a well-to-do master-mason from the outset of his career, prevented from attaining who knows what heights only by his genial obsession with music and consequent failure to cultivate 'the art of enriching himself by business'.[1] He had indeed a deep interest in music, as his own father had had and his son was to have, but he was largely a self-made man, starting out with the modest good-will established by his father in the building trade, but with virtually no money, and through successive stages as single-handed worker, employer of two men, then of six, then of nine, rising from near-penury to the ownership of several houses, a dozen cottages, a sizeable piece of land, and a brick-yard. When he died his personal estate was valued at £850, the equivalent of well over £10,000 at today's ever-changing rate. In 1870, therefore, when Thomas Hardy junior met Emma Gifford, his father was financially better off than hers. But it would never do to admit to the daughter of retired solicitor, gentleman of leisure John Attersoll Gifford, or later to the world, that master-mason Thomas Hardy had risen from next to nothing; he must appear to have started at the level on

22

which he finished, and to owe it only to his disrelish for professional application that he had not advanced to still greater success.

Thomas Hardy senior was handsome – the camera shows that – and something of a charmer. Whether, as local rumour had it, he exercised his charm on the village girls to the extent of finding their seduction no problem is a matter lacking proof, but highly probable. Country life at the time – and the Puddletown area of Dorset was emphatically no exception – included a great deal of promiscuity, which means that Thomas Hardy senior would see nothing heinous in a few cheerful deflowerings, nor the girls in being deflowered. On a slightly more respectable level, it was a widespread custom in rural areas for a man to make sure, before marrying, that his bride was capable of producing another generation to take over the work. What we do know for certain is that Thomas senior seduced Thomas junior's mother, for young Thomas was born only six months after his parents' marriage.

Jemima Hardy, the mother in question, provoked her son in after-years to even greater dissimulation about her than about his father. His maternal grandmother, Elizabeth or Betsy, was the daughter of a prosperous yeoman-farmer of Melbury Osmund named Swetman; evidently a remarkable woman, with a penchant for clothes and for books, which she not only acquired but read, she made the cardinal mistake (unless one believes that love overrides all) of marrying George Hand, a lowly working man with few assets and fewer prospects. Her father promptly disowned her. After celebrating his married state with the procreation of seven children Hand died, leaving widow and brood dependent (for Swetman did not relent) on the less than modest support of the Melbury Osmund Poor Law authorities. At the age of about thirteen Jemima went into domestic service, and later became a cook, working in various Dorset houses and, briefly, in London.

She was, without question, a remarkable woman. In addition to mastering the art of cookery she learned something of glove- and dress-making, and became as well read as her mother. Early experience of adversity fashioned the sternness she had inherited from her Swetman grandfather and the courage of her mother into a character of great power, so that

23

throughout her life she was able to dominate her household, including her son Thomas – especially including her son Thomas – in almost every aspect of their lives. It is significant that of the two brothers, Thomas and Henry, and the two sisters, Mary and Kate, Thomas was the only one to marry and, except for a short period when Mary taught in Berkshire and Kate near Sherborne (following a season of training at Salisbury), the only one to live even briefly more than two miles from the Bockhampton cottage.

The cottage also included among its occupants during Hardy's early years his father's mother Mary, *née* Head, widowed in 1837. Born at Fawley, Berkshire,[2] in 1772 and an orphan by the age of five, she was brought up by her maternal grandfather until she was thirteen – a period of such intense unhappiness that once she had left Fawley she could never be persuaded to return.[3] From 1785 until 1799 when she appeared at Puddletown, there is a mysterious gap in our knowledge about her, though from researches recently carried out by Robert Gittings it seems she may have spent part of the time in Reading House of Correction facing a charge of theft that could have resulted in her being hanged. Freed of this, she probably made the move from Berkshire to Dorset in the employ of a family that owned property in both counties. There were at least two of these, for one of which Hardy's father later carried out work.[4]

If Gittings's findings are valid, Mary Head Hardy had a 'past' that excelled even Jemima's in its need for concealment. But she had an enormous influence on Hardy's development, her immense fund of anecdotes, legends, folklore and personal experiences firing his imagination and supplying him with material for prose and verse that was to last him throughout his literary career. Less happily, the gruesome streak in many of her stories also influenced him, fanning his predilection for the macabre to the point of implanting in him a permanent fascination with death and despair. This tendency may almost be said to have started at birth, when he was all but discarded as stillborn. Before he was eight we find him lying in the sunshine and deciding he had no wish to grow up or make any new friends. At his first school his melancholy demeanour, as he sat in his allotted place at the end of a bench, tempted the other boys in the row to slide suddenly along and push him on to the floor.⁵ On his twenty-fifth birthday he wrote in his diary: 'Not very cheerful. Feel as if I had lived a long time and done very little.'⁶ In 1887 he wrote to his friend Edmund Gosse: 'As to despondency, I have known the very depths of it. You would be quite shocked if I were to tell you how many weeks and months in bygone years I have gone to bed wishing never to see daylight again.' In his sixties he was convinced he stood in grave danger of dying before he had completed *The Dynasts*. This was hardly the temperament to find harmony with the ebullient Emma and her confidence in God.

More favourable to their enjoyment of one another was the Hardy family's love of music. Thomas's grandfather had played the cello or 'bass-viol' as one of the church musicians at Puddletown, where by old tradition the violin was prohibited as the Devil's instrument, and later had continued his playing at Stinsford, reorganising the musicians there and in due course reinforcing them with his two sons. The sons also learned secular music, and, like the players in many other churches, varied the Sunday hymn-playing with the performance of lively dance-music at weddings, Christmas parties, and like functions. Jemima Hardy, though not a player – she used to sigh wistfully over the 'quaint old piano' on which her children practised – was also 'musical to a degree' in Hardy's words, and with such parents it is not surprising that he himself was highly musical. Hymns, marches, and the dance-tunes played by his father were his first introduction to melody, together with the songs his mother sang. Of the dance-airs he names four: 'Enrico', 'The Fairy Dance', 'Miss Macleod of Ayr', and 'My Fancy-Lad' or 'Johnny's Gone to Sea'; of Jemima's songs, also four: 'Isle of Beauty', 'Gaily the Troubadour', 'Why Are You Wandering Here, I Pray?' and 'Jeannette and Jeannot'. None of these is among the equally few titles cited by Emma from the Gifford repertoire, but since both families sang and played much else, a great deal of it widely popular, it is a fair conjecture that when Thomas and Emma met they had many pieces in common. Widespread popularity was not confined to the fashionable London 'hits' disseminated by the railway; the old country songs, taken from county to county by itinerant ballad-mongers, were sung, often with altered words, in places far from their source.

After he had been a year at the little school in Lower Bock-hampton Hardy was judged strong enough to walk daily to a Dorchester school kept by one Isaac Last in Greyhound Yard. The school was owned by Nonconformists, and Last himself was a Congregationalist, but there was no attempt to interfere with the pupils' religion, and the young Hardy continued to be a regular Church of England worshipper at Stinsford. During this period his death-wish nearly came true when, while swimming one day in the Frome, he was caught in the rush of water at one of the weirs and all but drowned.[7] In 1853 Last was able to start his own school, private and fee-paying, where Hardy was able to stay for the remainder of his schooldays, learning mathematics and Latin. In 1855 his mother arranged for him to have private lessons in French, at about the time when Emma must also have been learning it. Which became the more proficient it would be hard to say. Hardy's lessons stopped when he entered business the following year, and although he took them up again in London during the 1860s it was only for 'a term or two'. No comments on his spoken French survive, and he left no French writings. Emma in the last years of her life used to discuss French literature in corre-spondence with her friend Alda, Lady Hoare,[8] and confessed to another friend that she read fiction (which included trans-lations of Tolstoy) only in French.[9] On the other hand two let-ters written by her in French in 1910 to Mlle Rolland, sister of Romain Rolland and the translator of *Tess*, are only just com-prehensible amid their grammatical and syntactical mistakes.[10]

Again like Emma, Hardy during these school years was earnestly exploring English literature. Because at St Juliot he introduced her to fields that were new to her, it is generally assumed that she was unread. We have already seen that this was not so, and in fact during their teens the Plymouth library facilities probably gave her some advantage over the boy de-pendent on his grandmother's old-fashioned collection, sup-plemented by what his mother could afford to buy. But both had to accommodate their reading to their musical activities, Hardy having taken up the fiddle-playing at village weddings and in farmers' parlours that his father had adopted in the old church-musician days.

At sixteen he left school and began work in South Street as apprentice in the firm of John Hicks, architect. By good fortune Hicks was himself well read and disposed to allow his employees all the reading-time their architectural duties could be made to furnish; and since the other apprentice, Henry Bastow, was also of a scholastic turn, and an argumentative Baptist, Hardy had plenty of opportunity to sharpen his wits.

Within weeks of his starting work, an event occurred that gave great stimulus to his fascination with the macabre. A public hanging took place outside the prison, and the youth was careful to watch it from a close vantage-point. Hangings, though less common than when Mary Head perhaps lived under the shadow of the noose, were still far from rare; but this one was to pass into history as a local *cause célèbre*. The 'victim' was a woman, Elizabeth Martha Brown, her crime the murder of her husband because of his infidelity. Martha Brown was strikingly handsome and commanded a good deal of public sympathy. Hardy was horrified by her execution. As the years passed his memory of it remained acute,[11] and undoubtedly inspired the execution of Tess, as another execution that he was to see only two years later – but this time through a telescope from the heath behind his birthplace – became blended with an anecdote of his father's to inspire the hanging in 'The Withered Arm'.[12]

But what is remarkable is that near the end of his life the features of the Brown execution that he recalled as vividly as any were the sound made by the woman's thin black silk dress as she was led to the scaffold and the outline of her figure as the dress, moistened by rain, clung to her body as she swung.

That amid the intensity of his revulsion the young man could notice such points is explicable only in terms of keen sexual awareness. Yet he was to write in his autobiography the passage so often quoted:

His immaturity, above alluded to, was greater than is common for his years, and it may be mentioned here that a clue to much of his character and action throughout his life is afforded by his lateness of development in virility, while mentally precocious. He himself said humorously in later times that he was a child till he was sixteen, a youth till he was five-and-twenty, and a young man till he was nearly fifty. . . .[13]

The passage is usually interpreted on a sexual basis, implying late puberty and late ability to accomplish sexual intercourse. Some have even gone farther and suggested the passage veils a confession of lifelong impotence – a charge strenuously rejected by others, though usually on the wrong grounds, such as the clause in Hardy's will of 1922 making provision for 'the first child of mine who shall attain twenty-one years'. This is a standard clause inserted by solicitors to cover all eventualities, without regard to individual probabilities, and proves nothing. Far more relevant to the problem is a letter written in 1923 by Florence Hardy to Dr Marie Stopes, the birth-control pioneer:

I find on talking to him [Hardy] that the idea of my having a child at his age fills him with terror. . . . He said he would have welcomed a child when we married first, ten years ago, but now it would kill him with anxiety to have to father one. However, I shall make use of your kind advice with regard to the alkaline douche, as I think it may be beneficial to health. . . .[14]

I interpret this to mean that the douche was no longer necessary as a birth-control measure because sexual intercourse had ceased owing to Hardy's fear of begetting a child. An earlier letter by Florence, to Lady Hoare in 1918, anticipates the second sentence in the passage just quoted:

Babies seem to choose to come where there is little room for them, and to carefully avoid going where their presence would be most eagerly welcomed. . . . How eagerly a baby would have been welcomed in *this* house – Max Gate – years ago![15]

The second Mrs Hardy was a woman who 'enjoyed' very poor health, but the two letters, and in particular the reference to the douche, do not suggest that she suspected herself of infertility. Neither, for that matter, do they suggest that she suspected Hardy's procreative powers. On the other hand one has to remember that he and Emma greatly wanted children; there is the well-known line in the *Life*, following the disclosure that

28

a runaway maid of theirs at Sturminster Newton was to have a baby, 'Yet never a sign of one is there for us.'[16] Although both wives were well into their thirties when they married, the double failure of motherhood makes it hard to clear Hardy of all suspicion of being the cause. Nor would he necessarily know if this were so. It is fully possible to enjoy apparently normal sexual intercourse while in fact the seed of the male is incapable of fertilisation; only recently have doctors come to realise how commonly this is the reason for a childless marriage.

That Hardy was not incapable of the sexual act is virtually proved by his second wife's observations – and when he married her he was already an old man. Moreover his recollection of the shapely corpse of Martha Brown is but one of many indications that he had a lifelong interest in sex, and not a few of the indications point to this having sometimes taken a practical form. So strong is this evidence that, if the reference to tardy 'virility' does have a sexual meaning, it must be taken as one of the many instances of Hardy's words concealing an unpalatable truth by proclaiming its opposite. But it is far from certain that the phrase does refer to sex; it is more likely to refer to Hardy's late assumption of a manly appearance. He grew up small in stature, of indifferent physique, and with an air of baby-faced naïveté to which his sensitiveness is shown by his early cultivation of a moustache, soon followed by a full beard.

Awareness of sex was implanted in him, to judge from his own words, long before puberty. When he was only five the 'big house' of Stinsford parish, Kingston Maurward, passed into the ownership of Francis Martin, whose wife, Julia Augusta, was childless. Through his father's professional contact with the estate it was not long before little Thomas became known to Mrs Martin, who forthwith allowed all her frustrated maternal instincts to concentrate on him. She would take him on to her lap and kiss and hug him as other emotionally baulked women fondle a lap-dog. When she decided to provide Stinsford with a school he was one of its first pupils. When, a year later, Jemima transferred him to Dorchester, Mrs Martin was seriously offended; and when, a year later again, the now ten-year-old boy was taken by a village girl to a harvest supper and Mrs Martin arrived there with her party she reduced him to tears by accusing him of deserting her and then allowed him, the mason's son, to dance with her little niece.

To what extent there were sexual undertones in the lady's excessive passion for this child of another class is a matter of opinion, though it is difficult to imagine her lavishing the same adoration on Mary Hardy, only a year younger. What is important is the sexual connotation given to the affair by Hardy. His account contains such phrases as 'he had grown more attached to her than he cared to own', 'his feeling for her was almost that of a lover', 'his lover-like promise of fidelity to her ladyship'.[17] To the end of his days he remembered the sensuous rustle of her silks, like that of Martha Brown's. The Martins soon left Kingston Maurward, and Julia and Thomas met only once thereafter, when she was in her fifties and he twenty-two. He notes in the *Life* that when he called at her London home the butler looked little altered, but 'the lady of his dreams – alas!'[18] If the image he had retained had been only that of a second mother, the change in her appearance would have meant little to him, and the recollection of a purely filial relationship would not have justified the mutual embarrassment he records.

During his teens he went through a series of generally ephemeral love-affairs of the sigh-from-afar variety familiar in adolescence. These blameless experiences are freely chronicled (except for suppression of names) in the *Life*, and many were recalled later in verse or their heroines used as characters in the novels. Their innocence has been linked with Hardy's lifelong dislike of being touched. But this applied only to the touch of *men* and, later, of servants; how else could it be reconciled with his enduring passion for dancing, in an age when the most popular dances involved a firm clasp of the partner? The poems contain many references to pleasure in the touch of women's hands or lips, from the hint of a farewell kiss for Emma at the end of their first meeting[19] to the holding of Agnes Grove's hand, a quarter of a century later, at the Larmer Gardens.[20] If the adolescent romances to which Hardy admitted in old age were somewhat ethereal, it does not follow that there were no others, no forerunners of the Sparks sisters.

A man who could compile an autobiography that omitted all mention of the most important love-affair of his youth, probably extending to a proposal of marriage, was quite capable of concealing teenage embroilments; and of one of these we have the evidence of strong family tradition, if not academic proof.

The tradition goes that one Christmastide during the 1850s, when Hardy was present at a festive gathering in the house of his relatives the Sparkses, he found himself alone with Rebecca Sparks, his cousin and Tryphena's eldest sister, and began to make some very forthright amorous advances. Whether or not Rebecca protested, someone interrupted them, a great rumpus ensued, and Hardy was forbidden the house. To assess the likely truth of this tale, it should be judged in the context of the environment in which he grew up, and this, as we have seen, was somewhat short of strait-laced. The Puddletown parish register records enough illegitimate births to tell its own story of the prevalent sexual freedom. The young Hardy cannot have been unaware of what went on. During his lonely prowls about the Heath he must have stumbled on sights that needed no explanation, nor can he have been ignorant of the amorous free-for-alls that followed some of the dances at which he and his father played, and which he was one day to exploit in *The Woodlanders* and *Tess*.[21] Against this background the Rebecca episode is easily credible, and it may not have been isolated. There will be those who say that a portrait is being painted of Hardy as a precocious young rake. On the contrary, in place of the usual drawing-room versions of his youth he is being shown as a normal product of his surroundings. There is no logic whatever in conceding the influence of the mysterious Heath, of his father's and grandmother's stories, of the hangings he saw, and then brushing aside any possible influence by the overtly libidinous habits of the country people among whom he grew to manhood.

Girls, however, filled only a part of his mind during his last school years and his time with Hicks. He continued to argue religion, to progress with his architectural training, to read omnivorously, to extend his study of the classics, adding the pursuit of Greek to that of Latin, and to give attention to painting in watercolours. In this season began his friendships with two men who became very dear: William Barnes the

Dorset poet, who ran a small school next to Hicks's offices, and Horace Moule, the highly talented scholar and literary critic who for sixteen years, from 1857 until his suicide, virtually controlled Hardy's intellectual development. It was Moule who introduced him to the new Radical weekly *The Saturday Review*, to whose pages are traceable not a few of the iconoclastic ideas that later so distressed Emma. Moule also advised him that if he were to succeed as an architect he should spend less time on the classics. Hardy took the advice, but the decision was a major step, for prior to it he had entertained ideas of becoming a don or even of entering the Church.

The mid-nineteenth century was the heyday of Victorian church restoration. During the eighteenth century and the Napoleonic wars the fabric of the country's Church of England buildings had become as dilapidated as the spiritual worth of their incumbents, and many architects were kept busy on an endless succession of orders to rebuild. Unfortunately their work was often done with boorish insensitivity to the finer points of the original craftsmanship and a complete lack of feeling for the past, and with a few distinguished exceptions they did more harm to England's church heritage than all the depredations of Elizabethan anti-Catholic precautions and seventeenth-century Puritan fanaticism put together.

No one was to become more distressed by this spectacle than Hardy,[22] but during his apprenticeship with Hicks he knew only that requests kept coming in from all quarters for help in arresting decay or even collapse. He thus had no lack of work and, since he quickly became good at it, no reason to fear his prospects. To save the long daily walk to and from his home, and probably to effect some independence from his mother, he ceased living at Higher Bockhampton during the week and took up residence in lodgings, and for a time in Hicks's own house. He made a few pleasure-journeys, one to Salisbury to visit his sister Mary, now at the Teacher Training College, and another to Somerset, where he sketched Glastonbury Abbey. Just when Emma's world was being shattered by the financial disclosures consequent on her grandmother's death, Hardy's world was showing him the vision of becoming a well-to-do country architect, perhaps Hicks's successor.

Against reason and against prudence, but with the support

of his parents, he decided in 1862 to seek architectural work in London. His motive was possibly not entirely professional. A pupil of Hicks whose time was nearly up when Hardy joined the firm remained there long enough to bring back spirited accounts of his adventures at some of London's famous (and infamous) dance-haunts during trips to the capital. For one with Hardy's interest in sex and girls this would be an exciting if frivolous extra reason for the move, and indeed the alacrity with which he visited the places described by his colleague bears out its attraction.

His father had procured him an introduction to a London architect, but it was through another introduction that in April 1862 he found himself in the employ of Arthur Blomfield, noted restorer, church designer, artist, actor, singer and wit. His offices at 8 Adelphi Terrace,[23] overlooking the Thames, were run on astonishing lines. There was little architectural instruction, the nine or so assistants and articled pupils progressing, like the children in a twentieth-century *avant-garde* school, at their own pace and to their own taste. Each day began with earnest discussion of the latest social scandals and the more lurid items of news. Practical jokes were played on eminent members of the Reform League, a body of political extremists that had its headquarters on the floor below. After he had worked at Blomfield's for some years Hardy began to treat his colleagues to short lectures, in office hours, on poets and poetry. Most remarkable of all, Blomfield encouraged his staff to sing frequent 'glees and catches' during the day, not just on an informal music-while-you-work basis but as a properly organised office choir, in which he himself took the bass part. Relating this, Hardy discloses that he himself 'could sing at sight with moderate accuracy from notation, though his voice was not strong'.[24] At Blomfield's request he sang on one occasion in the church choir of St Matthias, Richmond.

The unorthodox pattern of this existence affected him in two ways. The unexacting nature of his duties left him with plenty of energy, physical and mental, to pursue his literary interests and self-education, and the racy talk of his colleagues, backed by the evidence of his eyes as he moved about London, suddenly laid before him a vast world, at once fascinating and fearsome, of which he could have envisioned barely a fragment from the reports of his London-visiting Hicks acquaintance. In consequence he embarked on a dualistic way of life that, had anyone (including himself) realised it, was perhaps the first indication of the tremendous strength of will hidden within the shy, babyish-looking country lad, seemingly so out of place among the sophisticated upper-middle-class public-schoolboys who graced Blomfield's premises. A lesser man would either have shut his eyes to all but London's intellectual amenities and concentrated on study, or let go his studies to enjoy the pleasures and seamier side of the metropolis. Hardy kept up both rôles, and although in five years it nearly wrecked his health its effect was to hasten his lagging progress towards maturity as neither rôle could have done on its own. In the passage in which he says that he remained a youth until he was five-and-twenty, it should not escape remark that he dates his arrival at manhood during this period in London.

Because of the importance of his intellectual pursuits to his career, most biographers pass only lightly over his more diversionary activities; yet it is the diversionary activities that give the better clue to the man Emma was to marry, and it is therefore fitting to reverse the normal pattern here. His arrival in London having nearly coincided with the opening of the Great Exhibition of 1862, during his first six months he paid visit after visit to it. Inspired by its art exhibits, he then moved on to explore the National Gallery picture by picture. He read, as usual, extensively. Horace Moule had given him a copy of Palgrave's *Golden Treasury*, a volume later much loved by Emma, in which he marked off the songs and ballads in just such a manner as she might have done. In 1862 Moule was admitted to the Inner Temple, which meant that Hardy saw him during most of his London visits as well as continuing to be directed by him from Dorchester. In about 1865 Hardy began to compose verses, which he submitted to various magazines with uniform lack of success. He succeeded slightly better with prose, finding a publisher for an architectural essay that had won a competition and also for a *jeu d'esprit* called 'How I Built Myself a House'. He widened his knowledge of serious music by attending operas and by buying himself a violin, which he played in his lodgings with a fellow-lodger who played the piano.

But the impact of this half of his new world can have been nothing to that of the other half, the London of pleasure, poverty and vice. This was still largely the London of Dickens, as it was that of Mayhew, Barnardo (he arrived there in 1866), Doré, 'Walter' of *My Secret Life*. Hardy cautiously concedes that he visited a few notorious haunts (in fact, those about which his colleague at Hicks's had told him): the Cremorne Gardens, the Argyle Rooms, 'Baron' Nicolson's establishment, Willis's Rooms; and admits that the conversation at Blomfield's included much about the activities of noted courtesans – though the ones he names, including that errant daughter of Plymouth, Cora Pearl, were at the time elsewhere. He does not, however, remind us that at the Cremorne Gardens, after the family parties had gone home, the dancing-partners who remained – an estimated 300-odd on an average fine night[25] – were almost all prostitutes, or that the Argyle Rooms, presided over by the notorious Kate Hamilton, though ostensibly a dance-hall for the well-to-do, were in fact London's premier venue for picking up better-class whores, or that Baron Nicolson's Cider Cellars were the scene of mock trials for prostitution in which homosexual actors in 'drag' represented the prostitutes. Even Willis's Rooms, the former Almack's, were not widely associated with decorum. But looking back on it all in the poem 'Reminiscences of a Dancing Man', a splendidly nostalgic account of these scenes of night life, Hardy betrays his full awareness of their real purpose:

> Whither have danced those damsels now!
> Is Death the partner who doth moue
>   Their wormy chaps and bare?
> Do their spectres spin like sparks within
> The smoky halls of the Prince of Sin
>   To a thunderous Jullien air?

When to the prostitutes who plied for hire in these and many other indoor places we add the far more numerous company who walked the streets, their numbers become so staggering that only by realising their essential place in a society in which sexual deviation by 'respectable' women was made almost impossible can one credit the figures. As one contemporary writer put it, the total was 'variously estimated, according to the opportunities, credulity, or religious fervour of observers, and the width of interpretation they put upon the word'.[26] The highest calculation, made in 1869 from data gathered by Henry Phillpotts, Bishop of Exeter, placed the numbers – in a city of which the adult male population was not much over a million – at 80,000, a figure accepted by James Beard Talbot, Secretary of the London Society for the Protection of Females, in his book *The Miseries of Prostitution*.[27] In 1857 Sir Richard Mayne, Chief Commissioner of the Metropolitan Police, had compiled returns giving a total of 9,400; but this covered only those prostitutes 'well and accurately' known to the authorities. William Acton, Deputy Keeper of the Marshalsea Prison, who conducted his own investigation into London prostitution and published Mayne's figures in the book that resulted, commented: 'I must observe that these returns give but a faint idea of the grand total of prostitution by which we are oppressed. . . . Were there any possibility of reckoning all those in London who would come within the definition of prostitution, I am inclined to think that the estimates of the boldest would be thrown into the shade.'[28]

The better-class streetwalker's beat had shifted from the Strand to the Haymarket, but it was still only a few minutes' walk from the Adelphi, and Hardy must have been accosted many times after leaving work in the evenings. Are we really to believe that a young man of such wide general curiosity and acute consciousness of sex never sampled the wares here or at the markets he admits to having visited? Without doubt his raffish colleagues periodically did so, and no doubt recounted their experiences the following day; nor does this imply any special viciousness on their part. Denied sexual outlets in other directions, most young men-about-town had occasional recourse to a harlot, and by the young male visitor up from the country it was customarily regarded as an essential part of his visit. Venereal disease was looked on as a sporting hazard and, although it was rife and largely incurable, even the habitual womaniser stood a fair chance of avoiding it in so large a selection of partners, a proportion of them always fresh to the game.

Quite aside from Hardy's curiosity and natural excitement at the new milieu, his background was scarcely calculated to make him regard a little sexual indulgence as particularly wicked; and that he did not do so is borne out by his cheerful portrait of a prostitute in 'The Ruined Maid', a poem he composed – significantly – in 1866, and perhaps in his allusion in his first published novel *Desperate Remedies* to 'lost women of miserable repute looking as happy as the day is long'.[29] Even the sequel to 'The Ruined Maid', 'A Daughter Returns', composed thirty-five years later, is less a serious condemnation than a tongue-in-cheek satire on the Victorian belief in the Wages of Sin.

There was, of course, the question of money. Most of the better-type women of pleasure confined their favours to rich clients prepared to spend in an evening what Hardy might earn in a month. But sometimes such women are irresistibly drawn to the spectacle of innocence (or apparent innocence), taking it as a challenge. On such occasions money and lavish entertainment are less important than bringing about the innocent's downfall. No poetic hint has yet been interpreted as showing Hardy to have had such an experience, but it is not to be ruled out. There are few hints about any facet of his private life during these five London years. Yet, quite aside from possible experiments in practical sex, he was not by a long way the man to have lived in an emotional void; and the conclusion generally drawn is that he had a love-affair, perhaps more than one, about which he chose in old age to tell posterity as little as he did about his love-affair with Tryphena Sparks. But an affair with whom? In August 1862, within a few weeks of his arrival in the capital, he took his cousin Martha Sparks, the youngest and, to judge from photographs, best-looking of Tryphena's three elder sisters, out for an evening at the Exhibition.[30] A solitary but apparently reliable reference discloses that at one time he thought of marrying Martha, but was forbidden by her mother on grounds of consanguinity.[31] This episode could have occurred while he was working in Dorchester, but he was only twenty-two when he left for London, and she was twenty-eight. A love-affair would have been one thing, but it is difficult to believe that the diffident young Hardy, scarcely launched yet into a career and mindful of the Rebecca episode (assuming it occurred), would have dared to propose marriage at this stage.

The alternative is that he continued after their first outing to see Martha in London, where she had employment as a lady's maid, and fell in love with her there. Besides being pretty, she was stylish (her job necessitated that) and evidently of some education, having learned French and been to Paris. Finally, amid the metropolitan strangeness she was a link with his own world and his own class. On the other hand her duties would have prevented her from meeting him oftener than probably once a week, leaving him plenty of time for all his other recorded (and unrecorded) activities. He may well have moved slowly up to the point of asking her parents if he might marry her, and been rebuffed. Martha was to become pregnant by, and eventually to marry, the butler at her place of work; but the pregnancy did not occur until 1869, two years after Hardy had returned to Dorset.

Another possible lover is the woman mysteriously known just as 'H.A.' In the four letters to his sister that Hardy reproduced in the *Life*, he refers to H.A. only twice: in February 1863 to say that she had been ill 'as I daresay you know' and to ask whether she had written to Mary yet; and in October 1865 to enquire whether it would be 'awkward' if he brought H.A. down for Christmas and Boxing Day. He was therefore in contact with H.A. for at least three of his five London years, and she was known to Mary, presumably through Mary's fairly numerous visits to London. Why H.A.'s advent at Christmas time should be awkward for Mary any more than for the rest of the family is a puzzle. To arrive home with a young lady (unchaperoned, apparently) for such a family festival as Christmas would normally mean that the girl was an acknowledged fiancée.

In the absence of other guides to Hardy's thoughts and actions we usually turn to his poems, but unless some buried clue still awaits detection there is not much help here. Gittings tentatively links H.A. with the deeply felt poem 'Neutral Tones', composed in 1867.[32] If the speculation is right, the poem confirms that Hardy and H.A. had a love-affair and commemorates its bitter ending. 'Neutral Tones', however, could also be applied to Martha, for the pond beside which the lovers have their final encounter could equally be on 'Egdon' or Hampstead Heath, or in Kensington Gardens. H.A. is probably the subject of 'Her Initials', a brief poem, dated 1869, in which the poet while turning some pages comes across 'two letters' (in the manuscript 'the initials') of a woman's name, and realises they no longer mean anything to him. Less probably, the initials could be those of Tryphena Sparks. Gregory Stevens Cox (son of James) links H.A. with the poem 'Retty's Phases', but the relevance is hard to see.[33]

Whoever she was, however, or whether not she but some other woman was involved, some time before 1867 Hardy appears to have had an affair of the heart that, as indicated in 'Neutral Tones', ended badly. Gittings offers the theory that the emotional shock may have been responsible for Hardy's loss of religious faith.[34] No doubt it played its part, but the loss of faith is likely to have been due to a complexity of causes, and if H.A. was the girl who caused the shock she did so after the process had already begun; for in 1865 he was still proposing to bring her home for Christmas, yet the previous August, when he had conceived the notion of matriculating at Cambridge with a view to 'combining poetry and the Church', the scheme had fallen through because he felt he could not honourably take Orders 'while holding the views which on examination he found himself to hold'.[35] A major cause of his change to unbelief was the increasing difficulty (which he never surmounted) of reconciling the existence of God with the presence of evil and suffering. When, in his unappeasable inquisitiveness, he left the bright highways for the dark alleys of London, he saw suffering such as made the worst poverty he had known in Dorset mild by comparison. There can be little doubt that the gradual effect of living in a city whose bright surface hid such putrescent depths ate like a creeping blight into his beliefs. In vain, in an endeavour to hold on to the faith of his upbringing, he began to 'practise orthodoxy' by attending Sunday evening service at Westminster Abbey: he found it merely 'a very odd experience'.

It should be remembered that he was far from alone in his doubts. This was the age of Darwin and John Stuart Mill, and, as Evelyn Hardy has neatly put it, the effect of these and other writers on their generation is comparable with that of Galileo and Kepler on theirs or the invention of the nuclear bomb on our own.[36]

The work for Blomfield entailed nothing creative, and the better post Hardy might have procured through his social contacts he never sought because, in his own words, he 'constitutionally shrank from the business of social advancement', causing himself to be 'quizzed by his acquaintance for his lack of ambition'.[37] His 'unfortunate shyness' also prevented him from seeking introductions to eminent poets then in London, such as Browning and Swinburne. By the end of 1866 his health had begun to break down, a misfortune he himself attributed to the presence of the insanitary Thames outside the Adelphi windows, but which others told him was caused by his habit of reading in his lodgings every evening instead of going out. (If this were so, his shattered romance must have brought about a marked change in his habits.) Whatever the reason – and it was probably the sustained effort to cram too much into his life – his condition became so noticeable that Blomfield suggested he should return to the country for a spell. Accordingly in July 1867 Hardy went back to Bockhampton, leaving his books in his lodgings. Hicks was only too glad to re-employ him, and superficially Hardy resumed where he had left off in 1862. His health soon mended and, since he was not required to attend the South Street office on a regular basis, he used his surplus time and energy to write his first novel, 'The Poor Man and the Lady'. This fact, together with a brief summary of his unsuccessful but not entirely discouraging attempts to sell the book to Macmillan and then to Chapman & Hall, and the information that he read a great deal, are all that the *Life* tells us about the second half of 1867 and the whole of 1868. Yet even the unambitious Hardy cannot have felt happy at going back five years in his profession. Nor are his parents likely to have been too pleased by his abandonment of his London opportunities; Mrs Hardy's reactions are probably accurately mirrored in those of Mrs Yeobright to the homecoming of Clym in *The Return of the Native*. Clearly, not the least reason for Hardy's decision to occupy himself with writing a novel was to find compensation for the generally bleak atmosphere surrounding his life and future.

But there was another compensation. Tryphena Sparks,

who reached the age of seventeen in March 1868, had done well as a pupil-teacher in Puddletown until the preceding February, when she was dismissed, apparently for neglect of duty.[38] Whatever the reason, she left Puddletown and, according to local tradition, taught in the small school at Coryates, a hamlet in Waddon Vale, midway between Dorchester and Weymouth. Here she would appear to have remained until her three years as a pupil-teacher were completed in November 1869. There is a letter, posted from Puddletown in August of that year, in which she says she is home for a month's holiday; she does not say from where, but the job must have been far enough away to necessitate living nearer than Puddletown, and in a letter from Plymouth, written six years later, she writes of having spent part of her holidays at Waddon and having stayed as the guest of Miss Samson, the woman known to have run the Coryates school.[39]

Events for Hardy meanwhile had taken an unexpected turn. In February 1869, though only fifty-three, John Hicks died, and his business passed to George R. Crickmay of Weymouth, who discovered that on the books were a number of unfulfilled orders for the restoration of churches. Being personally much occupied with a large housing project in Weymouth itself, Crickmay left most of the church work to Hardy, who carried it out so well that in June he began a three-month stint in the Weymouth office that in fact became prolonged until February 1870. Thus he found himself in lodgings at Weymouth at the same time that Tryphena was apparently teaching in nearby Coryates.

There is strong reason to conclude that this was the culminating period of their romance. Whatever flights of imagination Miss Deacon's investigations may have led her into, most scholars now accept the truth of her basic premise that a romance of some sort did occur, though probably slightly later than she and her collaborator, Terry Coleman, suggest.[40] Certainly the laws of probability favour the premise. If we accept the evidence, Hardy had already cast favourable eyes on two of the Sparks sisters (it is an odd coincidence that the one he missed out was called Emma), and Tryphena, like the others, bore the family features that he saw in his much-adored mother. Moreover Tryphena had in a marked degree

41

the characteristics that were to draw him to Emma Gifford – vivacity and a sense of fun. This is conclusively proved by the breezy style of her letters. But how deeply the two were attached, or for how long – these are much harder questions to answer. The manner of Hardy's attachments, throughout his life, was to fall in love with great intensity for a very short time and then, if he continued to associate with the beloved, to do so on a basis of intellectual friendship. It is invariably overlooked, when comments are made on the cooling-off (at least outwardly) of his love for Emma around 1890, that the attraction had lasted far longer than that of any other woman in his life before or after.

Although the poem 'In a Eweleaze Near Weatherbury' (see below, page 46) indicates that the romance began during the summer of 1868, if Hardy and his cousin saw much of one another before the last month of that year it must have been very clandestinely, for after what we are presuming to have been his relationship with the two elder sisters, Maria Sparks, their mother, would have kept Tryphena under very close surveillance. But in November Mrs Sparks died. Long afterwards Hardy wrote a poem, 'Mother Won't Know', in which he depicted the follies of a family liberated by death from the control of a strict mother. It is likely, therefore, that his meetings with Tryphena increased during the winter of 1868–9; and now, in June, here they were, both living away from home, within three miles of one another, and even with a railway link.[41] Yet there is no positive proof that the meetings occurred. Hardy, unquestionably, enjoyed himself at Weymouth, but he would have enjoyed himself independently of Tryphena, for the town, first popularised by George III, offered boating, swimming, dancing, and the general animation of a seaside resort in the season. The *Life* and a group of poems specifically associated with Weymouth in 1869 testify to his happiness during his term there; but to determine whether Tryphena contributed to his euphoria we are driven to the usual expedient of trying to read between the lines – especially the verse lines.

The first thing to notice is that Hardy gives just over one page of the *Life* to these nine months, and that the only specific act he mentions – joining a quadrille class – did not take place until November. Of what he did during the summer, except go swimming and boating, he says nothing. This may be because, outside his work, he really did do nothing else, or it may be a Hardyan silence to conceal something he did not, even in old age, wish to make public. He entered the quadrille class at the persuasion of a new office colleague who had joined Crickmay 'in August or September'. Did this young man himself not discover the quadrille class until he had been in Weymouth several months (and this is to assume that his home was not there), or did Hardy delay joining the class until Tryphena had completed her third year of pupil-teacher training – also in November – and gone home? One certain fact is that she herself could never have joined the class with him: one of the requirements of her probation was that she should at all times show impeccable moral rectitude (a further reason for rejecting any idea that a moral lapse was responsible for her dismissal at Puddletown), and this quadrille class was not just a place of dancing – bad enough in the eyes of the school's Nonconformist sponsors – but, in Hardy's words, 'a gay gathering for . . . love-making by adepts of both sexes'.

The same need not to tarnish her name means that, if she and Hardy consorted at this period, any love-making would have had to be conducted where there was absolutely no danger of her being recognised. Nevertheless, there must have been many opportunities in the sheltered countryside and even on the lonelier parts of the coast; and if they were seen merely walking together in Weymouth exception could hardly have been taken to a decorous meeting of cousins. Whether Hardy proceeded as far as asking for an official betrothal and giving his partner a ring, as family tradition asserts, research has yet to prove. Long afterwards the story reached Florence Hardy, who apparently believed it since she passed it on to Irene Cooper Willis, her eventual trustee and collator of the correspondence now in the Dorset County Museum.[42] The customary version is that Hardy gave Tryphena the ring and she later returned it to him, whereupon he gave it to Emma. But Miss Willis, quoting Florence, states merely that Thomas 'broke off an understanding that there had been between him and a girl of his own countryside and bestowed upon Emma the ring intended for her', which is tantamount to saying that

Tryphena never actually received the ring.

The story that Tryphena had a son by Hardy rests almost wholly on the testimony in old age of her daughter by her eventual husband Charles Frederick Gale; and the supporters of this evidence are at pains to stress the reliability of the old lady during her first interviews with enquirers before she started to become senile. But this is largely irrelevant; the factors that really determine the credibility of the story are seldom even touched upon. One, already discussed in these pages, is the possibility that Hardy, though not impotent in the sense that he could enjoy a sexual relationship, was infertile. Another is that with his immense love of children it is most unlikely that he would have managed to keep secret the fact that he had a child of his own, if only because he would at some time or another have wanted to make contact with his son. At the very least the son, duly disguised, would have featured in a crop of poems, whereas the believers in his existence can cite none that are not of the most dubious validity. Finally, and fatally for the child theory, it is quite beyond any rational belief that Tryphena could, in the world in which she moved, have kept the secret of a pregnancy and birth from being discovered by the successive authorities that examined her credentials for teaching in the Nonconformist school at Coryates, entering a teacher-training college in London, and being awarded a headmistress-ship of major importance in Plymouth. The past history of candidates for these posts was gone into with all the thoroughness of detectives investigating a murder. Even those who reject Coryates are left with the other two tests; and, if it is conceded that Tryphena did teach at Coryates, there would not have been time for the pregnancy between leaving the Puddletown school and beginning there.

None of the poems to which Hardy attached the name 'Weymouth' or the date 1869 or 1870, or which have since been identified as belonging to the group, extols happy times with a lover, but there are three that treat of a lover's sudden disillusionment or a quarrel. These are 'At a Seaside Town in 1896', in which the lover, feeling he is giving too much attention to the attractions of the town, resolves to think more about his beloved, only to find that she no longer means anything to him; 'At Waking', a poem of great power and clearly

44

genuine feeling in which the lover, waking at dawn, sees his beloved as 'but one of the common crowd . . . a sample/Of earth's poor average kind', and is so appalled that he tries to deny the vision; and 'In the Vaulted Way', telling of a farewell meeting at which the girl bewilders her lover by kissing him affectionately despite words the previous night that had 'burned/My fond frail happiness out of me' so that she leaves him sad and bewildered. Bailey suggests that the first poem may refer to Tryphena either in the flesh or as a symbol of Hardy's consciousness that he was not sufficiently concentrating on writing the new novel *Desperate Remedies* on which he had now embarked: if this is so the last lines must allude to a temporary loss of inspiration.[43] But with this proviso all three poems imply that a serious rift occurred between Hardy and some girl at Weymouth, presumably Tryphena. Once again the cause is something about which we are reduced to speculation, but by far the most probable is resentment by Hardy at Tryphena's determination to place her career before marriage and go to London for training. Even today such a decision might well cause resentment, and in the mid-nineteenth century it must have seemed outrageous, an utter betrayal of love.

We can imagine that he upbraided her bitterly, and that the robust Tryphena responded in kind, so that he really believed she no longer meant anything to him. Yet, as so often between lovers, a tender kiss was enough to set him in a turmoil of doubt again; and that he still placed a measure of hope in her down to the moment of meeting Emma is shown, as will become apparent, in two of the poems he wrote about his first journey to Cornwall. In consequence it would be unwise to read too much into his description of the quadrille class. After the Cremorne Gardens and the Argyle it must have appeared tame enough, yet he may have consoled himself for Tryphena's departure with a flirtation, 'innocent' or otherwise. The 'experts in love-making' would scarcely have deserved the epithet if one of their number could not have captured the ever-susceptible Hardy. One of the Weymouth poems may refer to some such minor romance: 'Her Father', in which a young man keeping a rendezvous with his girl in a busy part of the town finds her there with her father and, baulked of showing his love in the parental presence, ends by wondering whether the father's love is not the worthier sort. 'The Dawn After the Dance', on the other hand, the only Weymouth poem alluded to in the *Life*, where Hardy says it is 'supposed, though without proof, to have some bearing' on the dances at the quadrille class,[44] does not appear to apply to himself at all, if only because it concerns two successive New Year's Eves and he was in Weymouth for only one.

We need to consider a little further the poem mentioned on page 42, 'In a Eweleaze near Weatherbury'. This has nothing to do with Weymouth. 'Weatherbury' is Hardy's name for Puddletown, and that the poem's subject is Tryphena is virtually proved by the appended date 1890, the year of her death. The argument that the main scene of courtship was Weymouth is not, however, invalidated; on hearing of his former lover's passing it would be natural for Hardy to think of the setting of their first avowals, rather than the region clouded by the memory of their final quarrel. 'The Mound', a late poem that is perhaps also a record of the quarrel, is sometimes supposed to be laid in the Puddletown area, mainly on the strength of an entirely uncorroborated illustration by Hardy to 'In a Eweleaze'; but it could just as well be near Weymouth. The lines in this poem in which the speaker says she will 'not be bound/For life to one man' consist closely with the suggestion that the dispute was over Tryphena's determination to set career before caresses.

One month after she had left home for Stockwell Normal College near Brixton, south London, Hardy returned arbitrarily from Weymouth to Higher Bockhampton. In the *Life* he states that he needed to be spared the distraction of the dancing-class to concentrate more closely on *Desperate Remedies*.[45] What reason he gave Crickmay for withdrawing from the Weymouth office he does not say, but they must have parted on good terms, for within a week of his arrival at home he received a letter from the architect asking whether he could go to Cornwall to see about implementing one of the church-restoration commissions that had been accepted by Hicks so long before. The church was close to the north coast, at St Juliot.

At first, preoccupied with his novel, Hardy declined; but Crickmay persisted, and the novel was almost finished. Hardy decided to send it off, less the final chapters, to the friendly Macmillan, and to set out for Cornwall. He had nothing to keep him at home. Even if we do not accept the poetical hints that relations with Tryphena had already cooled, she had moved out of his orbit, gone to London. Thus the stage was set, the last stage-direction given, for the meeting of the two whose lives were to remain linked for forty-two years, and in the memory of the survivor for sixteen more.

The old-fashioned picture of the pair stresses their differences in social class, in background and temperament, in education, in religion, but declares that in the field of sex they shared an equal innocence. The truth is that Emma, the town-bred girl, though undoubtedly a virgin, probably had as wide a knowledge of the 'facts of life', and as great a degree of broad-mindedness, as any country girl, while Hardy, the country boy, pretty surely had as much sophisticated sexual knowledge and experience as any young man-about-town.

CHAPTER THREE

From St Juliot to St Peter's, Paddington

ONLY DEVON lay between Dorset and Cornwall, but the young architect – he was now twenty-nine – found the journey disjointed, uncomfortable and tiring. The bitter difference between illusion and reality that was to characterise the whole four-year courtship began, in a manner of speaking, even before he and Emma met, at any rate in his retrospective vision; for no contrast could be greater than that between the cold rise before dawn, the bag-laden trudge to Dorchester station, the three crawling trains (Dorchester–Yeovil, Yeovil–Plymouth, Plymouth–Launceston), the dreary sixteen-mile horse-and-trap drive over the solitude of Bodmin Moor, and the rosy recollection of forty-four years later.

> When I set out for Lyonnesse,
>   A hundred miles away,
>   The rime was on the spray,
> And the starlight lit my lonesomeness
> When I set out for Lyonnesse
>   A hundred miles away.

When he at last reached St Juliot Rectory, it was to find that the Reverend Caddell Holder was in bed with gout, and since his wife chanced to be tending him at the moment it was her sister who waited to receive the visitor in the drawing-room. From this point onwards we have three records of what happened: Emma's account in *Some Recollections*, Hardy's

48

laconic diary notes, and the spate of poems he composed after her death. It will be noticed that two of these records were set down more than forty years after the events of which they tell, and in an emotional atmosphere that must have made them appear to the writers like a faraway sunlit landscape seen across a barren, shadowy waste. Moreover they are records of young love – well, fairly young – remembered in old age, not described while it was still being experienced. The difference in the two treatments is therefore significant: Emma's the simple narrative uncomplicated by any hint of hindsight or consciousness of irony; Hardy's a poetic evocation tinged, in all but the earliest compositions such as 'When I Set Out for Lyonnesse', with an increasing awareness that even such love as blossomed at St Juliot can never be without its difficulties, misunderstandings, certainty of change if not of transience. The pages of *Some Recollections* devoted to Emma's first meetings with Hardy contain fewer words than his corresponding poems, but they are enough to make clear the dissimilarity in character between the man and the woman; nor does it matter that they are dissimilarities between two people now in old age, for the gulf is plainly lifelong and fundamental. When they first roamed the wild cliffs or picnicked in the Valency Valley or made music round the Rectory piano, what they found they had in common was enough to hide the underlying disharmony; and when afterwards this gradually came to light both he and she proved too firmly moulded to make the adjustments that, under the stimulus of affection, a younger couple might have made.

Again, had those first four courtship years been spent continuously in proximity, with daily or near-daily meetings, at least a glimpse of fact might have loomed through the gold-tinted mists of myth. But Hardy's visits to St Juliot were spaced out between much longer periods of separation, and except when through the agency of Miss D'Arville they enjoyed a few days together in the neighbourhood of Bath, once when Emma paid a short visit to her brother Walter in London at a time when Hardy was there, and once when she made a momentous journey from St Juliot to Bodmin, she never travelled anywhere to meet him. Absence makes not only the heart grow fonder, but also the judgement kinder.

They exchanged letters, probably many, although later they both took care that all were destroyed; and these must have etched still deeper the false picture, Emma's correspondence having no purpose but to dwell on the common interests that bound her to her Man of Destiny, his because he knew how much that was likely to disturb her he had to hide. Peering back with aged but clear vision across the years, she recalls that when she saw him she was 'immediately arrested by his familiar appearance, as if I had seen him in a dream'.[1] And in a dream she continued to see him, until too late.

To some extent the same may be said of him. Few conditions make a man more susceptible to love than the void caused by a romance that has just ended, even when he is reluctant to admit its end. One other poem concerned with his first journey to Cornwall contains hints that until the very moment of meeting Emma he retained a hope that the breach with Tryphena might not prove final. In 'The Wind's Prophecy' the first half of each stanza describes the stages of the route, the second how his heart is filled with the love he is leaving, all unconscious of the new love to which he is drawing near. One couplet runs:

> 'I roam, but one is safely mine,'
> I say. 'God grant she stay my own!'

The confidence in the first line is betrayed by the doubt in the second. In short, Hardy the man of ever-changing loves was ripe for a new encounter, and from the minute he met Emma it seems fairly certain that Tryphena remained in his reckoning only as an embarrassment. Not only is there no firm evidence that he ever visited her at Stockwell, but, as Gittings has shown, he seems to have taken pains to be in London when she was on holiday in Puddletown and in Bockhampton or St Juliot when she was in London;[2] and the Sparks family tradition that, after completing her training, she chose a headmistress-ship in Plymouth because it lay on the route to Cornwall is well outside the convincing vein of the other Sparks traditions. The offer was such an astounding opportunity, a girl of her ambition would probably have seized it even if the school had been in Northumberland. Furthermore, it is very unlikely that by the time she needed to make the decision she would not have perceived, had she and Hardy still been in touch, that his thoughts had veered elsewhere.

In later years Emma referred more than once to her growing shyness, but the fact that she wrote of it as a new development shows that she was not shy as a young woman. Dinner was already laid when he reached the Rectory on that first occasion, and evidently she lost no time in discovering that he liked music, for despite his tiredness and the need to spend some time in Caddell Holder's sickroom after the meal there was music-making before the visitor was allowed to go to bed. He does not mention music on the second evening, but on the third 'the two ladies sang duets', and on the fourth and last there was further music. Thus was established, within hours of their first contact, the most enduring of the links between them, the one means of communication that towards the close might, as Emma realised, have mended the long failure to communicate that was the essence of their estrangement.

Hardy names two of the songs the sisters sang in duet, but gives no clue as to what other melodies filled the Cornish night air: perhaps country songs, perhaps drawing-room ballads, perhaps even operatic arias – to the English and Irish opera composers mentioned in the first chapter as in vogue during the mid-century Hardy's London diary adds the current European favourites, Rossini, Donizetti, Meyerbeer, Verdi, Bellini. Financial stringencies would have prevented both Helen and Emma from buying copies of many of the successes that had appeared since their Plymouth days, but they included such subsequent evergreens as Tchaikovski's 'Chants Sans Paroles' (1868), Brahms's 'Hungarian Dances' (1866) and 'Lullaby' with English words (1870), Balfe's 'Killarney' (1861), Foster's 'Beautiful Dreamer' (1864), Ascher and Guernsey's 'Alice, Where Art Thou?' (1864), and three of the most magnificent Strauss waltzes. Hymns composed between 1860 and 1870 included Lyte's 'Abide with Me', Reginald Weber's 'Holy, Holy, Holy Lord God Almighty', Neale's 'Jerusalem the Golden', and an English translation of the German carol 'Heilige Nacht'. It was also the decade in which the British, as well as the Americans, first heard 'John Brown's Body' to the tune of Julia Ward Howe's 'Battle Hymn of the Republic'. For England's battle hymn, the Reverend Sabine

Baring-Gould's 'Onward Christian Soldiers', the breathless public had to wait until 1871.[3]

One would dearly like to think that Hardy, mindful of his prowess at Blomfield's, joined in the St Juliot singing, possibly with a rendering of 'Champagne Charley', published in 1867; but there is no record that he ever sang in Cornwall except in church, or at any time gave Emma a gift of sheet music.

A good deal was fitted into his first, four-day visit: drawing and measuring at the church, a drive with the two ladies to Boscastle, Tintagel, and Penpethy slate quarries (commemorated more than half a century later in the poem 'Green Slates'), an expedition with Emma to Beeny Cliff – he on foot, she on horseback – a walk to Boscastle down the Valency Valley accompanied by Helen and Emma for 'three-quarters of the way' (they may have turned back on account of Emma's lameness, though it does not seem to have handicapped her on similar occasions), a trip to Boscastle in the chaise during which they walked up the steep hill to spare the horse, a quiet evening in the garden. When Hardy came to leave, half an hour before dawn on the Friday morning, it was Emma, not his hostess, who kept striking a light throughout the night in case she should fail to rouse the servants in time to get him ready.[4] The poem 'At the Word "Farewell"' sharply etches the scene at their first parting:

> She looked like a bird from a cloud
>   On the clammy lawn,
> Moving alone, bare-browed
>   In the dim of dawn.
> The candles alight in the room
>   For my parting meal
> Made all things withoutdoors loom
>   Strange, ghostly, unreal.
>
> The hour itself was a ghost,
>   And it seemed to me then
> As of chances the chance furthermost
>   I should see her again.
> I beheld not where all was so fleet
>   That a plan of the past

Which had ruled us from birthtime to meet
    Was in working at last:

No prelude did I there perceive
    To a drama at all,
Or foreshadow what fortune might weave
    From beginnings so small;
But I rose as if quicked by a spur
    I was bound to obey,
And stepped through the casement to her
    Still alone in the gray.

'I am leaving you . . . Farewell!' I said,
    As I followed her on
By an alley bare boughs overspread;
    'I soon must be gone!'
Even then the scale might have been turned
    Against love by a feather,
– But crimson one cheek of hers burned
    When we came in together.

From the last two lines it would seem that, abandoning both his diffidence and the Victorian rules of propriety, he actually kissed the cheek of his acquaintance of four days. Even if, as he concedes in the *Life*, the incident may belong to his second visit, the boldness was considerable. Whether he was really in love yet – one must always remember those rose-tinted spectacles supplied by the years – we cannot tell; but in a letter written in 1918 to Mrs Florence Henniker he included 'At the Word "Farewell"' among poems that he declared were 'literally true',[5] and Bailey's argument that its probability must be offset against the fact of the engagement to Tryphena becomes meaningless if we accept that, in spite of lingering hopes on the way to Cornwall, the romance had virtually ended in Weymouth. We are left with the truth already stated, that no man is better disposed to fall in love than he who has just seen a love-affair turn to dust.

Not the least interesting lines in the poem are those in which the poet speaks of a Plan predestining from birth his meeting with Emma. Evelyn Hardy declares unequivocally that he had no such conviction, but was merely echoing Emma's own attitude; and in view of his love-life prior to 1870 this appears very likely.[6] But there can be no doubt of Emma's sincerity. Against her provincial experience this architect who had worked in London, who had seen plays and operas on the London stage, had been to London concerts, who wrote poetry and prose, must have seemed like a being from a superior world, the most 'civilised' person she had met since leaving Plymouth; and he must have brought a nostalgic pang for the lost life in that city. The fact that he had had virtually nothing published yet merely put him in the same category as herself, also an aspiring writer; and there was his ability to *talk* books; despite her twenty years of avid reading, beside the results of his prolonged 'cramming' she must have felt herself a tyro in literary experience, with just enough of it to make him warm to her as a kindred spirit.

No doubt he delighted in enlarging her literary horizons; no doubt he delighted in playing on her obvious admiration for many things about him. By now he must have acquired a fair knowledge of how to make himself attractive to women, and here was a woman who notwithstanding her years had as far as we can tell never previously loved a man, so that she had no standards of comparison. Not that he was her superior in every aspect: any danger that she might lose her self-esteem was obviated by his wonder at her skill on horseback, his awe of 'her' incredibly savage black-cliffed coast, his total inability to match the exuberance of her chatter as her thoughts 'hopped like a bird on a bough' in the words of a later friend[7] – though this inconsequentiality of style deceived him, as it has deceived others to this day, into underestimating the mental ability behind it:

> It was what you bore with you, Woman,
>   Not inly were,
> That throned you from all else human,
>   However fair!

> It was that strange freshness you carried
>   Into a soul
> Whereon no thought of yours tarried
>   Two moments at all.

Perhaps, even so early as at their first meeting, she sensed her class superiority, albeit we may be sure he kept as quiet about his family background as about Tryphena and the other women in his past. And there was something else he kept quiet about, of far greater bearing on their future harmony than the not very unusual fact of his having had, by the age of twenty-nine, several love-affairs. This was his loss of religious faith. No one knows at what point he revealed to Emma that he was an agnostic. With his diligent study of the Bible, ability to recite large sections of the church services by heart, and intimate knowledge of church music, he could keep up the deception without difficulty, even in a clergyman's household, and the likelihood is that he kept it up for several years. In the summer of 1872 we find him reading one of the lessons at St Juliot, a function that even the easy-going Caddell Holder would hardly have assigned to a known unbeliever.

When Hardy departed on that March morning, therefore, he left no blemish to mar his new friend's golden dream. She must have hung on the arrival of his first letter as only a lover can, for if he left Lyonnesse with magic in his eyes there is small doubt that his Iseult, as he was long afterwards to call her, had magic in her own:

> When I came back from Lyonnesse
>   With magic in my eyes,
>   All marked with mute surmise
> My radiance rare and fathomless,
> When I came back from Lyonnesse
>   With magic in my eyes!

Among those who surmised, though not necessarily mutely, must have been his observant mother, but he lost no time in going down to Weymouth, now safe from Tryphena. Hardly had he set to work on the church drawings he had brought back than Macmillan rejected *Desperate Remedies*. Hardy chose to try it, still incomplete, on Tinsley Brothers, a firm to whose list he thought it better suited. At the beginning of May, William Tinsley agreed to publish it, subject to some alterations, if Hardy would contribute £75 towards the cost. He accepted, and in mid-May went to London again. He was still far from deciding to become a full-time author, but he seems to have regarded himself already as a freelance architect, airily throwing over Crickmay's work and taking on assignments for Blomfield and another London architect, Raphael Brandon. Why he should have gone to London is unclear. Mrs Bromell, Tryphena's daughter, told Lois Deacon that it was in pursuit of Tryphena, but if so he waited a very long time before stirring himself, and, as already stated, there is no evidence that they met now or wanted to meet. On the contrary, his only discoverable motives, feeble though they may sound, were to be in a better position to obtain books to send Emma and perhaps to resume contact with Horace Moule, now again in the capital. That he told Moule of his 'vague understanding' with Emma is further testimony that she, and not Tryphena, now filled his thoughts.[8] The poem 'Ditty', bearing the initials 'E.L.G.' under the title and in effect an ode to her, was composed at this time.

On 8 August he left Brandon as abruptly as he had left Crickmay and made a second trip to St Juliot in fulfilment of a promise given during his first, and therefore by inference for purely social reasons.[9] The visit was in his own words 'a most happy one', and more than any of the others contained incidents made famous through his verses and his and her sketches of one another. The cold weather of March had given place to the hot weather of high summer, and the 'young lady in brown' had become a vision in lightweight pale blue, which he thought suited her complexion far better. Her appearance, as shown in the well-known portrait now in the Dorset County Museum, has already been described; and the assumption that it had changed little throughout her twenties is corroborated by a letter written to her in 1872 by an otherwise unidentified M. Hawes of Twickenham.[10] He or she thanks

. . . dearest Emmie for your very sweet photo and letter full of romantic ideas – the former is such a pretty picture besides being a beautiful likeness, you are not a bit altered and do not look a day older. They say a practical mind keeps one young. I am sure you do not look more than 18. I am not quite used to your style of hair yet, but it gives you the look of the old pictures in Hampton Court.

The climatic link between the March and August visits is

56

that from well before the former until the middle of the latter no rain fell – a drought that was to remain unsurpassed until 1976, more than a century later. Perhaps the long spell of dryness benefited Emma's lameness, for they appear to have both gone about on foot more than in March. Even when it did rain at last, in their delight in being together they carried on much as before, as witness his sketch, dated 22 August 1870, showing Emma sitting in a downpour on Beeny Cliff. They drove a good deal with the Holders, visiting Bossiney, Tintagel and Trebarwith Strand to the south, The Strangles and Bude to the north. They also sometimes visited a local clergyman and his family – perhaps the Serjeants of St Clether, the 'Face at the Casement' household. But there is no suggestion that they ever went to call on Caddell Holder's family at Llanteglos-by-Camelford, or Emma's much-loved Uncle George and family at Launceston, or the other Serjeants at St Benet's. If she had been on her own, these omissions might be put down to a lover's wish to keep her beloved all to herself; but she was already sharing him with the Holders, and why should his host and hostess keep him away from their friends and relatives? There may be some simple explanation, but pending its discovery it does not present a happy augury, particularly when to the list of the unvisited are added John Attersoll Gifford and his wife at Kirland.

However, these puzzling failures did not impede the growth of their mutual fascination. 'We grew much interested in each other,' she notes in *Some Recollections*, 'and I found him a perfectly new subject of study and delight and he found a "mine" in me, he said. He was quite unlike any other person who came to see us, for they were slow of speech and ideas!'[11] No wonder her new suitor found it easy to conceal the perils latent in their association: he was the shining pool come upon suddenly in an endless desert, and the thirsty traveller does not probe to see what lies under the dazzling surface. But he was prudent in his actions as well as in his words. In recent years, with the onset of his unbelief, he had given up going to church, but now, on Sunday, 14 August, he was careful to accompany Emma both to morning service at St Juliot and evening service at Lesnewth, across the Valency Valley.

To the second Cornish visit belongs the incident of the

picnic tumbler lost in the Valency River, commemorated by him much later in the poem 'Under the Waterfall' and at the time by a sketch of Emma attempting rescue. They read poetry together, especially Tennyson and Coleridge, who had been among her favourites at Plymouth, but not, we may be sure, his own favourite, the erotic Swinburne. He instructed her in what to read during his absences, including Dante beloved of his mother. The outside world impinged on their consciousness in the grim news of the Franco-Prussian War, supplied to them in a regular flow of articles from Moule. Work also impinged: Hardy had brought the manuscript of *Desperate Remedies* away with him, and at last he began to make the alterations requested by Tinsley. Though he may have felt the novel was destined to be the first of many – and this is far from certain, poised as he still was between literature and architecture – he cannot have foreseen the far-reaching results his task was to entail in another direction. Emma offered to make him a fair copy of the work, and so launched herself upon a stream of activity that was to last a quarter of a century, provoke her contemporaries (to say nothing of posterity) into a turmoil of argument over its extent, and play an integral part in the history of the Hardys' marriage relations.

That she quickly became very much more than a mere amanuensis is hardly in dispute. From 1870 onwards she acted as his research assistant, cutting from newspapers items that she thought would be of value and noting the titles of books likely to prove useful as source-material.[12] From the outset, too, she must have acted, almost willy-nilly, as his sub-editor; J. I. M. Stewart points out that Hardy's manuscripts from which she made her copies were often corrected to such a degree that she was forced to use her discretion on what was the final construction and sense.[13] This led her to make suggestions, some of which he found helpful even at the height of his powers, as when he adopted her proposal that Angel Clare should give Tess his ancestral jewellery.[14] By then she was also carrying out research in the field, and may have started it much earlier. The Hardys' American friend Rebekah Owen recorded in her diary for 1892 that during an excursion to Wool Manor – the 'Wellbridge Manor' of *Tess* – Emma related how, a few years before, she had obtained entry by a ruse, presumably to report to Hardy on the Turberville portraits.[15] After their marriage there was no novel of his up to the time of *Jude* except *Far from the Madding Crowd* of which she did not share in the preparation, in however minor a rôle. In 1940 her nephew Gordon Gifford wrote to *The Times Literary Supplement*, giving as his authority that he had lived at Max Gate and knew what went on there, to state that *Jude* was the 'first of the Hardy novels in which she had not assisted by her counsel, copious notes for reference and mutual discussion'.[16] In 1910 Emma wrote to Lady (Alda) Hoare: 'My husband's books have not the same kind of interest for me as for others. I know every word of the first edition – in MS sitting by his side.'[17]

No wonder people who became aware of this assistance half-believed she wrote the novels in their entirety or, more maliciously, accused her of believing it. Dr Fred Fisher, who was physician to the whole Hardy family at Bockhampton and to Thomas and Emma from soon after their establishment at Max Gate in 1885 until his retirement in 1910, wrote to the journalist T. P. O'Connor:

Of course, I knew the novelist's first wife very well. She was very clever . . . and for a long time I suspected her of writing the famous novels. Later on she told me he always submitted them to her, and she gave me the impression she revised them pretty freely.[18]

After O'Connor had published the letter without permission, the embarrassed doctor wrote indignantly to Lady Hoare in an attempt to retract his assertion, but it seems fairly evident he had meant what he said to O'Connor; and his belief was far from unshared. Emma was certainly in no great haste to deny the impression she gave, especially after Hardy had begun to turn to younger literary women for advice, but her most-quoted affirmation of her rôle is, I think, misunderstood. Again it is O'Connor who tells us of a conversation between himself, Emma and an unidentified lady, during which Emma is supposed to have interrupted a eulogy of Hardy by this lady with a ridiculous story of how she and Jemima Hardy would each attribute to the other the credit for writing Hardy's novels. Emma is then alleged to have pointed to her 'ample bosom' and said to the lady, 'I have it all here, but I have not the power of expressing it', adding: '[Hardy] is very vain and selfish, and these women that he meets in London society only increase these things. They are the poison. I am the antidote.'[19] It is extremely difficult to conceive of such an exchange between Emma and Jemima, or of Emma asserting that there had been one: just possibly Jemima may, during their brief season of friendly relations, have remarked that she did not know what Hardy would do without Emma's help, and Emma may have retorted that *she* did not know what he would do without his mother's fund of tales and country lore. The next observation is always taken as meaning that locked in Emma's breast were all the qualities needed to write novels as fine as Hardy's, if only she had the requisite power of expression. But since she immediately went on to criticise his society friends it seems far more credible that her meaning was 'Why, in his vanity, does he selfishly turn to these women, when I have within me all the counsel he requires, lacking only the power to express it as well as they?' In view of the part her poor powers or oral expression will be shown to have played in the tragedy of her wedded life, the remark thus interpreted becomes deeply poignant rather than absurd. After all she had done for him, the protest was understandable and probably justified. And in so far as his dancing after society women was threatening his marriage, at least in his wife's eyes, they were indeed the poison, she the antidote.

At the same time it must be conceded that she did, apparently, come to believe (perhaps not until after his prose-writing had ceased) that she had *inspired* his novels. She herself wrote a tale called 'The Inspirer', the subject of which was a wife who inspired her author-husband's fiction; the manuscript is now lost and the date of composition is unknown. Edward Clodd, a close friend of Hardy for many years, entered in his diary for 1913 that he had been told by Hardy, during a visit to Clodd's home at Aldeburgh, of 'the illusion [Emma] nursed that she had written his novels because he got her to copy his MSS'.[20] Hardy had just been studying certain secret diaries of hers (see page 135 *et al.*), discovered by him after her death, in which he may well have found the source of this remark. But the extremity of bitterness that we know motivated these journals, which he subsequently burned, leaves a persisting doubt as to what she really believed in calmer moods.

I have already mentioned the deceptive effect of Emma's scatterbrained style of chatter. Many no doubt have genuinely thought her lacking in the brain-power to be able to help on a serious literary plane. But her letters to the press, the best of her private correspondence, her published articles, and to a lesser extent (because it is much less mature) her unpublished novella 'The Maid on the Shore' all testify to her being no literary nincompoop, unqualified to comment on her husband's work even if he did brilliantly outshine her. If he himself preferred to disparage her mental powers in some of his poems, he went on accepting her help year after year, and when finally she ceased to be admitted to the inner processes of creation it was not because of any decline in her ability.

There are several possible explanations for her continuing to help: vanity, because she felt it identified her with his work; a refusal to believe that she could not eventually modify his 'pagan' outlook and its reflection in his writing; affection, which saw in her assistance a means of holding him when he began to slip away; and a degree of tolerance and broadmindedness much in excess of that generally credited to her. The truth may contain an element of all these. As late as 1906 she besought the Reverend Richard Bartelot, newly appointed to the living of St George, Fordington (Max Gate was in his parish) to 'come to tea once a week to try and make Tom more religious'.[21] Yet in none of her surviving letters is there any support for the adverse reviews of so many of his books. Her views on marriage probably became uncompromising only in measure as she saw Hardy's attitude erode their own union. And there is nothing in her writings or reported remarks to suggest that she was a disciple of Mrs Grundy. For one thing she was too fond of children: passionate child-lovers are seldom prudes.

Had she been as scandalised as some of the reviewers by the sexual aspects of *Desperate Remedies* she would not have continued to make a fair copy, knowing that her own hand was furnishing sinful material for others to read, nor would she have encouraged Hardy to write further novels. True, the celebrated lesbian scene between Mrs Aldclyffe and Cytherea was beyond doubt outside her understanding in 1870. Some biographers, such as Hawkins and Guérard, whom he quotes, maintain that it was outside Hardy's. 'The extreme frankness and clumsiness of this scene', writes Guérard, 'is the strongest evidence that Hardy had no idea what he was writing about.'[22] But the scene is the reverse of clumsy, and the 'frankness' is prudently offset by references to Mrs Aldclyffe's *mother*-love. Hawkins comments that Guérard's observation seems justified by Hardy's 'comically prim little summing up':[23] 'This vehement imperious affection was in one sense soothing, but yet it was not of the kind that Cytherea's instincts desired.'[24] The remark is surely ambiguous enough to be as applicable to lesbian as to maternal love. The episode suggests an amalgam of a homosexual anecdote told to Hardy, probably at Blomfield's, with personal recollections of Mrs Julia Martin's infatuation with him as a little boy. Mrs Aldclyffe's cry, 'Now kiss me. You seem as if you were my own, own child!' could have come straight from Mrs Martin's lips, and so could other Aldclyffe utterances.[25]

Hardy must have known that Emma would be unaware of the meaning of what she was being asked to copy in this particular *Desperate Remedies* scene, or he would not have risked distressing one with whom he was now seriously in love; but he appears to have been confident of her attitude towards the more understandable sexual side of the book. While making his alterations for Tinsley he complimented her by recasting the heroine, Cytherea, in her exact likeness as he saw it at that time:

Her face was exceedingly attractive, though artistically less perfect than her figure, which approached unusually near to the standard of faultlessness. But even this feature of hers yielded the palm to the gracefulness of her movement, which was fascinating and delightful to an extreme degree. . . .

Her hair rested gaily upon her shoulders in curls, and was of a shining corn yellow in the high lights, deepening to a definite nut-brown as each curl wound round into the shade. She had eyes of a sapphire blue, though rather darker than the gem ordinarily appears; they possessed the affectionate and liquid sparkle of loyalty and good faith as distinguishable from that hard brightness which seems to express faithfulness only to the object confronting them.[26]

Here are the seeds of the beautiful lines of more than forty
years later:

> O the opal and the sapphire of that wandering western sea,
> And the woman riding high above with bright hair flapping free –
> The woman whom I loved so, and who loyally loved me.

It is not known exactly when he returned to Bockhampton
from his second Cornish visit, but it was probably before the
end of August. He knew he would have to wait a long time
before he could make a living from literature. On the other
hand, with that immensely high hurdle, the acceptance of a
first novel, safely cleared, architecture seemed a dreary alternative. No doubt he had a fresh set of questions about Cornwall from his mother to answer, and the proximity of
Puddletown cannot have been very soothing. If he had found
his relatives there an embarrassment before, they must now
have appeared a menace. But, while he spent an anxious
autumn finishing his literary alterations and checking the
packets of fair copy that kept arriving, there was no anxiety in
Emma's feelings. In October she wrote that all around her
seemed a dream, their love the reality. (In March it had been he
who constituted the dream.) She finished her task by the beginning of December, and Hardy received a Christmas present in
the shape of Tinsley's notification that the story was now
accepted. The same month saw Tryphena's return home for
Christmas after completing a highly successful first year at
Stockwell. Hardy could scarcely leave Bockhampton before
the seasonal festivities, but January 1871 found him in
London, nominally for the absurd reason that he needed to
pay Tinsley the £75 in cash. He admits in the *Life* that after
paying out this sum he had less than £50 left in the world; to
incur the expense of the London trip was therefore little short
of madness, except that it took him out of reach of Tryphena.[27]
When she went back to college, he went back to Dorset.

He spent the rest of the month and part of the next taking
down ballads – doubtless with the singing sisters of St Juliot in
mind – from old people, since the young were turning to other
music. He does not name his ballads for us, nor did he do anything to preserve them, though he may have used the words of

some in *The Return of the Native*. It is a pleasant conjecture that one or two may have found their way to St Juliot and reappeared in Emma's marathon last piano performance at Max Gate. (See pages 219–20.)

Desperate Remedies was published, without the author's name, in March 1871. The first reviews were mixed, but not on balance discouraging, until in April the *Spectator* condemned it so trenchantly that the reviewer even included Tinsley Brothers in his censure. Hardy read the review sitting on a stile near Kingston Maurward House, on the route he had trodden so often in his Dorchester school and office days. He never forgot that moment, which had the effect of adding one more to the list of occasions when he wished he were dead.[28]

The latter part of the review was, in truth, not uncomplimentary, but the first part was enough for Hardy. Too late he saw that the lesbian scene and other 'daring' aspects of the book damned it at the outset as a candidate for family reading and therefore for the libraries. His vision of making at least enough money by it to justify a formal proposal of marriage vanished into the distant trees as he sat on the stile. The kindly Moule sent him a note advising him to ignore the *Spectator*, but Hardy must have longed for Emma's consolation while not daring to seek it with financial failure as his only courtship gift. He accordingly adopted a ruse. Getting in touch with Crickmay, he found that the St Juliot restoration work was at last ready to go ahead, and offered to go down there and supervise the start. Crickmay agreed and, in May 1871, Hardy paid his third visit to Cornwall. Emma herself laid the foundation stone of the new tower and north aisle, her brother-in-law exhorting the watching schoolchildren to remember the event and speak of it to their descendants. Looking back in 1911, she wondered if any of them had; but when Hardy appealed after her death for anyone who recalled those days to come forward no one came.[29]

Even the work on the church, which should have given him modest cause for pride, probably added to his depression. Just when he started to regret the vandalism of so much nineteenth-century church restoration is uncertain, but in addition to the builder's destruction of the medieval screen, the rehabilitation of which Hardy had carefully planned, Crickmay's designs entailed the usual lavish discarding of salvageable stonework. On all counts Emma alone stood between her suitor and complete despair, and she proved impressively equal to the burden. Neither he nor she gives any details of activity related specifically to this time – the *Life* dismisses the whole visit in one line – but from her general comments on his sojourns at the Rectory we can infer that, except for rather more time spent at the church, they resumed the pattern of life they had enjoyed the previous August. This was only his third trip to Cornwall in more than a year, but by taking up at each reunion precisely where they had left off the time before, they could build up an illusion of more frequent contact. It was all part of the greater illusion that they were getting to know one another.

Fortunately there was no misconception about her present power to comfort him. She helped him to collate the best parts of the *Desperate Remedies* reviews to send to Tinsley (there were no press-cutting agencies in those days), and encouraged him in a project to write a short, purely rustic novel while plodding on with the dull but at least remunerative work for Crickmay, whose commissions-in-hand ranged from building new church schools to enlarging Weymouth's residential area. By the time he set out for Dorset again at the beginning of June he had recovered his morale, if not his happiness; nor was the former shaken even when he saw *Desperate Remedies* already remaindered on Exeter station bookstall. During the rest of the summer he divided his time between architecture and writing the new novel, *Under the Greenwood Tree*.

It is now fairly widely accepted that the book's heroine, Fancy Day, was drawn with Tryphena much in mind: the physical appearance, the character (prudently shorn of Tryphena's earthiness), the vocation, all strongly suggest Hardy's former lady-love. Asked long afterwards by an interviewer whether he thought Fancy Day would have made a good wife, he replied: 'I have known women of her type turn out all right, some of those early examples of independent schoolmistresses included.'[30] Those who claim that in 1871 he was still involved with Tryphena as well as with Emma see part of their evidence in *Under the Greenwood Tree*. But it is equally permissible to take a reverse view. If Hardy had now finished with Tryphena, he could make literary use of her without emotional upset – as throughout his career he made use of people and incidents from life – to provide a ready-made heroine for a book that he wished above all to complete quickly. Far from indicating that Tryphena was still in his heart, Fancy Day suggests a kind of farewell tribute; for by 1871 only one woman occupied Hardy's heart – Emma Gifford.

There being no option clause in the contracts of those days, he sent the completed manuscript to Macmillan early in August. Between then and October he presumably continued his architectural work; and it was once more in his official capacity as architect that he revisited St Juliot early in October. By now he had become less resigned to his long absences from Emma's side; at some time during 1871 he composed the poem 'The Minute Before Meeting', in which a lover contrasts the brevity of his meetings with his loved one to the dreary months of separation. He had good reason to lament the infrequency of her company, for during this exceptionally anxious period she seems to have been – even at a distance – his driving force. Nevertheless, they were not always apart at the times suggested in the *Life*. According to that volume, he was at Bockhampton when he heard from Macmillan that *Under the Greenwood Tree* would be reconsidered in six months' time, interpreted this as a rejection and more or less decided to abandon writing, but resolved to consult Emma first 'by letter' on the decision.[31] She immediately urged him to continue with what she felt was his true vocation, whereupon her unselfishness in counselling the less lucrative course moved him in honour bound to opt for architecture. That some such exchange took place there is no reason to doubt, but it took place face to face at St Juliot, to which Macmillan's letter had been forwarded and from which he wrote to Tinsley casually mentioning his completion of 'a little rural story' and announcing that he had begun a new 'plot-novel' without the crime element of *Desperate Remedies* – his first mention of *A Pair of Blue Eyes*.[32]

Although there is evidence that Jemima Hardy took her share in urging her son not to abandon writing, and Horace Moule advised him not to confine himself exclusively to architecture lest the fine drawing-work strain his eyes, at this point it was Emma and no one else – least of all his uncertain and despondent self – who saved Thomas Hardy for us as a writer. A lesser woman, intent only on marriage, would have thought only of the course likeliest to bring in the money; and one of the ironies that beset their lives no less than those of Hardy's fictional characters is that when, ultimately, her sacrifice was rewarded by the influx of more money from writing than he would probably ever have gained from architecture, their relations had become too strained for either of them to enjoy it.

One may ask how near they were at this time to a formal engagement. The matter is of some moment, as we shall see, in relation to events the following year. In his chronicle of this October, Hardy uses the phrase 'architecture being obviously the quick way to an income for marrying on'. Since he failed to remember whether he had been at St Juliot or Bockhampton during the great debate, 'marrying' may be a similarly inaccurate pre-dating of his proposal; on the other hand, his praise of Emma's unselfishness implies that at least their previous 'understanding' had developed into a tacit acceptance that marriage was their destiny. In the poem 'The Seven Times', which commemorates Hardy's journeys to Cornwall before his marriage and one after Emma's death, the stanzas treating of this visit in autumn 1871 and the next in August 1872 run:

'I journeyed to the place again the fourth time
    (The best and rarest visit of the rare,
As it seemed to me, engrossed about these goings),
        And found her there.

'When I bent my pilgrimage the fifth time
    (Soft-thinking as I journeyed I would dare
A certain word at token of good auspice),
        I found her there.'

The bracketed lines of the second stanza above (the sixth in the poem) are always interpreted as meaning that Hardy's proposal of marriage was made in the summer of 1872. But the second line of the preceding stanza could also refer to the proposal, especially as we know of no other explanation for it. The lines in the following stanza would then mean that during his

1872 journey Hardy was meditating on his intention of asking John Gifford for Emma's hand, provided she thought the moment propitious. 'At token of good auspice' is nonsense applied to a proposal of marriage; he had been having more than two years of such tokens. We shall come in due course to the disastrous outcome of his attempt to do the right thing by John Gifford; but 'Soft-thinking', taken to mean 'tender thinking' in relation to a proposal, can also mean 'thinking in my soft innocence'.

Unless Hardy is to be credited with duplicity shameless even for him, his position in 1871 makes it less likely than ever that he had not yet severed relations with Tryphena, or that so intelligent a woman would not have sensed yet that something was wrong. At all events, he showed a measure of conscience in not entirely relinquishing, without second thoughts, his chivalrous feeling that he should go on with architecture precisely because Emma bade him go on with writing. Having once more set negotiations with a publisher in train, he returned to Dorset on 30 October, his work on the church completed, and continued activities for Crickmay until he saw an opportunity for a more promising post in London. Here he took inexpensive lodgings over a tailor's shop in Paddington and continued to grind away at *A Pair of Blue Eyes* in the evenings, changing its setting to north Cornwall and remodelling its heroine – as he had done with Cytherea – to resemble Emma. At this time the story was called 'A Winning Tongue Had He'.

Meanwhile Tryphena Sparks, going from success to success, had emerged from her second year at Stockwell with such distinction that, thanks to this and her unspotted moral record, she was able despite her youth (not yet twenty-one) and some stiff competition to obtain the post of headmistress at the very large day school for girls in Plymouth, at a salary (with supplements) of more than £100 per annum. By contrast Hardy was shortly to receive £60 from Tinsley for *Desperate Remedies*, leaving a loss to him on the book of £15. His earnings from architecture are not recorded, but cannot have been high in view of his still very modest rank in the profession.

But better things were on the way, for in April 1872 Tinsley offered him £20 for the copyright of *Under the Greenwood Tree*, which he accepted. Emma during these months was helping her relatives in preparation for the reopening of the restored church, also in April. The newspaper account states decorously that at the morning service there was a much more numerous congregation than could have been expected; but Emma forty years later recalled that she had been more impressed by the huge crowd waiting *outside* the church for lunch to begin.[33] The patron of the living, the Right Reverend Richard Rawle, came all the way from his living in mid-Dorset, buoyed up no doubt by the thought that he had just been appointed Bishop of Trinidad; but neither Crickmay, the chief architect, nor Hardy, his man on the spot, put in an appearance. The builder's charge for the work was £1,164 14s 0d, the architect's £76 9s 0d. Rawle generously paid more than £900 of the total; Caddell and Helen Holder contributed £60 19s 6d. The list of minor contributors is interesting: Miss Gifford produced 10s of her own money and 8s 10d from the sale of sketches; Crickmay gave £5; Captain Holder, as already stated, £1 1s; 10s came from Thomas Hardy, and the same amount from Henry Jose; Emma's brother Walter contributed 5s, their mother 10s; and there is an intriguing item, 'Collected by Mrs Gifford, Bodmin, £6 3s 0d.'[34] Did that sum include anything from John Attersoll Gifford?

Under the Greenwood Tree was published late in May 1872.[35] Reviews were good, so good that without waiting to see the sales (which was just as well) Tinsley, mindful of Hardy's reference to a 'plot-novel', on 8 July asked him if he would care to turn it into a serial for the firm's monthly publication *Tinsley's Magazine*, with book publication in the usual three volumes to follow. For this Hardy would receive £200. It was the turning-point for which he had hardly dared to hope and for which Emma had without doubt regularly prayed. With Hardy's earnings as an architect – which he was bolstering up by doing work for several London firms, including Blomfield's – marriage was suddenly a practical possibility. Yet there is no indication that even at this stage he told anything of his intentions to his family, though one may suspect he had said something to his trusted confidante, his beloved sister Mary, who would sooner have laid down her life than betray his secret.

It is equally hard to estimate how much Mr and Mrs Gifford knew at this time. Obviously the Holders could scarcely avoid being *au fait* with the situation, but to what extent the household at St Juliot was on good terms with that at Bodmin is another matter. The events of high summer 1872 are customarily reconstructed by Hardy's biographers on a false premise – namely that, because the first (September) instalment of *A Pair of Blue Eyes* bears an instruction to send the proofs to Kirland Manor, Hardy must have stayed there in August as guest of the Gifford parents.[36] The *Life* is evasive in the manner usual with its compiler when he had something to hide; and what he had to hide is assumed to be an unpleasant interview with John Gifford. The account mentions neither Mr and Mrs Gifford nor even Emma, nor states where Hardy stayed; merely that he 'drove' to St Juliot and 'paid a visit' to Captain and Mrs Serjeant at St Benet's Abbey. To discover where he really was we have to turn to an article published in the *Bodmin Guardian* for 28 January 1928, where among the tributes that followed Hardy's death there appears a report of an interview with Colonel Sir William Charles Eldon Serjeant, Kt, CB, Kt of Grace, OStJ, QC, the younger son of Emma's friends and in 1872 about fifteen years old. The report reads:

Sir William Serjeant, of St Benet's Abbey, points out that a considerable number of instalments of 'A Pair of Blue Eyes' Hardy's first novel, which originally appeared in 'Tinsley's Magazine', was written in a summer-house in the grounds of St Benet's, then the residence of Sir William's late father, Captain Charles Eldon Serjeant. At this time Hardy was engaged to Miss Emma Gifford, whose father resided at Kirland. This lady, who had beautiful light golden hair and blue eyes, was very accomplished and taught Sir William drawing and water-colour painting as a little child. She was the inspiration of 'A Pair of Blue Eyes.' A few years later Mrs Hardy's only brother, Richard Gifford, became a master at Dr Drake's school, Ledrah House, St Austell, where, says Sir William, 'I received my first idea of "education" – chiefly in the art of "boxing" and in "Rough House", by the way—'.

There are of course, a number of inaccuracies, obviously due to faulty recollection after the lapse of more than half a century: the novel was not Hardy's first; Richard was the eldest of three brothers. But there can be little doubt that the main substance of Sir William's reminiscence is correct. At a first reading the paragraph could be taken to mean that Hardy *and* Emma stayed at St Benet's at this time. In 1872, however, Sir William was fifteen, hardly a 'little child'. It seems therefore that the reporter means to say Emma *had* taught the boy drawing and painting during a previous visit – probably during her recovery from nursing Helen after the accident to the gig. In any case, as will shortly be made clear, Hardy's stay in August 1872 lasted at the most three weeks, hardly time enough for much artistic instruction.

We are left with the question of how the visit came about, and how it can be reconciled with the instruction to send the first proofs to Kirland. A likely, if up to now unproven, sequence of events may have been as follows.

Accepting the sixth stanza of 'The Seven Times' as referring to an intention to approach Mr Gifford for Emma's hand (as a consequence of the sudden improvement in Hardy's finances), he would obviously have disclosed his intention to her in advance, and just as obviously she, knowing her father, would have decided to go to Bodmin in person, rather than write, to learn if the 'auspice' were indeed good and send 'token' to her suitor accordingly. This was the journey commemorated in 'I Rose and Went to Rou'tor Town'. The poem makes it plain that something went terribly wrong. Either Emma was deceived by her father's manner into thinking all would be well, and only when he saw Hardy for the first time did she realise her mistake; or for some reason she left her journey to 'Rou'tor Town' (Bodmin) too late to prevent Hardy from setting out after she had found that the auspice was far from good, so that all she could do was to await his arrival and the inevitable clash; or she may have met him at Bodmin Road station, warned him that to show up at Kirland would be most unwise, and whisked him off to St Benet's without his having met her father at all.

On balance, the second possibility best fits the poem, the second stanza of which (it is Emma speaking) runs:

> When sojourn soon at Rou'tor Town
> Wrote sorrows on my face,
> I strove that none should trace
> The pale and gray, once pink and brown,

When sojourn soon at Rou'tor Town
Wrote sorrows on my face.

This very much suggests the unhappy Emma, having sounded
the ground and found it treacherous, hiding her dismay as best
she could while she awaited Hardy's coming. But, whatever
the exact circumstances of John Gifford's outburst against the
marriage, it was obvious that Hardy could not remain at Kirland. In 1920, Vere H. Collins, during a talk at Max Gate,
asked Hardy point-blank to explain the word 'evil' in the lines
that open the last stanza:

The evil wrought at Rou'tor Town
On him I'd loved so true
I cannot tell anew. . . .

Hardy's answer was 'Slander, or something of that sort . . .'.[37]
After such an upset with her father Emma may have felt dis-
inclined to take Hardy immediately back to St Juliot (though
they were to stay there before his return to London), and her
good friends the Serjeants, living only a few miles from Kirland, were the obvious alternative. She had stayed with them at
least twice before; and they were eccentric enough to accept at
short notice and with undiminished warmth a fiancé who had
just been virtually thrown out by her father. It is in tune with
her strong and independent character that the scene at Kirland
clearly failed to shake for an instant her intention to go on with
the marriage.

The stay at St Benet's, however, was shorter than Sir William implies. Hardy left London on 7 August, travelling to Plymouth by sea (as he was to make Stephen Smith do in *A Pair of
Blue Eyes*) but almost certainly *not*, as suggested by some writers, visiting Tryphena there. By 30 August he was at St Juliot,
for on that date he sent from there his outline for the October
instalment of the serial, due to appear in the magazine on 15
September. Any hesitation felt by Emma about the Holders'
reaction to events at Bodmin must have already dissolved; perhaps letters had been exchanged. In a mere three weeks at St
Benet's, Hardy's 'considerable number' of instalments written
in the summer-house was therefore only the one instalment for

October, though it consisted of five chapters, which may have confused Sir William; furthermore at the outset Hardy must also have corrected the September proofs he had had sent to Kirland, and which were presumably brought over by Emma or a servant. For there seems no doubt that Emma visited him at St Benet's. It was evidently from here, not from Kirland, that they set out on the walk described in the poem 'Near Lanivet, 1872', which he always in after life insisted was literally true. The 'stunted handpost' about which there has been some controversy, stood, on Hardy's own avowal,[38] somewhere on the old Bodmin–St Austell road. It appears to have been either at Reperry Cross or at Treliggon, the 'rival' site first noticed by Kenneth Phelps.[39]

There was a stunted handpost just on the crest,
    Only a few feet high:
She was tired, and we stopped in the twilight-time for her rest,
    At the crossways close thereby.

She leant back, being so weary, against its stem,
    And laid her arms on its own,
Each open palm stretched out to each end of them,
    Her sad face sideways thrown.

Her white-clothed form at this dim-lit cease of day
    Made her look as one crucified
In my gaze at her from the midst of the dusty way,
    And hurriedly 'Don't,' I cried.

I do not think she heard. Loosing thence she said,
    As she stepped forth ready to go,
'I am rested now. – Something strange came into my head;
    I wish I had not leant so!'

And wordless we moved onward down from the hill
    In the west cloud's murked obscure,
And looking back we could see the handpost still
    In the solitude of the moor.

'It struck her too,' I thought, for as if afraid
    She heavily breathed as we trailed;

Till she said, 'I did not think how 'twould look in the shade,
  When I leant there like one nailed.'

I, lightly: 'There's nothing in it. For *you*, anyhow!'
  – 'O I know there is not,' said she . . .
'Yet I wonder . . . If no one is bodily crucified now,
  In spirit one may be!'

And we dragged on and on, while we seemed to see
  In the running of Time's far glass
Her crucified, as she had wondered if she might be
  Some day. – Alas, alas!

If the walkers had been discussing Mr Gifford's hostility, the sadness of Emma's face in the second stanza immediately has point; so does her gloomy speculation in the penultimate stanza. So soon after the 'evil wrought at Rou'tor Town' her position against the handpost might well have seemed a portent that spiritual crucifixion was only just beginning. Yet here, too, we have a puzzle. In 1934 Sir Arthur Quiller-Couch, opening a garden fête at Lanivet, recalled that whenever Hardy had paid a visit to Cambridge 'he always used to spend an hour or two in my room, tapping me for reminiscences of Lanivet for the reason that, as a guest of St Benet's, he spent his honeymoon there'.[40] The Hardys spent their honeymoon in France, so obviously the word was a slip for 'engagement'. But could Hardy really have looked back on this anxious – and brief – period at St Benet's as one of such happiness? Or did he and Emma spend a longer, unrecorded period there during late 1873 or 1874? There is the unsolved mystery of why the memorial tablet to Emma, placed in St Juliot church in 1913 under Hardy's direction, states that she lived at the Rectory from 1868 to 1873; for she did not get married until September 1874. A greater part of the time than she states may have been spent in London with her brother Walter, at whose house she stayed to establish her residential qualification; but surely not all of it. The established annals of their lives allow plenty of opportunity for both her and Hardy, who depicts himself in the *Life* as having spent the first half of 1874 quietly writing at Bockhampton, to have passed a leisurely period with the understanding Serjeants; and this is not to overlook Hardy's letters

74

to Leslie Stephen, proving him to have been at Bockhampton at certain dates.

I have called the Serjeants eccentric. Captain Charles, Hardy's host, white-hatted in an epoch when all men's hats were black, divided his time between collecting carriages (horse, not railway) and making speeches with a view to entering Parliament 'where, however,' in Quiller-Couch's phrase, 'he never arrived'. One suspects that the household was really run by his wife Jane, although all that appears to be known about her is that she lived to be ninety. There were three daughters and two sons. The eldest daughter, Alexandra, before ending her days in Bodmin asylum, used to take items of family plate and jewellery out of the house and give them to random villagers, who always returned them surreptitiously to the Abbey. The other two daughters, Sarah Flamank and Jane, both married and promptly vanished without any discoverable trace. Sir William's elder brother Charles died at fifty-five without leaving any impression on the few who might still remember him.

Sir William himself, on the other hand, is well remembered in both Lanivet and Bodmin. He studied law and had a distinguished army career, fighting in several African campaigns including the Boer War, and playing a part in organising Lord Haldane's reforms. During the First World War he inaugurated the Pioneer Corps. But it is his home life that stayed in people's minds. It appears uncertain whether he married once or twice, but one wife was a Sicilian of great beauty and skill as a violinist, who after some years suddenly left him. They had no children, but an adopted daughter, Ruby, also apparently of foreign birth, since her surname before adoption was Vaglica. In spite of the remunerative china clay deposits discovered during one of Emma's visits, the estate under Sir William was always in debt, and shrank steadily as he sold off pieces to keep afloat. This did not prevent him from ordering the planting of twenty *million* bulbs to augment the splendour of the woods and grounds. As an artist he learned well from Emma's tuition, twice becoming a medallist before he was twenty. A painting by him was on sale at Lanivet's village store as recently as 1977. For forty years he also contributed articles on shooting and fishing to the *Field*, the first said to have been written when he

was fourteen. If this was so, he was already a published writer
when Hardy was at St Benet's working on *A Pair of Blue Eyes*,
but there is no hint that Hardy helped him with the pen as
Emma had helped him with the brush. Perhaps the successful
youth felt he did not need Hardy's help. Later, alongside such
sober works as a drill manual, he wrote a preface to a new edition of Bonatus's *The Astrologer's Guide*, and a treatise *Spirit
Revealed . . . A Revelation of the Latter Days*, which contains
passages so closely similar to Emma's later religious essays
that the book must surely have been well known to her.[41]
During the First World War the Colonel also presided over the
local tribunal to examine conscientious objectors; on arriving
for each session he would remove his loaded revolver from its
holster and lay it on his desk, muzzle towards the applicant. He
died in 1930, and having quarrelled with the Rector of Lanivet
was buried in the neighbouring parish of Roche.[42] As befitted a
person of considerable local eminence, his funeral was well
attended and fully reported, but the list of mourners does not
include one relative.[43]

As if to confirm that Hardy was still *persona grata* at St
Juliot, it was on the first Sunday after their move there at the
end of August that Caddell Holder invited him to read one of
the lessons. Working as fast as he could on the serial, Hardy
made plentiful use not only of real places (discreetly disguised)
but also of real happenings that he and Emma had experienced. For the second and last time a heroine was modelled on
her appearance, and this time partly on her personality as well.
Even some of Elfride Swancourt's dialogue is based on
Emma's remarks, as Gittings has demonstrated by comparing
a fragment of a letter from Emma to Hardy (preserved only in
quotation by him) with an observation by Elfride to Knight.[44]
Much more is to be learned by comparing Emma with Elfride
than by the endless attempts to identify Hardy with either
Knight or Smith. Sometimes a poem confirms the validity of
the comparison. In the novel, when a group from the Rectory
walks to 'West Endelstow' church, 'Elfride was nowhere in
particular, yet everywhere; sometimes in front, sometimes behind, sometimes at the sides, hovering about the procession
like a butterfly'.[45] In the poem 'After a Journey' Hardy says of
Emma:

Where you will next be there's no knowing,
Facing round about me everywhere. . . .

All in all, a graceful tribute by Hardy to his fiancée, one
might think; yet even in this there were portents. Emma was
now in her thirties, but to attract the reading public Elfride had
to be made a dozen years younger. Almost at the outset of the
book we are told that 'Elfride's presence was not powerful, it
was weak. Some women can make their personality pervade
the atmosphere of a banqueting hall; Elfride's was no more
persuasive than that of a kitten.' Applied to Emma this is not
only unflattering but grossly untrue. Hardy may have denied
that he was describing her in this passage, but she must
have wondered, later if not – with the blindness of love – at the
time.

Biographers are confused in the matter of Parson Swancourt. Some maintain that he is drawn from John Gifford;
others point out that the opening chapters had already been
written when Hardy set out from London for his first meeting
with Gifford. Strong tradition in the Holder family has it that
the parson is closely founded on Caddell Holder.[46] This may
indeed be true, but there is no suggestion that the genial
Holder ever voiced the snobbish sentiments expressed by
Swancourt. These are pure John Gifford, and obviously the
outcome of Hardy's recent disastrous encounter – or possibly
near-encounter. True, the first hint of them occurs in Chapter
3, written before the disaster; but at this early stage they took
the form of a relatively harmless enthusiasm for genealogy.

The novel also offers a clue to Jemima Hardy's reaction to
her son's engagement. This occurs in the passage in which Mrs
Smith, Stephen's mother, on hearing of his intention to marry
Elfride, warns him that the girl is 'throwing herself at 'ee' and
tells him to wait a few years when he may 'go higher than a
bankrupt parson's girl'. Supporters of the belief that this
shows Emma to have 'thrown herself' at Hardy cite in evidence
a long paragraph from a letter written by Florence Hardy to
Rebekah Owen on 24 October 1915. Since the paragraph is
certainly a corrective to the rosy accounts of the Hardy–Emma
courtship given in *Some Recollections*, the *Life*, and Hardy's
poems, I quote it in full:

I cannot really believe those days in Cornwall – at St Juliot – were really so free and happy. Her [i.e. Emma's] father at that time was a bankrupt – and I hear since had been struck off the rolls – another brother had shown signs of insanity – and another was bringing the whole family into disgrace. One sister had married the old clergyman to escape the life of companion to an exacting old lady – and she was trying to marry her younger sister – the late Mrs. T.H. – to any man who would have her. They had nearly secured a farmer when T.H. appeared. And she was nearly thirty then. And the sisters had violent quarrels. Of course the whole situation has been much idealised. I expect though the poor girl liked being in the Rectory as it must have been an improvement on her truly horrible home – with the father's drunken ravings – once in Plymouth he chased the mother into the street in her nightgown.[47]

In fairness to Florence it must be stated that she wrote during a period of extreme strain and trial, when Hardy's unremitting eulogies of his first wife, often delivered in front of Florence to greatly embarrassed acquaintances, were almost more than she could endure.[48] As so often in such polemics, there is just enough truth in some of the assertions to make readers ignore the known or likely inaccuracy of others. For example, Gifford is not listed in the records as a bankrupt nor as having been struck off the rolls. Confining ourselves to the point at issue, Jemima Hardy may nevertheless have used the word 'bankrupt' in her exasperation just as Hardy made Mrs Smith use it. That she *was* exasperated is a near-certainty. The thought of her son daring to choose a wife not pre-selected by herself must have seemed an act of base treachery, particularly if she had hitherto supposed that he was just having an affair with this woman in Cornwall as he had had with so many others. Of course she accused Emma of throwing herself at Thomas! But the simple fact is that if Emma had been merely bent on bettering herself, instead of being in love, she would scarcely have committed herself to a man of Hardy's income and prospects prior to 1872. As for the Holders forcing her hand, if that had been so surely she would have been married at St Juliot, whereas in the event Helen and Caddell did not even attend her wedding.

Hardy returned to London early in September with only writing now in mind. An excellent offer of architectural work was declined and, finding the metropolis suddenly ill-suited to concentration on Cornwall, he went home to finish the serial at Higher Bockhampton. Critics who find the second half of the book (before the peremptory ending) better than the first attribute the fact to the customary beneficial effect of his home on Hardy's work. But this time it cannot have been very soothing. Whether or not he had broken the news of the engagement to his mother yet, the certainty of disapproval from one he loved and respected must have been an ever-present disturbance, and there was also John Gifford's opposition to be reflected upon at greater leisure now. If Hardy's work improved, it can only have been due to the stimulus of realising that from now on it was Emma and himself against both sets of parents – or at least against the dominant partner in each set, for Mrs Gifford's and Thomas Hardy senior's views on the engagement have never been discovered.

For Emma it was an equally difficult time. Long engagements were not uncommon in Victorian days, but a long engagement during which the prospective bride did not see her betrothed from one month's end to another, conscious all the while of her father's hostility, was somewhat less common. There were letters to be written and read, help to be given on topographical points, the parish work to do and Fanny to be exercised, but Emma's faith in her absent man is remarkable. Even if she still knew nothing of his earlier loves, she was no fool, and a man of thirty to whom London was as familiar as Boscastle to her, and who by now must have demonstrated his experience in love-making, was not calculated to reassure the mind of a distant lover.

As it happened, Hardy for once gave no grounds for anxiety. His literary fortunes continued to improve. In November 1872, *Under the Greenwood Tree* was read by Leslie Stephen, editor of the *Cornhill Magazine* and among the most esteemed men of letters of the era. Learning from Moule that Hardy was the author, he invited him to contribute a serial to the *Cornhill*. Though still only halfway through *A Pair of Blue Eyes*, Hardy could not afford to let this chance of real prestige slip by. Explaining that he could do nothing for the present, he nevertheless sent in a thematic outline of a proposed story and even gave it a title – *Far from the Madding Crowd*. If his romance with Tryphena had done nothing else for him (and it probably improved his knowledge of the ways of women), it would have justified itself by indirectly furnishing him with the basis of what was to prove his first financially successful book; for Bathsheba Everdene, though in person and character a reflection of one of Hardy's aunts, in her capacity as a woman farmer was drawn from Catherine Hawkins, widowed owner of a farm at Waddon, close to Coryates where Tryphena, on the balance of evidence, had taught in 1869.[49]

In December, Tryphena and Hardy possibly met at a family gathering, for they were both in their respective homes over Christmas. She had come up from Plymouth for the wedding of her sister Rebecca, a puzzling match that has baffled the Sparks family ever since. Not only was Rebecca more than forty, but three days after the wedding she abandoned her husband, a local saddler, and accompanied Tryphena to Plymouth, there to remain. A silly story has been invented that she was really Tryphena's mother; it is much more likely that, having her full share of peasant regard for money, she found that her new husband had less than she had supposed, and attached herself while the going was good to her only relative with a respectable income.

And a respectable income was what Hardy still needed if he were to marry without seeming to justify some of John Gifford's objections. The heady euphoria induced by Tinsley's £200 for *A Pair of Blue Eyes* was quickly modified as Hardy realised that it was one thing to have sufficient prospects on which to base an engagement, and another to be sure of enough hard cash to support a wife. In mortal fear lest Leslie Stephen lose interest in the *Madding Crowd* project, he rattled away so fast at *A Pair of Blue Eyes* that the book version, duly revised, was published before the serial had finished running. For the first time Hardy's name appeared as author. Like its predecessor, the book had a good press but indifferent sales. In June, having managed to send Stephen a little more material, Hardy went to London to show the city to his brother Henry. After Henry had left, Thomas, who had dined in London with Horace Moule, went to Cambridge where Moule was now working to see a little more of him. It was their last meeting: three months later the forty-year-old Moule, man of great talent and greater charm, but an alcoholic and a depressive, committed suicide. Their last talk together Hardy later commemorated in the poem 'Standing by the Mantelpiece', and the sight of the coffin being brought back to Fordington church he recorded in 'Before My Friend Arrived'.

Not dreaming he had seen his friend and mentor for the last time, Hardy returned from Cambridge to London and went on to Bath, where Emma was staying with her elderly friend Miss D'Arville, to whom he had been introduced at St Juliot. It was the lovers' first meeting for more than nine months. The trio explored Bath, and then Hardy seems to have gone alone with Emma to Clifton, Chepstow, Tintern and the Wye Valley. To have no chaperon was a bold undertaking even if they were now openly engaged, and is one of the many illustrations of Emma's lack of narrowmindedness in many respects. On 2 July he went home to Bockhampton, where he remained, hard at work on *Far from the Madding Crowd*. In September he attended Moule's funeral, and at the end of the month he sent Stephen the first twelve chapters of the serial, on the strength of which Stephen commissioned the rest.

Now for the first time Hardy began to experience just what editorial intervention could mean. Fortunately Stephen was brilliant at his task, and Hardy a writer who throughout his life was willing to accept suggestions. The result was that following emendations to scene after scene a far better book emerged than the one Hardy had originally written. What interests us here, however, is what Emma thought of her exclusion. She knew Hardy was at work on another novel, but no chapters came her way for copying, no requests for ideas. She was to regain her position later, but if she had known in 1873 that she was being replaced by the infinitely more accomplished Stephen it could have deprived her of the confidence to resume her help, and one of the forces that kept the marriage together until the mid-1890s would have been lost. Hardy's statement in the *Life*[50] that he told her nothing of the nature of the story in order to give her a pleasant surprise is as improbable as Gittings's suggestion that he 'felt awkward' about a brisk exchange of letters with St Juliot under the eye of his mother.[51] He had been exchanging letters and packets of manuscript ever since he was occupied with *Desperate Remedies*. Of equally scant validity is the speculation that he was reluctant to bring Emma in on the creation of a novel dealing mainly with the working-class people of his own environment. The same class of people, drawn from even closer to his home, had filled the pages of *Under the Greenwood Tree*. Hardy's motive remains obscure, but his exclusion of Emma may be added to the list of ill-omens that preceded his marriage; for it was the first sign of his capacity, destined to become so evident at Sturminster Newton, for withdrawing into the world of his current literary preoccupation at the expense of all consideration for the needs and feelings of his wife. Possibly Emma felt a presentiment of what was to come; her comment when she did at last read the serial – in print – was 'Your novel sometimes seems like a child, all your own and none of me'.[52] The presentiment would have been all the more disturbing if she had known that her supplanter was a free-thinker.

It was unfortunate that Hardy's next journey to Cornwall followed hard on his long-postponed first meeting with Stephen. The sage invited him to lunch, where he met Mrs Stephen and, more notably, her sister Anne Thackeray – the first of the 'literary ladies' who were to beguile Hardy for the rest of his days. The talk at the luncheon-table and afterwards was pitched at the highest intellectual level, and much of it was contributed by the garrulous Anne. Going immediately from this window on a new world to spend Christmas (for once) at St Juliot, Thomas must have noticed the contrast. But the effect should not be overstressed. To say only how elementary must have seemed the literary talk at the Rectory, how naïve Emma's attempts at writing, is to ignore that Hardy was in love, and delighting in it. Far from behaving disdainfully, he is likely to have been full of his latest experience, his pride in being commissioned to write by the distinguished editor and savant, of penetrating his sophisticated circle. He must surely have regaled his hosts with an account of Leslie Stephen's odd appearance and odder ways, and have responded to their inevitable excitement at his good fortune. Moreover, in the Stephen household he was a pigmy; in Caddell Holder's he was a giant. That he did not regard Emma's capabilities as entirely contemptible even beside those of the dazzling Miss Thackeray is demonstrated by his reversion to using her help for his

next novel, *The Hand of Ethelberta*, in the form of borrowing
entries from her diary (see page 86); whether she also fair-
copied this novel we do not know, since the manuscript has
been lost. He was not bound to this course. He had already
broken with one fiancée; with both pairs of parents set against
his present engagement, he could no doubt have found diplomatic means of breaking with another. Instead, with whatever
consequences to them both, he stood by her and eventually
drew her with him into those literary salons that were as far removed from the drawing-room at St Juliot as from the parlour
at Higher Bockhampton.

Nevertheless, however loyal his conduct at this time – and it
is loyalty for which he is seldom given credit – it was founded
on yet another illusion. He might enthuse to Emma about his
new world, but unless he was deliberately smothering a doubt
his belief that his entry into the topmost literary circle would
leave their relationship unaffected shows that it was his turn to
be naïve. Whether in this she was more discerning than he,
whether it crossed her mind that his latest experience, like the
book that had occasioned it, was all of him and none of her, we
cannot tell, because in any case love and loyalty would have
smothered the thought.

He went home on New Year's Eve 1873–4, and on the way
saw a copy of the *Cornhill* containing the first instalment of *Far
from the Madding Crowd* on the same Plymouth station bookstall on which he had seen the remaindered *Desperate Remedies*. He was surprised and fascinated to notice that the
illustrator was a woman, Helen Paterson, and even more surprised by the accuracy of her rendering of an area of life with
which she would normally have no contact. He spent the first
half of 1874 working industriously at Bockhampton, his mind
now bent on marriage before the year ended, while in March
Emma entered her fifth year of waiting for her 'destiny' to
fulfil itself.[53] Periodically he emerged to meet the Stephens,
and by degrees met other members of the *haut monde* of letters, including, in May, his illustrator Miss Paterson. She, too,
was shortly to be married, and it was typical of Hardy's inability to meet any attractive woman without mentally associ-
ating himself with her in a kind of Ethel M. Dell romance that
in 1906 he wrote to Edmund Gosse suggesting that 'but for a

stupid blunder of God Almighty' he would have married Helen instead of Emma.[54] He also composed a poem, 'The Opportunity (For H. P.)', with the same theme. In fact he and Miss Paterson met just once.

On 17 September 1874 he did marry Emma, at last, in St Peter's Church, Paddington. Two members of her family were present, none of his.

CHAPTER FOUR

St Peter's, Paddington, to Max Gate

NONE OF THE FOUR PARENTS was present at the wedding, only one of the seven brothers and sisters. The ceremony was performed by Emma's uncle, Canon Edwin Hamilton Gifford, at the time Rector of Walgrave in Northamptonshire, Honorary Canon of Worcester and St Albans, and Examining Chaplain to the Bishop of London. He had himself been married for the second time in 1873. This was the uncle who ten years later was to become Archdeacon of London and Prebendary of St Paul's, and to whom Emma was so often proudly to refer as a counterweight to her ungodly husband. Canon Gifford at least seems to have felt no reservations about the match, to judge from the friendliness of his letters agreeing to officiate.[1] The other relative present was Emma's youngest brother Walter, with whom she had been staying to establish residential qualification; he gave her away and signed the register, the second witness being the daughter of Hardy's landlady.

Many theories have been advanced as to why the wedding was in London and why the two families almost boycotted it. Conceivably Emma thought St Juliot too near Bodmin and feared an interruption by an enraged father in the proper style of Victorian melodrama; perhaps she simply did not wish to expose the Holders to recriminations from Kirland, even persuading them against attending the wedding in London. On Hardy's side the absence of support is harder to understand: surely his beloved Mary – quite used to visiting London on her own – should have attended, and apart from the family there

85

were his London friends and former colleagues, though his natural diffidence probably kept him from informing any of these. The bridal pair's own accounts are worse than laconic. Although Emma considered the wedding to be the point towards which God had been guiding her throughout her thirty-four years, her only comment on it is to praise the weather; and Hardy allocates just two sentences of the *Life* to cover wedding, honeymoon, and installation in their first home.

They spent the wedding night at the Palace Hotel, Queensway, and the next day moved on to Brighton where Hardy wrote, briefly, in pencil, and on a half-sheet of note-paper, not to his mother or to Mary but to his brother Henry, to inform the family that the wedding had been performed and that he had sent off an announcement to the *Dorset County Chronicle*. He even denied, in effect, that a honeymoon was taking place at all, adding to his laconic wedding information 'I' (not we) 'am going to Paris for materials for my next story' (*The Hand of Ethelberta*).² Fortunately from among the vast number of documents lost or destroyed Emma's honeymoon diary has survived. It is simple, refreshingly enthusiastic, packed with sharply observed details, and amusingly illus-trated with mostly postage-stamp-sized drawings. In Brighton they attended concerts together – something they never relin-quished throughout the darkest days to come – went to church, and Emma found herself fascinated, as so many have been, by the famous Aquarium. Hardy bathed in a rough sea, and it was still rough when they crossed to Dieppe. But by the time they reached Rouen she had recovered from an unpleasant dose of seasickness sufficiently to take a deep interest in the first evening's dinner menu at the Hôtel d'Albion. Later the cham-bermaid, with the indifference of French chambermaids to what might be going on in a honeymoon bedroom, entered without knocking, to find them both at desks writing.

From Rouen they continued to Paris, which they first saw by moonlight and, as the days passed, proceeded to explore with presumably, on Hardy's part, less of an eye to what might interest his bride than to what might be useful for the new book. Emma's sketches never included herself, so that when she says that whether by day or by night everyone gazed at her and adds 'Query – Am I a strange-looking person – or merely picturesque in this hat – Women sometimes laugh a short laugh as they pass. Men stare; some stand, look back . . . look curiously, inquisitively – some tenderly . . . Children gape too,' we are left tantalisingly unable to judge, even from a thumb-nail sketch, whether all the attention was justified. Charac-teristically, the diary contains many allusions to children, one compliment to Paris cats, and a reference to 'little birds dust-ing themselves' round her stone bench in the Tuileries Gar-dens. The voyage home was again rough, and Emma was again seasick. How Tom fared on either voyage she does not say; for a wife on honeymoon she says very little about Tom.

But she says more than he. In those two sentences in the *Life* Paris is not even mentioned. Norman Page, in an interesting article on Emma's travel diaries,[3] suggests that Hardy's silence is due to embarrassment 'in view of the later fortunes of the marriage', but there could be a more immediate reason: sexual difficulties. Unlike many unfortunate Victorian brides, Emma, as we know, must have had some idea of what to expect in bed, even if her mother had been too saintly to tell her and her sister too frustrated; and Hardy was a very long way from the inexperienced John Ruskin, who thought his wife was deformed because she had pubic hair. But many factors can prevent sexual accord. The poem 'Honeymoon Time at an Inn' gives a possible hint of something amiss at Rouen. The open-ing stanzas run:

At the shiver of morning, a little before the false dawn,
    The moon was at the window-square,
    Deedily brooding in deformed decay –
    The curve hewn off her cheek as by an adze;
At the shiver of morning a little before the false dawn
    So the moon looked in there.

Her speechless eyeing reached across the chamber,
    Where lay two souls opprest,
    One a white lady sighing, 'Why am I sad!'
    To him who sighed back, 'Sad, my Love, am I!'
And speechlessly the old moon conned the chamber,
    And these two reft of rest.

The poem then describes the fall of an old mirror from the mantel and how, as the bridegroom tried to dissuade the bride from picking up the pieces, she voiced her dismay at the ill portent, a portent which the Spirits confirmed. But the first two stanzas describe the feelings of the couple in bed *before* the mirror fell. Phelps has taken the trouble to ascertain that while the Hardys were in Rouen the moon's phase was such that its appearance and time of passage would have been exactly as set forth in the poem.[4] There may be allusions to sexual difficulty in other poems, too darkly wrapped for anyone to have yet interpreted them.

Emma's diary offers no inference of dismay or disillusion on this score, but humiliation (if the shortcoming were hers), loyalty (if it were Hardy's), and in either case general delicacy, would all have prevented her.

They returned to London on 1 October. After Paris it struck Emma as dirty, an impression enhanced by the heavy rain. She had liked Paris. In spite of a sturdy Protestant disparagement, in the diary, of the French priests 'whose age can be known by their harshness and closeness of expression, like concealed, concentrated wickedness, like liquid become a hard substance', she liked the capital, as she liked France, with an affection that was never to diminish. After the carefree days of sightseeing, the plod round London's south-western suburbs in search of lodgings would have depressed anyone. At last they installed themselves at St David's Villa, Hook Road, Surbiton, an address calculated to prolong the depression. Hardly were they settled in than they were called upon by Emma's father, an astonishing event after his absence from the wedding. How the visit went is something we should much like to know, but to his dying day he never repeated it. It can surely not have taken place after he had written his notorious letter (if he did write it: we have only the word of Florence Hardy,[5] never at her most reliable when treating of the Giffords) calling Hardy that low-born churl who has dared to marry into *my* family', so perhaps it was at Surbiton rather than at Bodmin that something occurred to occasion this step which he must have known would virtually cut him off from the Hardys for ever. Yet it is surprising that Emma's mother never managed to sneak away for a brief reunion with her daughter, and more surprising that they were never visited by the Holders nor went again to St Juliot. What happened to change Caddell and Helen from being still happy to receive Hardy on three more occasions after the scene at 'Rou'tor Town' to boycotting the wedding and never again having personal contact with the pair until Emma went, alone, to see Helen about the time of Caddell's death in 1882? As to the withdrawal of the Gifford parents, it has not been noticed that this was the second time in three generations that such an event had occurred in Hardy's innermost circle: Jemima's maternal grandfather had similarly declined to have anything further to do with his daughter after she, too, had 'married beneath her'.

John Gifford did bring one visitor, if not his wife, to Surbiton: Annie, the small daughter of Emma's cousin Robert William Gifford Watson, who was overseas in his capacity as Governor of Lagos. If it be true that the honeymoon had shown up sex difficulties, the newlyweds must have wondered anxiously, as they made the little girl welcome, whether they would know the joy of parenthood themselves. In November, *Far from the Madding Crowd* was published as a two-volume novel, and except for a catty outburst by Henry James in the New York *Nation* (the book had come out simultaneously in America) attracted good reviews, followed this time by rapidly mounting sales. It also attracted a letter from Julia Augusta Martin which, Hardy being Hardy, 'revived throbs of tender feeling in him, and brought back to his memory the thrilling "frou-frou" of her four grey silk flounces when she had used to bend over him, and when they brushed against the font as she entered church on Sundays'.[6] One hopes that Emma's skirts, as she moved through the leaden respectability of Surbiton, produced an equally alluring sound.

Early in December Leslie Stephen, duly encouraged, asked for another serial for the *Cornhill*. Hardy was in a quandary. He did not wish to become type-cast as a writer about rustics, which some of the reviewers clearly already considered him, yet as a married man dependent on his pen he had for the first time to give serious consideration to pleasing a wide public. Anne Thackeray thought he should resume and extend his contacts with London society. Emma, enjoying her position as the wife of a really popular novelist, thought so too. A complete veil is drawn over their activities during their five and a half months at Surbiton. We do not even know how or where they spent Christmas; it is improbable that he had introduced Emma at Higher Bockhampton yet, although in another half-dozen years his sister Kate was to write to them both as though Emma had been a member of the family for decades.[7]

In March 1875 he took the plunge, moving their little household to Newton Road, Westbourne Grove, an area already familiar to him, much closer to the West End; and in the same month he offered Stephen the opening gambits of *The Hand of Ethelberta, A Comedy in Chapters*. A comedy it may be, but the theme, in a nutshell, is the concealment of humble class-background by a writer (in this case a woman) eager to make progress. Having used up the Bockhampton characters familiar to him, plus Tryphena, he now based his 'downstairs' characters on the Sparks family and much of his below-stairs 'copy' on what he had learned from Martha.[8] Ethelberta herself, in appearance, is a kind of Emma–Tryphena fusion. Following his wont, he saved time and mental energy by utilising his own experiences, including those of his honeymoon, in some instances drawing, as already remarked, on Emma's diary. Thus for this novel she furnished help in yet another guise.

They spent only three months at Westbourne Grove, long enough, Hardy felt, to give him the background for the London chapters of *Ethelberta*: not the background already familiar through his London years as an architect, but the world brought close by his association with the Stephens – the world of high society. At the end of the third month they warehoused their possessions – contained in four packing-cases, of which two and part of a third held books – and betook themselves to Swanage, the next area involved in the novel. On the way they paused for three days at Bournemouth, where Hardy composed a poem into which more has been misread than into any other written by him. 'We Sat at the Window' relates how 'we' – Emma and he – confined to their lodgings by pouring rain, bereft of books or other diversions, sat disconsolately gazing out of the window. This is the last stanza:

We were irked by the scene, by our own selves; yes,
For I did not know, nor did she infer
How much there was to read and guess
By her in me, and to see and crown
　　By me in her.
Wasted were two souls in their prime,
And great was the waste, that July time
　　When the rain came down.

This is invariably interpreted to mean that already the marriage was beginning to pall, the differences between husband and wife to distort the harmony of St Juliot and Paris. But it does not require great insight into human nature, nor any rare degree of personal experience, to know that in the happiest of love-affairs there comes a moment, sometimes only to one lover at a time, but more often to both at once, when suddenly everything seems flat, lustreless, love a mockery, the partner an unglamorous, even not very likeable person, the whole world as sour as vinegar. The moment passes, affection returns, tinged perhaps with a little sadness at the realisation that such lapses can occur in paradise, but with the sadness offset by a slightly deeper understanding.

No circumstances are likelier to precipitate this transient mood of disillusionment than a wet day away from home, deprived of every comforting possession. It is hardly surprising that Emma and Thomas were 'irked . . . by our own selves' (the manuscript more accurately reads 'irked . . . by each other'), but far from chronicling the first perception of incompatibility Hardy regrets that the opportunity was not taken to realise how much each inwardly held for the other. He was probably 'edgy' on that day of rain; he had not particularly enjoyed his first encounter with high society, yet he expected that his reading public would look to him to continue writing about it. There was also the problem, familiar to every author, of reconciling time spent in essential human contact with time spent in writing. But he still thought enough of Emma for what he was to call 'their happiest time' (even if it was primarily *his* happiest) to lie ahead, and she was still happy enough at Swanage to embark on a short novel or novella of her own.

They found lodgings, which they were to occupy for ten

months, in West End Cottage, on the hillside towards the back of the town as it then was. The owner was Captain Masters (the 'Captain Flower' of *Ethelberta*), first coxswain of the Swanage lifeboat and, although Hardy may not have realised it until too late, a distant family connection. John Hardy of Puddletown, the author's great-grandfather, had two sons, John and Thomas. From the latter descended the Hardys with whom we are concerned, from the former the many Hardys who still inhabit Swanage. Of one of these, Mr A. G. L. Hardy, Captain Masters was the great-uncle.[9] So hyper-sensitive was Thomas Hardy at this time to the niceties of class, had he known in advance of the distant kinship he would probably have sought rooms elsewhere; for Masters himself was no doubt quite aware of it, and can have seen no reason for not drawing Hardy's attention to the bond. Possibly it was this revelation that made Hardy decide the time had come to present Emma to his family. Typically, he makes no mention of the important event in the *Life*, but from Emma's diary we learn of a picnic at Corfe Castle (not until September, although the move to Swanage had been made in July), at which were present herself, Thomas, and his two sisters Mary and Kate. Apparently the meeting went off very well, Emma describing it as 'a splendid day'. The sisters' opinion is not on record, but from the cordiality of their subsequent letters they evidently liked Emma. Nor is there any record of Emma's first meeting with Hardy's parents.

While Hardy spent the months writing his novel, Emma tried her own hand at fiction in 'The Maid on the Shore', which Hardy-writers insist on calling a novel although it is no longer than a number of his short stories. 'The Maid' shows most of the faults common to the novice, although in judging, for example, the sugar-and-water language used to describe the heroine it should be remembered that a century ago magazines were full of such stuff. The story is also strongly derivative from *A Pair of Blue Eyes*. Yet it is not without its merits, and it is to Hardy's discredit that whereas he was ready in later years to help the no less immature efforts of other women aspirants, including Florence, he never acknowledged Emma's help by offering her the smallest literary assistance. It was left for Florence herself, when she first knew Emma, to attempt to place

'The Maid on the Shore' for her; and Florence's motives were by no means disinterested. If Hardy had applied a fraction of the editorial improvements to this tale that he exercised on Florence's books for children, Emma might have seen it in print. A single quotation will serve to show at one and the same time Emma's notable power of description and the minor stylistic and syntactical gaucheries that Hardy's experienced hand could have so easily have corrected:

They went long drives together, the roads were monotonous when giving no glimpse of the neighbourhood it is true; there were no buildings whatever, save occasional Dissenting chapels. Sometimes they passed through a poor hamlet, where miserable cottages and dirty yet healthy children might be seen. It was a relief when they drove through a village with a church, always in these parts called in addition to its name, church-town. No trees hid the scarcely cultivated lands; low hedges were protected by notched slates set on end, for the prevention of half starved sheep straying from the stony fields; dreary interminable roads they were, stretching for miles until stopped abruptly by a vast straggling, bleak moorland, where a broad track passed as a roadway through it; far away pools glistening, and locally prized hills giving distant beauty. Over all the exhilarating compensating North coast summer air blew, usually with a touch of keenness in its softness here on the moorland, turning to biting bitterness in the winter season. Occasionally there were beautiful glimpses of the sea at turnings of the road.

Alas, there is little in either the novella or the diary to indicate Emma's personal feelings in 1875. She made a number of sketches, including one of Masters in his boat (not the life-boat), recorded a pleasant steamer-trip, and described the environs of Swanage in her customary evocative manner. But after her account of the picnic and scenery at Corfe the diary peters out. In the *Life*, after repeating one or two of the Captain's anecdotes Hardy confines himself to remarking that they walked daily on the cliffs (no pony here, it seems, for the periodically lame Emma) and on the shore, and listened to the contrasting sounds of the sea breaking on Durlston Head and a thrush singing. In the poem 'Once at Swanage' he describes a rough sea they watched by moonlight, standing hand-in-hand.

The spray sprang up across the cusps of the moon,
 And all its light loomed green
 As a witch-flame's weirdsome sheen
At the minute of an incantation scene;
And it greened our gaze – that night at demilune.

Roaring high and roaring low was the sea
 Behind the headland shores:
 It symboled the slamming of doors,
Or a regiment hurrying over hollow floors. . . .
And there we two stood, hands clasped; I and she!

 Bailey sees in the poem a 'sinister symbolism', the last line suggesting the couple united against some unknown threat to their happiness, one day to be realised in Emma's 'delusions'.[10] Maybe, but to me this seems a typical case of reading far too much into some of Hardy's poems. Is the poet never to be allowed to mean exactly what he says and no more? The moon, Bailey points out, is always a sinister symbol to Hardy. So it is, but greenish moonlight on a stormy sea is a sinister sight to most of us, and as for standing united against the threat of future madness, a simpler explanation of the hand-in-hand attitude is that the married couple were still sufficiently in accord to react to the awe-inspiring scene with this common and spontaneous gesture.

 A little further light on the Swanage period comes from the account of a return visit made by the Hardys with their new American friends Catharine and Rebekah Owen in September 1892. The occasion was a meeting at Swanage of the Dorset Field Club, of which Hardy was a member and therefore absent from his guests most of the time, leaving them to his wife to entertain. Emma talked freely to Rebekah about her stay in Swanage – the inference being, though Rebekah does not say so, that she regarded it as a happy time, but disliked talking about *The Hand of Ethelberta* because it had 'too much about servants in it'. They visited West End Cottage, still occupied by the Captain's widow, of whom Emma observed that she stole, but was 'fairly pleasant' while the Hardys were in residence. Emma confided that she felt frequent impulses to record her impressions of places, as she felt many fancies

94

thronging her brain, but could not find the energy to commit her impressions to paper.

Although the insight it affords us into Hardy's mind, particularly on the class question, makes *Ethelberta* of great interest to the modern student, the tale was not a success. Emma was not the only reader to find 'too much about servants in it'; others resented the abandonment of the pastoral atmosphere; others again noted Hardy's inability to write about salon society with the conviction that he brought to village life. The book version completed, the Hardys moved in March 1876 from Swanage to Yeovil, itself in Somerset but a good centre for house-hunting in north Dorset. Unsuccessful in this, in May they rather suddenly went abroad again, this time to Holland, up the Rhine into Baden and the Black Forest, then back via Strasbourg and Metz to Brussels and Antwerp, whence they crossed to Harwich on yet another rough sea. Once more Emma's travel diary has been preserved, for the plain reason that she turned her honeymoon diary back to front and used the spare pages. The frugality learned at Bodmin died hard.

The most interesting aspect of this second travel chronicle is not the expected succession of sharp observations and explanatory drawings, nor even the pointed reference again to babies, but the hints that Hardy was not always the perfect travelling-companion. There was an incident at Cologne when he lost his temper over a brandy-flask, no mention of sympathy when she was 'very weak and ill with an ulcerated throat' at Strasbourg, and – the most significant – she had barely had time to recover from that ailment when he submitted her to an ordeal that would have tested the strength of a woman in full health and untroubled by lameness. The occasion was his wish to make a thorough examination of the field of Waterloo, and it is illuminating to give her account of the day in some detail.

At Brussels they took a tram to the station, then a train to Waterloo. Here they walked a mile to the Hôtel du Musée, climbed the steps of the Lion Mount to survey the battlefield, lunched, looked round the museum, and set out on foot for Hougomont where they inspected the kitchens and chapel. From Hougomont they walked to La Belle Alliance, then to La Haye Sainte to look over the farmhouse room by room. Here they were given some 'light cake' and a child gave Emma some flowers, after which they walked back through Mont Saint Jean and Waterloo. For good measure they inspected the Hôtel des Colonnes in which Victor Hugo finished writing *Les Misérables*. Finally they had a long walk back to the station for the Brussels train. 'These villages', Emma wrote, 'very long and roughly paved.'

She experienced 'great fatigue', which not surprisingly persisted the next day, 'and Tom was cross about it'; so cross, in fact, that he dragged her off on a tour of a lace-making factory, walking there and back, followed by a drive round the city. His insensitivity on this occasion, though it involved a more physical matter, was of exactly the same type that later made him ignore her loneliness at Sturminster Newton, spurn her in favour of other women, publish poems about his early love-affairs, and show no appreciation of her literary help. It was not intentional cruelty; he would have been shocked (as after her death he *was* shocked) to realise that he was being cruel at all. It was rather as though all his perceptiveness, his finesse were reserved for the characters in his novels. 'He understands only the women he *invents* – the others not at all,' Emma was to write to a friend nearly twenty years after her private Battle of Waterloo.[11] In her bitterness she exaggerated, but not by much.

Despite her fatigue in Brussels, she made her usual careful notes on what she saw, and it is worth remarking that she describes religious paintings, even those wholly Roman Catholic in theme, without prejudice. As in her appreciation of Continental church architecture, she confined her strictures to those who officiated in the buildings. Yet the acrid flavour of the latter stages of the holiday persisted, for at the end of it she wrote: 'Going back to England where we have no home and no chosen county.' Hardy probably felt the truth of this himself, the more so as his family had begun to make unflattering comments on the couple 'wandering about like two tramps'.[12] For both of them, in fact, the Bohemian existence that at St Juliot Emma had deemed proper for a romantic author and his consort had palled badly, not helped by the poor showing of *Ethelberta* after *Far from the Madding Crowd*. Moreover, Hardy, the largely self-taught, felt a desire to stoke up the educational fires and brew himself a further mess of intellectual pottage, for which a settled home was the best environment.

Fortunately they had been back at Yeovil less than a fortnight when he heard of a pleasant unfurnished house to let at Sturminster Newton, a comely townlet on a hill above the Dorset Stour. He took it immediately, and they rushed off to buy furniture at Bristol, spending a hundred pounds in two hours. (This, on the heels of a Continental holiday, is an indication of the profit *Far from the Madding Crowd* had brought its author.) Riverside Villa occupied, and still occupies, a pleasant site at the top of the gentle descent to the river, on the bank of which it had its own boathouse. The villa, with its cheerful barge-boards, is complacent and comfortable-looking rather than beautiful, but it must have seemed exquisite to the nomads. Not only was it their first real home, but also the first place in which the longed-for birth of a baby would not have been tempered by anxiety for its welfare amid hired furniture and an all too likely atmosphere of hostility: lodging-house owners are not noted for welcoming babies. The Hardys must have known, too, that the removal of these disadvantages had come at something near the eleventh hour; when they moved in Emma was well into her thirty-sixth year. Sturminster provided virtually the first and last opportunity, and Hardy's already-quoted comment on their servant's expected baby, 'Yet never a sign is there of one for us', must be taken in this context.

Denuded of the aura with which Hardy's term 'idyll' has invested it, the Sturminster period was really one of contrasts. Against Hardy's well-known afterthought addition to his diary, 'Our happiest time', should be set the neglected sentence a few pages earlier in the *Life*: 'It was their first house and, though small, *probably* that in which they spent their happiest days' (my italics).[13] Unlike the other, this is not a diary quotation, and it is as though, with maturer reflection over the years after the diary entry and even the interpolation were penned, Hardy had realised that the skies were not always halcyon above the Vale of Blackmore that spread beyond the Stour outside the villa windows.

On the credit side there were the novelty of having a home, the hope that it might see the coming of a baby, the pleasantness of the countryside and small but active market-town, and the greater pleasantness of its social life into which the

Hardys appear to have been warmly received. The leading family, the Dashwoods, owners of most of Sturminster and many other properties, welcomed the newcomers to their exquisite seventeenth-century home, Vine House, where they met the Dashwoods' relatives the Warrys and Knowleses, and many friends. Here was a new kind of society for Emma to enjoy, neither the London high society of recent discovery nor the large-town society of Plymouth, but the leading social element of a small country-town. Her Continental diary, like its predecessor, peters out soon after the return to England, but we can learn a little of how the days passed from the *Life*, and a little more from correspondence. Hardy informs us that they rowed on the Stour almost as soon as they had arrived, surprised their maid (the one who was to have the baby) with her lover but failed to prevent her running away, visited an unnamed lady at Stalbridge, had the Dashwoods to tea, attended a concert, watched games and dancing on the green, and finally enjoyed the hospitality of Vine House for their last night before they left Sturminster for London. The most important revelation, however, is of something that did not take place at Sturminster, namely that they spent Christmas 1876 at Higher Bockhampton. This is the first mention of a meeting between Hardy's parents and their daughter-in-law. Perhaps it was in fact the first, perhaps Hardy had profited by the success of the Corfe Castle picnic to brace himself for an earlier introduction.

From the surviving handful of letters written by Mrs Dashwood – also an Emma – to Emma Hardy after the Hardys had left the district, all dated between 1878 and 1883, it is deducible that our Emma rarely acquired so congenial a friend.[14] Mrs Dashwood expressed deep interest not only in Hardy's work but in Emma's writing ambitions too; she received magazines from her, and issued repeated invitations to the Hardys to revisit Sturminster, which she referred to as 'this gay city'; and from her manner of discussing the marriages, travels and other interests of her relatives she must have made Emma feel herself one of them. But possibly the greatest bond between them was painting. Emma Dashwood's maiden name was Knowles, and there is in the possession of the Knowleses today a copy of a rare printing of the poem usually known as 'Stanzas Written in

Richmond Churchyard' by their forebear Herbert Knowles, who died in 1817, aged nineteen. The poem, here called 'Laura', extends over forty-nine pages, the wide margins of which are exquisitely illuminated with flowers, landscapes, animals and human figures, painted in very rich colours by Emma Dashwood.

Yet there is no evidence that the Hardys ever did return to Vine House, nor the Dashwoods fulfil their intention of visiting the Hardys. Like the Serjeants and (in later years) Emma's great friend and confidant Alfred Pretor, the Dashwoods died or disappeared with no direct heirs. There are still family papers with the Warrys and Knowleses, but none bearing on the Hardys' brief time at Sturminster, nor is there any trace of the 'illumined album' that Emma Dashwood was given soon after they left and for which she requested their photograph.

Yet, in spite of the agreeableness of Sturminster and the warm friendships made there, a less 'idyllic' side to Emma's life existed. The question of money, of which there seemed to be no lack at the time of the furniture-buying, suddenly became insistent. Ever since finishing *Ethelberta* Hardy, with ample help from Emma, had been carrying out his intention of studying and note-taking. No further novel was planned or commissioned. Not until January, inspired by the Christmas visit to his native heath, did he decide on a book of which the hero should be the Heath itself, the other characters' lives to be lived amid it and dominated by it: in short, *The Return of the Native*. But after *Ethelberta* editors, including Stephen, were chary, and it was November 1877 before the story was accepted by Chatto & Windus for their magazine *Belgravia*. By a piece of tardy good fortune Hardy also placed it with Harper of America, a firm that was to serve him well for many years. However, during more than a twelvemonth it must have appeared to Emma that after their brief taste of mild affluence they were about to slip back into the straits that had so delayed their marriage.

To sharpen her anxiety she had (notwithstanding the Dashwoods) much loneliness to bear. Briefly though the period is covered, Hardy records a significant number of activities pursued without her: a walk to Marnhull (the future 'Marlott' of *Tess*), a brief excursion to London, a visit to Shroton Fair, during the return from which he probably caused her great alarm by getting lost in the fog, a short stay in Bath with his father, who wanted to try the waters for his rheumatism, a drive with the coroner to an inquest in another village. And these were only the highlights of his expeditions on his own, as the poem 'The Musical Box' shows. In this he returns at dusk from a walk by himself (one of many such is implied) to find Emma waiting for him in the porch 'with high expectant heart'. But inside the house a 'mindless' musical box is playing, and as he hears her welcoming laugh he ignores its 'thin mechanic air', in such contrast (though this the poem does not say) to other evenings when she had played and sung living music.

> Lifelong to be
> I thought it. That there watched hard by
> A spirit who sang to the indoor tune,
> 'O make the most of what is nigh!'
> I did not hear in my dull soul-swoon –
> I did not see.

What he did not hear and did not see was that not only his many expeditions alone, but also his preoccupation with his inner world, were not the most tactful or affectionate formula for preserving his wife's happiness. In 'Overlooking the River Stour' he realises, with hindsight, that in his rapt concentration on the beauties of nature spread out before the villa, even though he but saw them through the window during rain, it never occurred to him that behind him there was something else deserving of his attention, in the person of his wife.

> And never I turned my head, alack,
> While these things met my gaze
> Through the pane's drop-drenched glaze,
> To see the more behind my back. . . .
> O never I turned, but let, alack,
> These less things hold my gaze!

The friendly circle at Sturminster might offer much entertainment, but a wife so lately wed, enjoying the wonder of her first real home, wants to feel the nearness of her husband. Yet

Hardy went on moving in his private dream-world, and for one evening when

> . . . two sit happy and half in the dark:
> They read, helped out by a frail-wick'd gleam,
>   Some rhythmic text. . . .[15]

there must have been many when he shut himself away, physically or spiritually, and the gleam in Emma's heart was frail-wick'd indeed. He might write, also of this time,

> And beneath the roof is she who in the dark world shows
>   As a lattice-gleam when midnight moans[16]

– but too often he failed to treat the gleam as one that beckoned. Nor could the new novel, 'the most pagan of all Hardy's books' in Evelyn Hardy's phrase, have given Emma much comfort. Despite Hardy's willing churchgoing, by now she must surely have been aware of his agnosticism, and here was a book that not only expressed revolt against the Christian ethic but emphasised the superior force and durability of Nature's unchristian, pre-Christian powers. At this stage of their marriage, when the pair should have been exerting their greatest effort towards imaginative understanding, learning to tighten the bonds that united them so that the divisive barriers should be compressed as nearly as possible into non-existence, above all learning to find consolation in one another for the absence of a child, the preoccupied Hardy did not grasp the need, nor the danger of ignoring it. 'The Sturminster Idyll. Our happiest time.' He really believed it.

Perhaps Emma too failed to grasp that authors under pressure – as Hardy certainly was – tend to put in longer hours than men who, once they have left their place of work at the end of the day, are cut off from it until the following morning; but once novel-writing had superseded note-taking he seems to have given her little to do. Only seven pages of *The Return of the Native* manuscript are in her hand;[17] its setting was such that he had no need of her research; he had come to a halt in his compilation of philosophical and other data; and on the leisure side there was little to occupy her when not seeing her friends, for there is no indication that any of the Sturminster households lent her a horse to replace the undoubtedly much-missed Fanny, nor that one could be hired.[18]

One of the sparse entries in her 'second honeymoon' diary records that Riverside Villa was visited once by her brothers Willie and Walter, but no testimony exists to a return visit by Hardy's family. The obvious conclusion is that the Christmas at Bockhampton had not been a success; on the other hand, after Thomas and Emma had left Sturminster for Tooting the *Life* records a cordial message for New Year 1879 from the Hardy parents, with hope of an early meeting, which took place – although not until the following August – when Thomas and Emma went to stay at the cottage and made excursions with Jemima to 'Portland, Upwey etc.' Finally there are Mary's and Kate's very friendly letters of the early 1880s, including one from Kate in March 1881 on behalf of Jemima who 'would like to have come as she says she wants to see you again' – the letter is addressed to Emma and Thomas jointly – and advising them both not to enter the sea or go boating (this was just after Hardy had had a serious illness), since they 'would be much safer on Rainbarrows or Carstairs'. That is to say, Jemima advises a further stay at Bockhampton rather than convalescence by the sea. The impression is of uninterrupted good relations until at the earliest well into 1881.

The move to The Larches, 1 Arundel Terrace, Trinity Road – now simply 172 Trinity Road – in the Wandsworth Common area of Tooting, south London, took place in the third week of March 1878. Several reasons have been advanced for the Hardys' departure from Sturminster. One tale is that Emma urged the step because she felt she cut a better figure in London: hardly probable, since Emma in London had been no one, but in Sturminster the Dashwoods and others made her one of the top social circle. Irene Cooper Willis, who quotes the ever-suspect Florence Hardy for this information, states that Florence linked it with an alleged comment by Emma's brothers that Sturminster was so out-of-the-way that the sight of a strange bird on the lawn was an event.[19] Again hardly probable; it was not events that were lacking for Emma, but the companionship and full attention – at least sometimes – of her husband. As for the bird, to a bird-lover such as she the sight of a strange species *is* an event. The truth is that, if Hardy wished to make progress, a London base had become necessary, or so it seemed; he would have moved from Higher Bockhampton in just the same way. In other respects he was probably sorry to leave the congenial Stourside town. Emma was no doubt sorry, too; she can have had little hope that London life could bring Thomas any closer. In the poem 'The Second Visit', composed near the end of his life and recalling a visit to Sturminster in 1916, he speaks of everything at the old watermill being the same as of yore yet different, including a woman standing on the bridge who was not 'the woman who to fond plaints replied, "You know I do!"' In other words, complacent and unsuspecting, he had been wont to ask Emma 'Do you love me?' as though nothing were amiss, and she had answered 'You know I do!' But there can have been no complacency about her assurance.

Their new home was a sad falling-off from the standards of its comfortable predecessor. It stood at the northern end of the terrace, exposed to the north and east winds so that in summer the rain blew in through the door-cracks and in winter snow carpeted the entrance-passage and covered the window-sill plants 'as if out-of-doors'.[20] Hardy later commemorated this unweatherworthiness in the poem 'A January Night (1879)', adding to his note on the subject in the *Life* the comment that he and Emma felt 'there had past away a glory from the earth'. Emma must have recalled a very different end-house of a row, 9 Bedford Terrace, Plymouth. Nor was Tooting, even in its less seedy days, the district to inspire a socially conscious woman. The trouble with west London south of the Thames is that apart from a few 'better' areas it has absolutely no personality, whereas south-east London exudes personality from even its seamiest districts.

The main compensation was the proximity, in a house called Knapdale, of Hardy's friend and counsellor Arthur Macmillan, to whose household Emma was quickly introduced. Knapdale was in one of the 'better' areas, facing the northern edge of Tooting Bec Common, and its large rooms, wide lawns and impressive trees perhaps made some compensation for the loss of the Dashwoods' far older and lovelier house in Sturminster. Yet once again there is no evidence that the Macmillans, any more than the Dashwoods, procured Emma facilities for riding, although the Common, then as now, abounded in riders. Because of her lameness it is improbable that she could walk much, or dance, or play any game more energetic than the croquet available on the Macmillans' lawn. No wonder she put on weight.

In a remarkably short time Hardy was dining with publishers, hobnobbing with literary celebrities, joining the Savile Club, in his own words 'by degrees [falling] into line as a London man again'.[21] Sometimes Emma accompanied him, but many of the gatherings were for men only, and she was left much alone. It is indicative of Hardy's strange blindness at times that even after her death, when he was jolted into remorse for the many ways in which he felt he had treated her unfeelingly, never in the *Life* nor in verse, including the purely egoistic Sturminster poems already quoted, did he express concern about the effect on her of the lack of his companionship. Her harsher critics say that he could no longer endure her company; but in the Tooting as in the Sturminster days this is belied by the number of events they *did* share, not all of them because they were obliged to.

By far the most important of these was the visit in August 1879 to Bockhampton.[22] Hardy went first, Emma followed a week later. After a few days they took lodgings in Weymouth (Hardy was still gathering *Trumpet-Major* material), where Jemima visited them and drove with them to some of the places Hardy needed to see. The association of the two Mrs Hardys is itself interesting, but much more so is what may have happened at Weymouth in one interpretation of the poem 'She Charged Me'.

She charged me with having said this and that
To another woman long years before,
In the very parlour where we sat, –

Sat on a night when the endless pour
Of rain on the roof and the road below
Bent the spring of the spirit more and more. . . .

– So charged she me; and the Cupid's bow

Of her mouth was hard, and her eyes, and her face,
And her white forefinger lifted slow.

Had she done it gently, or shown a trace
That not too curiously would she view
A folly flown ere her reign had place,

A kiss might have closed it. But I knew
From the fall of each word, and the pause between,
That the curtain would drop upon us two
Ere long, in our play of slave and queen.

Critics differ on whether the scene is Weymouth or the woman of long years before Tryphena, but they all agree that the accuser is Emma, although her mouth was not, unless when taut in anger, a Cupid's bow. In all respects but this the poem strongly suggests that it refers to Emma learning for the first time about Tryphena. The 1879 sojourn in Weymouth was extremely wet,[23] ten years had elapsed since Hardy and Tryphena had been in the town together, and if we are right the 'folly' had 'flown' before he met Emma. That she tended to be jealous is an established fact, and if jealousy of an *affaire* long over and done with appears unlikely it may have provoked her to wrath by having been so long concealed. Nor would it assist Hardy's case that he was currently inviting further jealousy by already embarking on his long programme of infatuations with younger and more beautiful women. The last two lines seem to presage the estrangement.

If this reading of the poem is correct, Emma must have learned Hardy's secret from his mother, either through some innocent reference – say, when they were driving near Coryates – on the very reasonable assumption that Emma by this time knew of the Tryphena engagement, or, if relations between the two Mrs Hardys were beginning to be strained, from a malicious desire by Jemima to sow discord in the matrimonial wellbeing.

Meanwhile *The Return of the Native*, which had been published in book form the previous November and finished its serial run in December, had had very mixed reviews and discouraging sales. It was perhaps as well that its author had embarked on his second prose-fiction activity, the writing of short stories, of which in the next two decades he was to produce nearly fifty. He also renewed his old interest in the theatre and with it, inevitably, his interest in comely actresses. One of the first with whose 'rivalry' Emma had to contend was Helen Mathews, a woman already thirty but endowed with the slender build, dark hair, and slightly whimsical expression that most commonly attracted him. Yet during 1879 and 1880 he found time not only to take his wife abroad, to Dorset, to Cambridge, and to such functions as they could both attend, but to do some of the simpler things that show sympathy between them to be far from lost. He notes a day's shopping with her, a visit to the Lord Mayor's Show, a quiet evening sitting in Hyde Park and watching the carriages pass. They were invited to various houses, including that of Mrs Procter, an elderly lady of many fascinating literary associations whom Hardy had first met at the Stephens' home but on whom he had never yet called. It was the first of many visits down to the time of her death, for according to the published version of the *Life* she 'showed a great liking for Hardy and his wife, and she always made them particularly welcome'.[24] But the original typescript, prior to Florence Hardy's customary excision of anything too complimentary to Emma, reads: ' . . . showed a great liking for Hardy and his wife, and especially for Mrs Hardy, which she did not show for every woman' – whereafter is added in Hardy's handwriting 'far from it'.[25]

Throughout the latter part of 1879 and the forepart of 1880 he toiled away at *The Trumpet-Major*, finding an editor to serialise it in the magazine *Good Words* and a publisher to bring it out in book form. But, as in his London days as an architect, his health began to deteriorate. He had had bouts of illness ever since the autumn of 1878, but now they increased; yet except when he was out of London he continued working. No sooner was *The Trumpet-Major* out of the way than he embarked on *A Laodicean*, and was fortunate in again interesting the American, Henry Harper, who by now had published three of his short stories. The visit to France brought no improvement in health, and the week in Cambridge during October 1880, when he and Emma 'received much hospitality', was almost more than he could endure. They must have been anxious days for Emma, but if her conduct when his illness finally broke is anything to go by she looked after him well, even playing along with his fantasies which, fed by his usual fascination with the grotesque and sinister, became quite alarmingly morbid. While in France he thought their hotel in Le Havre old and gloomy, the landlord's and landlady's expression sinister, the waiter peculiar, the chambermaid full of foreboding. He later recalled telling a stranger on their coach that he carried his money in ordinary banknotes. Emma helped him search the bedroom (which had a blood-red carpet and a battered wall that looked as though a struggle had taken place there), and when they found a lumber closet with a mysterious second door at the back of it she aided him in stacking their luggage so that the closet could not be opened. Then they lay down (still dressed, apparently), keeping the light on, and waited until eventually they fell asleep. It is most unlikely that she believed in any of this nonsense, but she was wise enough not to upset her husband further by ridiculing him, instead following his whims at the expense of comfort and early sleep.

The return to Tooting all but coincided with the book-publication of *The Trumpet-Major*, but the Hardys were concerned only with Thomas's health. They sent for a doctor who happened to live opposite, but although this worthy diagnosed internal bleeding he had no idea of how to stop it. Emma therefore appealed to the Macmillans, who sent their own doctor. He ordered Hardy to lie in bed with his feet higher than his head until there was an improvement. But the weeks, then the months, passed, and meanwhile he was committed to continuing *A Laodicean* for *Harper's*, the first three instalments being already in print before he fell ill and serialisation being scheduled to start in December.[26] Consequently in addition to looking after him Emma undertook to write down the story from his dictation. They had no nurse; she had to perform every service for him, and the winter was bitter – it was in January 1881 that the snow carpeted the front passage; and she had also, one suspects, especially in the earlier and most painful stages of his illness, to help him with the story in a rather greater capacity than that of plain amanuensis. The narrative, which not surprisingly plummets in quality after the point it had reached when Hardy fell ill, shows that he racked his brains for material from what he had seen and read and done; and it would be astonishing if Emma did not offer suggestions.

In February, feeling that the climb back to health was not going too well, he took advice and called in one of the leading surgeons of the day, Sir Henry Thompson, whose field was diseases of the bladder. Thompson decided against operating. In the 1880s the operation would not have been easy, but whether Thompson was right is debatable. Hardy was evidently suffering from calculus, or stone, in the bladder, and the specialist's decision condemned him to painful and periodic inflammation of that organ for the remainder of his life. What makes the matter important for us is the question of whether the affliction affected his sexual capability; for he may have found the act of intercourse so liable to bring on a painful attack as to amount to a form of impotence. This would be consistent with the nature of all his subsequent infatuations, all of which followed the same pattern of intense ardour, absurd sentimentality, rapid cooling-off, and no suggestion at any time of physical adultery. But if it were so he must have mastered the handicap in old age, for there is no hint of it in Florence's letters to Doctor Stopes quoted in Chapter 2.

By 10 April 1881, Hardy had recovered far enough to go out for a drive with Emma and the Macmillans' doctor, and by the end of the month he had finished *A Laodicean* in his own hand. Two days later he and Emma called on Sir Henry Thompson for a final check, and a few days later still he went walking for the first time since the autumn. But his experience had convinced him that London was too much for his physique. Moreover, it had not, after all, proved essential to his writing. And the lease of The Larches had already had to be extended by three months. The second half of May was therefore spent in house-hunting once more in Dorset, a quest that resulted in their moving on 25 June to Llanherne, The Avenue, Wimborne Minster,[27] not far inland from Poole. Here they had a pleasant and well-stocked garden, something that must have pleased Emma, all her life a keen gardener, even more than it pleased Hardy.

So relieved was he to feel well again, and to be back in semi-rural Dorset, that his normal vulnerability to hostile criticism was proof against poor reviews and even poorer sales of *A Laodicean*, in sad contrast to the good press he had had for *The*

Trumpet-Major. The Wimborne period lasted exactly two years, during which he wrote one novel, *Two on a Tower*, and various poems and short stories. Once, not long after their arrival in Wimborne, Emma broached a plan for a book on Dorset to be written by Hardy with illustrations by H. J. Moule. Both men were attracted by the idea, but it was never implemented. Also soon after their arrival, they saw from the small conservatory of their new home the latest comet (Tebbutt's) on which a substantial part of the plot of the new novel was to hinge. Within a few weeks they were driving about the countryside noting features that would be useful. How helpful Hardy found Emma on these excursions it is difficult to estimate, but the date is only a few years before her enterprising visit to Wool Manor on behalf of *Tess*, and her activities included the compilation (a quarter of a century before Hermann Lea) of a comparative list of real and 'Wessex' names.[28] As with *A Laodicean*, it is hard to believe that during these drives she contributed no ideas of her own.

In August, they suddenly set off on a fortnight's tour of Scotland and the Lake District, and in December they visited London, where Hardy was able to arrange for serial publication of *Two on a Tower* in the *Atlantic Monthly*. In between times Wimborne offered them a fuller social life than they had expected, including Shakespeare readings, invitations to dinner, and a New Year's Eve ball at Canford Manor, the seat of Lord and Lady Wimborne. Curiously, although this social activity continued throughout their residence in the town and is fairly fully chronicled in the *Life*, a solitary invitation to Llanherne to tea is the only mention of reciprocal hospitality; yet Emma was to receive such warm commendation from many quarters for her hospitality and *savoir-faire* as a hostess both at Max Gate and in London that one would have expected her to play hostess sometimes at Wimborne. The explanation for her failure cannot have been domestic discord. If indeed 'She Charged Me' refers to her anger in 1879 at belatedly learning of the Tryphena engagement, she must have got over it, for Hardy ends his account of events during 1881 by observing that 'the year ended with a much brighter atmosphere for the author and his wife than the opening had shown'.[29]

On one of the exploratory journeys in preparation for *Two on a Tower* his sister Kate had been with them, so that at least in the early part of the period there was no disharmony yet between Emma and his family to upset him and make him misanthropic. All in all, Emma's much fuller life after the loneliness of Sturminster and Tooting prior to Hardy's illness, together with the spiritual drawing-together that the months of anxious nursing must surely have brought about, seem to have temporarily reversed the incipient deterioration of the marriage. We are left with the conclusion that Hardy recorded only the one visit of friends to Llanherne because he did not feel the house to be grand enough for most of his new circle. It was not just a question of the external appearance – and Llanherne was a passable, if undistinguished, building – but it is unlikely that the Hardys had added much yet to the modest tally of furniture bought for Riverside Villa. Similarly he had, apparently, invited no one to The Larches, being at pains to make people think he lived cheek by jowl with the Macmillans' dignified mansion – which in fact was a good mile away – instead of in a ramshackle terrace house much nearer Wandsworth Prison. He would have had little difficulty in persuading the sensitive Emma to curb her hospitable instincts in the interests of gentility. In the matter of snobbishness they were always at one.

In August 1881 a fillip was given to their social pretensions by a marriage that was to have much bearing on their relationship with the London *haut monde*. In 1873 Emma's uncle, Edwin Gifford, the canon who had performed the Hardys' wedding, married the daughter of his friend Bishop Jeune of Peterborough. Now in 1881 his wife's brother, Francis Jeune, married the widow of a certain Colonel Stanley, brother of Lord Stanley of Alderley. Mrs Stanley had been one of the most distinguished London hostesses, and as Mrs Jeune she had no intention of abdicating the rôle. Her connection with Emma may have been tenuous, but it was sufficient for the Hardys to procure a meeting with the Jeunes, at which Mrs Jeune seems to have conceived an instant liking for them that was to last through many years. There is no hint, either in Hardy's many allusions to her or in her own memoirs, that this aristocratic lady – her family had been leading landowners in

Scotland, her husband was to become Sir Francis Jeune and eventually Lord St Helier – ever 'looked down' on the humbly born Hardy (and, as his fame grew, his origins became harder and harder to conceal); but so ingrained was her upper-class outlook that, although on another page she gives a most kindly and totally unpatronising portrait of him, she writes with pride of her 'audacious' and 'hazardous' experiment of mixing the top stratum of society with 'such well-known representatives of literature, art, and politics as Sir John Millais . . . Mr Thomas Hardy . . . and others'. And she goes on to speak with approval of the 'new element' that was 'intruding itself' into the old social stronghold.[30] Although genuine affection took over, at the outset it was less the remote family connection that opened the august Jeune doors to the Hardys than their hostess's daring wish to mix the classes, provided that the lower class had certain credentials.

From now on the *Life* is heavily larded with social-diary entries that appear to have little purpose beyond demonstrating how illustrious was the circle in which Hardy now moved; few of the figures are brought to life by even the single phrase with which he could, when he chose, transform a name into a person. However, amid the endless chronicle of dinners and 'crushes' he does mention other things: for 1882 he records that he and Emma went to Liverpool to see a stage adaptation of *Far from the Madding Crowd*, took a turn round Dorset, Devon, and Wiltshire during which Emma 'with her admirable courage' wanted to walk rather than continue aboard a coach that was being pulled by a sick horse, called on William Barnes, now at Came Rectory, spent some weeks playing at 'housekeeping in the Parisian bourgeois manner' in a Paris flat, and attended a series of lectures on first aid. In all these activities, as well as their London visits, he and she were together; and their harmony is the more notable because it showed no faltering in measure with the progressively more unflattering picture of the Church that appeared in *Two on a Tower*.

Yet even in their closeness at this time there is mystery. At the end of November 1882 Emma received a letter from her sister announcing the death of Caddell Holder. Hardy, not yet engrossed with Society, devotes nearly two pages of the *Life* to an obituary of the good Rector, praising him in the most affectionate terms.[31] But he fails even to mention that Emma went to see her sister, either shortly before or soon after Caddell's death, still less to explain why he did not accompany her. That she did visit Helen during this time of bereavement is known only through a letter written the following year by Mrs Dashwood.[32]

Two on a Tower was published in volume form in October 1882. To what extent it really distressed Emma we can, as so often, only guess. Despite those scholars who see in her letters merely the spelling mistakes and sometimes questionable syntax, she was a good correspondent, and not above revealing her heart and inmost thoughts to those she felt would sympathise; but by a strange mischance the letters of hers known to survive include no more than three written before she took up residence in Max Gate at the age of forty-four. After her death Hardy, and later Florence and Irene Cooper Willis, destroyed most of her diaries and the letters she had received, but they could not control the letters she had sent, and it is ironic that Fate should seem to be observing Hardy's behests by obliterating all traces of her letters to her parents and brothers, the Holders, the Launceston Giffords, the Archdeacon, the Dashwoods and Warrys, the Serjeants, her closest confidant in middle age Alfred Pretor, and most of her other friends.

So we do not know what she felt. But if the hope of re-Christianising Hardy were at least an element in her continuance of help – and another element, surely, was affection – she can be said to have had some justification in the fact that he was never an out-and-out rationalist in the manner of his friends Leslie Stephen and Edward Clodd. He might write in old age 'I have been seeking God for fifty years, and if he existed I think I should have found him', but he was ever the agnostic, not the atheist, always just near enough to the fold, Emma must have felt, to be one day lured back inside it.

Just as he had felt he produced better work in Dorset than in London, so he now conceived the notion that he would produce his best again only by returning to the area he knew best, that of Bockhampton and Dorchester. Accordingly the agreeable life at Wimborne must be ended, and in the interests of English fiction the Hardy waggon must be once more set rolling; for, if Emma had a mission, so had he. In fact the idea of a return to Dorchester was not nearly so sudden as the *Life* implies. For a year or so he had been sounding out the possibilities of acquiring a piece of land on which his brother Henry could build a house to Thomas's own design. But when he and Emma left Wimborne in June 1883 he had not yet found a site, and they moved into an old house at 7 Glyde Path Road, a little turning off Shire Hall Lane. The address is confusing, for Shire Hall Lane has itself since been renamed Glyde Path Road and the original Glyde Path Road has disappeared, its site being now partly occupied by the new brick County Laboratory adjoining Colliton House.

Gittings has suggested that the two years (June 1883–June 1885) spent in Glyde Path Road are the period during which Emma's good relations with Hardy's family changed to hostility.[33] In support he quotes a paragraph from a famous letter by Emma to Elspeth, the newly married wife of the author Kenneth Grahame, who had sought her advice on how to cope with a marriage that was already proving far from easy.[34] The letter, however, which will be quoted here too in due course, was not written until August 1899, more than sixteen years after the move from Wimborne, and although Hardy's choice of Dorchester for a permanent home without thought for his wife's views may have diluted the Wimborne contentment, as long afterwards as 1891 Hardy could write from London to Emma at Max Gate that Polly Antell, Jemima's niece then living with her uncle and aunt in the Bockhampton cottage, might be appointed 'our agent' for paying the gardener.[35] Whether this was a request to Emma to get in touch with Polly or just a notification that he himself intended to do so, it shows that the parental home and its occupants were still a subject that could be mentioned naturally to his wife. It also shows that Emma, whether or not she had met Polly, knew who she was; and this is the only known breach by Hardy in the wall that he carefully maintained between Emma and his cohort of 'lowly' relatives, the Antells, Hands and Sparkses, who populated half Puddletown so dangerously near to Bockhampton.

Weber, who gives no source for his information, states that during the Glyde Path Road period Emma was still making 'infrequent visits' to the cottage, which means she must indeed have met Polly and made the rest of Hardy's wall extremely difficult to keep up.[36] For this reason the infrequency of the visits is more likely to have been due to his dissuasion than to a quarrel between Emma and the rest of the family. The ease of his reference to Polly seven years later does not indicate that, however few the contacts between Emma and his family had become, there was even then any bad feeling.

Emma must have watched with sinking heart and rising dismay the shaping of what was clearly intended for her permanent home: the bleak and remote site eventually chosen, the unattractive exterior of the building, the awkward layout within. A woman much less given to attaching importance to environment might have quailed. Those who are privileged to enter Max Gate today – and it should be stressed that it is not open to the public – with its many improvements made throughout the years and above all with the thoughtful and charming décor by which the present tenants[37] have almost magically uplifted it, need to exercise considerable imagination to visualise the dark, gloomy, damp and impractical house into which Hardy introduced his wife. In spite of the improvements, and the decorative flair of today's occupants, the interior plan remains inevitably fussy and awkward, and if Emma took any comfort at all from the gaol in which she was to spend the larger part of each of her remaining years it must have lain in reflecting how amply it justified her advice to Hardy to give up architecture as a career.

To be fair to him, he was undoubtedly ignorant of her distress, and also of the dangers he courted in placing himself almost under the shadow of his powerful mother. Undoubtedly too Emma showed her eagerness to fill properly the rôle of successful author's consort, and for him proper fulfilment meant allowing the successful author to take the lead in all things. She had been his contented companion in Wimborne: how much more should she be so in a town he knew and loved so much better. And because Dorchester was *his* town it was for him to choose the spot where they should live, and for him and his relatives to create the house of which she would be the privileged mistress. He did not realise, nor did she, that the woman who had been a source of strength and wise counsel while he was still a vacillating struggler was by reason of that same strength less adept at playing second fiddle to the man whose struggle had been won. So Hardy forged ahead with his plans, assuming, as Victorian husbands usually did, that what was right for him was right for her; and when in the *Life* he notes that the 'removal to the county town, and later to a spot a little outside it, was a step they often regretted having taken' it does not mean that he had consulted Emma, but that because he regretted the step it followed that so did she.[38] Three times at least, between 1900 and 1910, she expressed in letters to Rebekah Owen,[29] her cousin Leonie Gifford,[40] and Lady Hoare[41] her unhappiness at having to live in Dorchester. If Hardy had known of this he would simply have regarded it as an outcome of their estrangement, never as a contributary cause.

During the two years at Glyde Path Road he divided his time between searching for somewhere to build, to be followed by supervising the work there, and writing his only novel with an almost wholly Dorchester setting, *The Mayor of Casterbridge*. The impressive characterisation in it, together with the enthralling evocation of mid-nineteenth-century Dorchester life, are generally regarded as a vindication of the choice of the town for his home. To some extent the benefits are undeniable; but Hardy was in any event advancing rapidly in the mastery of writing, and in his determination to increase his literary significance he would without much doubt have produced an outstanding novel while living anywhere that gave him easy communication with Higher Bockhampton. Against the immediate benefits to his work of the return to Dorchester must be set the long-term effect of the strain it imposed on his marriage.

Of the Glyde Path Road house the *Life* says nothing, of the social life within it little more. If Emma seldom accompanied Thomas to Bockhampton, his relatives do not seem to have visited his own home at all, and this strengthens the idea that he was anxious to discourage any development of contacts between them and Emma. To have spent the odd Christmas at the cottage was one thing, or to have joined forces on jaunts round Weymouth, but any trend towards 'dropping in' by either side was too dangerous. That Hardy was reliving an old anxiety while compiling the *Life* is indicated by the almost complete absence from the relevant chapter of any mention of his parental home or its occupants, and of course none at all of his Puddletown relatives, although the period saw the death of two of his Sparks cousins, Tryphena's sisters Rebecca and Emma.[42]

He records a visit by his good friend Edmund Gosse, but is silent on the children's tea-party that Emma and he, the childless couple, gave and which Major H. O. Lock long afterwards remembered having attended in a blue Little Lord Fauntleroy suit.[43] He notes that he and Emma visited William Barnes and heard him preach, but tells us nothing about her reactions to his sudden fascination with circuses, a form of entertainment against which she held strong humanitarian views. He briefly reports a holiday he took in August 1884 in the Channel Islands, but does not explain why he was accompanied by his brother Henry instead of his wife. Six months later he was off again to stay with Lord and Lady Portsmouth and their family at Eggesford House, near Chudleigh in north Devon. Remarking only that 'Mrs Hardy was unable to accompany him',[44] he does not state that the reason was illness, which we learn only from a letter published elsewhere,[45] nor why he deserted his sick wife to make this quite unnecessary visit, the tactlessness of which was not mitigated by his ardent reports of the beauty of the young women at Eggesford.

By April, Emma had recovered enough to accompany him to London for what was to become their annual appearance during the Season. By June, Max Gate was near enough ready for him to superintend the removal of their furniture into it. He tells us he went down from London to do this, but not whether Emma went with him, remained behind, or had preceded him to Glyde Path Road to see to the packing-up. The house in Glyde Path Road was said to overlook the County Gaol; on 29 June 1885 Emma and Thomas slept for the first time in the gaol he had specially built her, and in the morning, presumably, the new gardener made the 500 motions with the pump-handle needed to supply the kitchen with water.[46] There was no bathroom.

CHAPTER FIVE

The Début of Max Gate to the Year of Tess

THE MOVE INTO MAX GATE coincides with the graduation of
the new Hardy who had been developing since the return to
Dorchester. There was *The Mayor of Casterbridge*, marking a
new phase in his career as a novelist; for the first time he owned
his own permanent home; he was now, with Emma, an established frequenter of London high society during the Season;
and in 1883 he had, as it were, proclaimed his new seriousness
in a curious poem, much esteemed by today's academics, 'He
Abjures Love'. This is not, as it sounds, a particular renuncia-
tion of Emma, but a repudiation of all his past loves – indeed,
of Love itself – in order to 'plumb life's dim profound' during
the 'few sad vacant hours' before the final 'Curtain'. The poem
was composed with great solemnity, and critics then and now
have for the most part analysed it in like vein. Evelyn Hardy
even sees it as revealing that 'lacking the consolations of religion . . . lacking, too, a detached philosophical attitude to the
inherently tragic and insoluble problems of life, Hardy's only
escape was to live as an avowed stoic'.[1] This may be a just reading of the poem's content, but what few of the critics appear to
see is the irony of the proclaimed intention compared with the
subsequent reality. Far from starting to live as a stoic, avowed
or otherwise, Hardy in 1883 was on the threshold of his busiest
period since youth of pursuing women he believed he loved. It
may be objected that this was only surface frivolity, and that
his turning away from Emma shows that deep in his soul he in
truth abjured love. But it is the argument of this book that deep

117

in his soul he never turned away from Emma, and that his pathetic preoccupations with other women were unconscious attempts either to eradicate her from his heart or to compensate himself for failure to re-establish his lost communication with her.

If it can be pinpointed, that loss probably dates from the moment when the site on which to build Max Gate was acquired. His inability to see how little the site would please Emma, his probable efforts to keep her away from his family while he was arranging the building work, his desertion of her to visit the Channel Islands, his insensitive excursion to Eggesford and behaviour when he got there, the fatalism and despair evinced in *The Mayor*, the rejection of love expressed in 'He Abjures Love' – all these must have spelled for Emma a fading of the pleasant *rapport* gracing Tooting and Wimborne that the ritual activities in London did little to counter.

If she had charged him with his growing neglect as she seems to have charged him at Weymouth with the concealment of his engagement to Tryphena, it might have launched a first-class quarrel, but at least Hardy would have realised her distress. That he never did so is revealed by poem after poem composed after her death, in which regret for his conduct is linked with protests that 'I never knew my crime'. But instead of having it out with him Emma turned in upon herself, became eccentric and in time bitter. The eccentricities extended to her style of dress, which as the years passed tended to lean more and more towards the fashions of her youth – not because she was by nature especially conservative, but from a comi-tragic attempt to re-attract the husband so increasingly susceptible to her younger rivals. It is not that she is likely to have feared his physical unfaithfulness. But there are other forms of infidelity no less wounding for being legally non-existent.

Even here Max Gate itself must take its share of blame. As Emma became gloomy so did Hardy, quite apart from his new intellectual seriousness. Five months after moving in he experienced a fit of depression that lasted three days; the end of the year found him 'sadder than many previous New Year's Eves have done'; he had sick headaches and more bladder trouble. No wonder the London Season and the smiles of beautiful ladies were a restorative to more than his intellect

Edwin Hamilton
Gifford, Emma's uncle
and the future
Archdeacon of London,
in 1862 (artist unknown).

Mrs Gifford senior,
Emma's grandmother, in
the portrait (by V. H.
Patterson, 1855) described
in *Some Recollections*.

(*left*) Emma Gifford in 1870: a detail of the portrait by an unknown artist given to the Dorset County Museum by Gordon Gifford.

(*below right*) No. 9 Bedford Terrace, Plymouth: the only survivor of the Giffords' five homes in the city.

(*below left*) Thomas Hardy in about 1870.

St Juliot Rectory today.

A sketch by Emma Gifford of the church at St Juliot before restoration.

St Benet's Abbey, Lanivet, today.

A rare photograph of Max Gate very soon after it was built. Note the still uncultivated garden and the absence of trees. The figure in the doorway is probably Thomas Hardy.

(*right*) Emma aged 55, photographed for *The Young Woman* magazine, 1895–6.

(*below left*) Rebekah Owen in 1879, aged 21, wearing the sun-hat described by Hardy in *Tess* and *The Well-Beloved*.
(*below right*) Emma Hardy photographed by Rebekah Owen in a churchyard.

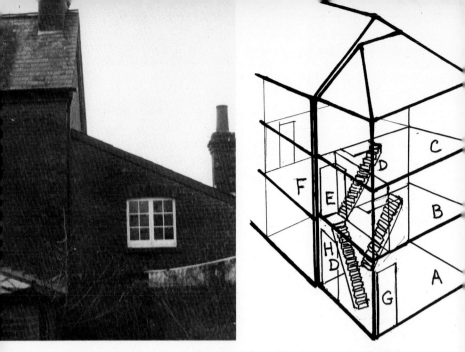

(*above left*) Max Gate, showing where Hardy proposed building a new second-floor room for Emma; (*right*) a diagram based on Hardy's sketch-plans in the Dorset County Museum. *Key* A apple store B man's room C new room for Emma D new staircases E new door into Hardy's study F Hardy's study G new garden door H existing garden door

Thomas Hardy: the 1906 portrait by Jacques-Emile Blanche.

Emma Hardy in her last years, with one of the Max Gate cats, photographed for *The Illustrated London News*.

(*above left*) Emma Hardy in 1908, photographed for *The Sphere*.
(*above right*) Florence Dugdale, sketched at Max Gate in
September 1910 by William Strang.

(*below left*) Gordon Gifford shortly before he volunteered as an
Army despatch rider, 1914.
(*below right*) Florence Hardy, Violet (Mrs Gordon) Gifford, and
her daughter Ethel in the garden of Max Gate about 1930.

Gordon
1914

and gradually obscured his deeper feelings for his (by Victorian standards) middle-aged and now portly wife. So they reacted adversely on one another, until by the time they had become adjusted to Max Gate and had mitigated its rigours by attracting their friends to visit them they believed that love was dead and withdrew into their shells.

Among the first visitors were Robert Louis Stevenson and his American wife, who afterwards made the following observation in a letter to her husband's mother:

Did I tell you that we saw Hardy the novelist at Dorchester? A pale, gentle, frightened little man, that one felt an instinctive tenderness for, with a wife – ugly is no word for it! – who said 'Whatever shall we do?' I had never heard a human being say it before.[2]

Fanny Stevenson was by most accounts so kindly as well as so intelligent a woman that one wonders whether to be more surprised at the uncharitable description of Emma (and the labelling of Hardy as 'frightened') or at the extraordinary reaction to such a commonplace expression as 'Whatever shall we do?' Gittings tries to explain away the whole observation by quoting a sour passage from the diary of Alice James in which Henry James's sister likens Fanny to 'an appendage to a hand-organ', endowed with 'such egotism and so naked!'[3] This, however, is as malevolent as the worst disparagements of Emma; contrast it with Edmund Gosse's view of Fanny in the *Century Magazine* during 1895: '[RLS] had married in California a charming lady whom we all learned to regard as the most appropriate and helpful companion Louis could possibly have secured.'[4] The 'appendage to a hand-organ' was, in fact, rather good-looking, and can scarcely have been motivated by jealousy; one is therefore driven to conclude that she really did consider Emma ugly. If so, she had an ally, also a woman and also American – most of Emma's more distinguished detractors were American, Irish or French. The novelist Gertrude Atherton, writing in her memoirs of an encounter with the Hardys only a few years after Mrs Stevenson's, evidently agreed with her: 'In Hardy's wake was an excessively plain, dowdy, high-stomached woman with her hair drawn back in a tight little knot. . . . No doubt Hardy went out so constantly to be rid of her.'[5]

Before judging the justice of this comment let us examine the circumstances of its delivery and the credentials of its perpetrator. Gertrude Atherton, a second-grade fictioneer who enjoyed a period of tepid fashionability, had been invited as guest of honour at a Society rout. What should occur, however, but the arrival of the infinitely more distinguished Thomas Hardy, just then entering upon his years as Mayfair's latest craze. Inevitably, if only *ex officio*, the wife of the great man moved within the same circle of limelight, and Gertrude Atherton found herself in relative shadow. The very acerbity of her comment indicates jealousy. It should be remembered too – as it seldom is about any of Society's more barbed comments on the Hardys – that this was the heyday of the 'catty' remark: Oscar Wilde produced some of his best dialogue by using such talk and sharpening it with his wit. Although only the comment on Emma is ever quoted, Gertrude Atherton's observations did not spare Hardy, either. He

drifted by, looking as little interested in his surroundings as usual. . . . He certainly never had the air of enjoying himself. One saw him in literary gatherings of every sort. . . . He never spoke unless addressed, and then as if his thoughts were far away. For my part I had avoided him after our second meeting. He was anything but great in personality.[6]

It happens that the few photographs we have of Emma include a portrait taken in about 1896. It shows a woman certainly not beautiful, but if anything rather better-looking than in the famous 1870 portrait-painting, still smooth-featured at fifty-six, and with a dignity not yet acquired in 1870: Raymond Blaythwayt, who interviewed Hardy early in the nineties for the magazine *Black & White*, thought her 'some few years younger' than her husband. The high stomach and stoutness, treated by many writers as though they qualified Emma for exhibition in a circus, were simply of the period – look at almost any group-photograph of middle-aged late-Victorian ladies of the better-fed classes and note how many are fat and clad in a style that a modern fashion-writer would call the high-stomach look. There were, after all, illustrious precedents: the dear Queen herself, and still more markedly the Duchess of Teck, mother of the future Queen Mary.

Gertrude Atherton's views on Emma's appearance involve a matter of opinion. Her final remark, that Hardy no doubt went out so often to be rid of Emma, is invalidated by the facts. Except when he attended all-male gatherings or they had simultaneous invitations to different functions, the Hardys in London society were almost always together, as they were when the American saw them. That Emma sometimes received invitations in her own right is proved by an entry in Hardy's diary (deleted from the *Life* by the vigilant Florence) that on 23 May 1894 he left a dinner at Lady Jeune's to 'pick up Em' from another dinner at Lady Lewis's.[7]

Having already interrupted the chronological record, it is perhaps suitable at this point to consider some of the other strictures on Emma collected by Carl J. Weber, together with one or two that he overlooked.[8]

Hamlin Garland, an American writer of almost endless trivia, is baldly stated by Weber to have visited Hardy's birthplace after Emma's death and been told by the tenant of the local belief that she had been much prouder of being an archdeacon's niece than of being Thomas Hardy's wife. What Garland himself, who visited the Birthplace more than a dozen years after Emma's death, wrote was that the 'owner' of the cottage, a Mr Pouncey, told him the first Mrs Hardy 'was, I believe, the daughter of a judge and the niece of an archbishop. It is said that she took more pride in being the daughter of a judge than she did in being the wife of Thomas Hardy.'[9] No wonder Weber frequently omitted to give the reference for his statements. The charge that Emma never appreciated Thomas's greatness is more explicitly made by Christine Wood Homer, who knew the Hardys well.[10] (It is a charge also levelled elsewhere against his mother.) Yet beside this must be set the comment of another old friend, Frances Mabel Robinson, to Irene Cooper Willis, that Emma 'had been the first in all the world to discover genius in this poor clerk sent down to examine the church',[11] and also the letters of Alfred Pretor advising her on the problems of living with a great man. Neither of these disproves the charges against Emma, but they provide an element of doubt.

T. P. O'Connor, in the closing paragraph of his obituary article on Hardy in the *Daily Telegraph*, remarks that his impression after talking with Emma during what appears to have been their only meeting (although he met Hardy a number of times) was that her 'whole bitter purpose was to discourage and belittle and irritate him' (Hardy).[12] Perhaps, if he met her at her most disillusioned and resentful during the last years, she did give him this impression. But O'Connor could perceive nothing of the emotional neglect, jealousy, wounded pride, religious frustration, and inability to communicate with her husband that underlay her attitude, nor appreciate the truth, as we have said, in her assertion that Hardy's Society women were poison to him, she the antidote. Indeed, how should he comprehend such subtleties, when at the beginning of his article he could write such nonsense as that Hardy's works show no interest in the world of London, that no fashionable people figure in them, and that he regarded his annual visits to the metropolis as something of a penance? O'Connor, whom a close relative of Lady Hoare called in an annotation to the Stourhead Collection at Trowbridge 'a cheap scandal-sheet journalist, not to be trusted for anything', was on the best reckoning no thinker, and lacked the insight, even if he had had the opportunity, to discern the real tragedy underlying Emma's attitude. The French artist Jacques-Émile Blanche, who painted Hardy's portrait in 1906 and twenty-two years later read the obituary, observed that, according to O'Connor, Emma would seem to have been Hardy's 'evil genius', but that he himself thought she had had little influence over him.[13] Blanche and his wife lived for some years in London, and knew the Hardys socially as well as professionally.

Widely quoted, again, is the story of a luncheon party given at Max Gate in 1893. One of the guests was Charles J. Hankinson, better known as 'Clive Holland', a close friend of Hardy and the subsequent author of two books about him. Hankinson took along with him 'Sarah Grand' (Mrs David C. McFall), a novelist whose book *The Heavenly Twins* had just been published. According to Weber, Emma praised the volume while Hardy 'looked on with a sardonic smile'. Weber goes on to relate what happened then,[14] but a slightly fuller version in the same vein is provided by W. R. Rutland, although, curiously, Rutland does not name Mrs Grand and so identify the occasion:

... a remark of Mrs Hardy's caused her husband to give expression to some very unorthodox views on conventional Christianity, and his abhorrence of religious pretensions which had no counterpart in the lives of the persons making them. We could see that Mrs Hardy was being shocked. Mme S. (another guest) was amused by Mrs Hardy's efforts to neutralise any unfavourable impression that may have been created by her husband's expression of unorthodox opinions. In the end Hardy himself appeared bored by the trend of the conversation into the 'safer' channels into which Mrs Hardy had steered it.[15]

Both this account and Weber's imply that Emma was angry, came near to making a fool of herself, and turned an agreeable atmosphere into one of tension and unpleasantness. But we also have Hankinson's own version.[16] After describing the conversation as an exchange of Hardy's heterodox opinions with Sarah Grand's more orthodox, he says he noticed that Emma was restive, though he fancied many of Hardy's views were advanced to invite dispute.

During lunch Mrs Hardy had several times intervened with a gentle denial that what her husband was saying was his real opinion; and Sarah Grand noticed this and smiled.
Once or twice, I remember, Mrs Hardy definitely intervened and said 'My husband doesn't think that at all.'
Then Hardy laughed.

Afterwards Sarah commented with pleasure on the lunch and the chance to talk with Thomas Hardy: 'Later she remarked how kindly and hospitable Mrs Hardy appeared to be. Adding, after a slight pause, "But perhaps a little too conventional for a man of the type of Hardy."'
The next day Emma wrote to the guests, including Hankinson, begging them not to take Hardy's expression of views too seriously.
If these two renderings of the same event illustrate how greatly truth is at the mercy of the observer, so can much depend on the tone and manner in which the spoken word is uttered. Many writers have repeated the novelist Desmond

MacCarthy's recollection of Emma once saying to him 'If you listen to what *I* am saying, you will find it as well worth hearing as Thomas Hardy's remarks!'[17] This may have been, as it is customarily interpreted, an illustration of Emma's jealousy and conceit. On the other hand, several who knew her, including T. P. O'Connor (for what he is worth) and Dr Fisher's daughter Cecelia, applied the adjective 'jolly' to her manner, and there are various instances of her displaying humour. Also, she complained on one occasion that letter-writing was her 'only resource for having all the say to myself, instead of listening "dumbly" to Thomas Hardy'.[18] It is therefore not impossible that MacCarthy took too seriously a semi-ironic protest that Emma, too, if only she could get a word in, was not devoid of interesting things to say.

Most of the derogatory remarks made by local Dorset people fall into the category of familiar malice expressed by certain of the less successful against anyone who has achieved a position of eminence they cannot hope to reach, particularly if it has been gained simply through a fortunate marriage. Of these comments the chronicler is more often Rebekah Owen than Carl Weber – though it is Weber who has preserved her remarks. Thus, according to her, a Mrs Sheridan thought Emma led Hardy 'a Hell of a life' and was 'half cracked'.[19] Theresa Featherstonehaugh found her 'a queer woman' and 'never thought her quite right in the upper story [*sic*]'. Mrs Moule said she was the Devil, and (writes Rebekah) 'Mr Moule's emphatic "Poor woman, she is phenomenally plain!" and his outbursts against her general unbearableness amuse us all'.[20] Miss Owen's amusement remained unchecked by any thought that she and her sister had received and were to continue to receive unstinted kindness and hospitality from Emma at Max Gate.

A rather different view of the half-cracked devil is taken by Isa MacCarthy, mother of Desmond, in several letters to Emma in 1902 and 1903, after her first visit to the Hardy home.

I shall never forget how cosy and welcoming the lights from your candles shone into the dark night as we came into your gates and although I felt very shy in my heart and full of fear *for myself* (longing to make a good impression) courage came to me at once from the welcome I received.[21]

Soon afterwards Mrs MacCarthy expressed her anxiety at Desmond's decision to become a writer. Emma's response has not survived, but on receiving it Isa MacCarthy wrote:

Your letter is most deeply interesting and I wish I could give you something out of myself too which might prove a worthy answer. I knew you would understand my anxieties and it touches me so much. . . . I am sure if ever I have the happiness of knowing you better I should learn from you much that would help me in the future.[22]

Another letter, devoted to a panegyric about the Dorset countryside, ends with the words 'Do forgive the burst of feeling. You have been so nice to me and kind I could not help writing it. . . .'[23] And in a fourth the writer refers to Emma's 'kind and affectionate heart towards everybody'.[24]

Nor were all the Moules of one opinion. Rebekah Owen also quotes a letter from Margery Moule concerning a visit she and her father had paid to Max Gate prior to Christmas 1896, when the Hardys were both 'very agreeable, very affectionate on Mrs Hardy's part. I devoted myself to her and left Thomas severely alone for a change.'[25]

Mrs Christine Wood Homer, to whose clear-eyed account of Emma I have already referred, confessed that despite all Emma's multiple oddities of behaviour she 'rather liked her', calls her 'poor dear Mrs Hardy' (this is after Emma's death), and sums up: 'It may well be she was deserving of pity and compassionate understanding rather than blame.'[26]

Another who thought of Emma as 'dear' was Albert Bankes, of Wolfeton Hall, Charminster, who was sorry that Hardy had three times refused a knighthood because Bankes would have so liked 'dear old Mrs Hardy' to be Lady Hardy.[27] True, he was something of a dear old soul himself – he even enjoyed Emma's poetry[28] – but the phrase suggests genuine affection.

And another person who thought Emma deserved pity was Florence Henniker, who paid her first visit to Max Gate expecting to pity Thomas Hardy but came away pitying his wife.[29] Frances Mabel Robinson, also already mentioned, was invited in 1939 by Irene Cooper Willis to write down her opinion of

Emma. After enumerating Emma's failings with a candour that would have been approved by Christine Wood Homer, Mabel Robinson summed up: 'Certainly she had not the intellectual value or the tact to hold the heart of her husband against all the world but she had loved him dearly and was a loveable, inconsequent little lady of whom we grew very fond.'[30]

Sir George Douglas observed a curious incident while the Hardys were his guests in Scotland in 1891. Emma was sketching, and Hardy ventured to criticise her perspective. She retaliated by criticising his novels, and Sir George noted that Hardy invariably referred to her criticism 'with a deference which it did not deserve'.[31] The extent and quality of Emma's help with the novels has already been discussed, but it is worth contrasting Douglas's opinion of her literary worth with that of Alfred Pretor a few years later. Pretor, a Cambridge don and a friend of both Hardys, became from 1897 onwards Emma's confidant and counsellor, to whom she poured out all her troubles in a vast exchange of letters.[32] She also persuaded him to write stories, to which she afterwards suggested improvements; and when some of his work had been accepted for publication she corrected his proofs. In 1899 his first volume bore the printed dedication 'To Mrs Thomas Hardy who suggested and encouraged the writing of these tales'. In a letter he told her: 'I value your criticism beyond measure.'[33]

According to Weber, Dame Rebecca West, as she afterwards became, once heard Emma say: 'Thomas Hardy, remember you married a lady.' But in 1973 Dame Rebecca told Robert Gittings in a letter that she had no recollection of Weber, and had heard the anecdote related by someone else.[34] The person who told it observed that Emma had uttered the remark in exasperation when Hardy appeared before her inappropriately dressed for some function to which they should have already set out. Both the offence and the rebuke, albeit not generally couched in Emma's terms, must be familiar wherever there is a married household.

These are some of the more familiar criticisms levelled against Emma, and less familiar words of praise. One or two more will be mentioned in their correct chronological settings. Life at Max Gate settled into a rhythm, if a dreary one. But there were compensations. Cats, to the number of four, became an established part of the household, and since the liking for them was shared by Thomas and Emma, may be reckoned among the sadly few common interests they retained until her death. After that, as if the cats symbolised too closely the departed mistress of the house, Florence quickly got rid of them.

There was also the large garden, the first of any magnitude that Emma had enjoyed since the Rectory garden at St Juliot (although there had been a small one at both Riverside Villa and Llanherne) and the first that, in so far as the law permitted women to own property, she could claim as hers. But the garden, like the cats, is in retrospect not without its sad symbolism too, for although to screen it from the cold winds and colder prying eyes Hardy personally planted round its perimeter 'two or three thousand' (so he claims[35]) little pines, Emma was dead before they grew large enough to afford her comfort, as he subsequently acknowledged in the poem 'Everything Comes'.

Finally there were the young Giffords. The children's party at Glyde Path Road testifies that the final extinction of hope for a child of their own had not weakened either Thomas's or Emma's delight in other people's children. In about 1885 or 1886 Emma's brother Walter – the one who had settled in London and attended his sister's wedding – sent his small daughter Lilian to stay at Max Gate. Although he had his own home and a steady job at the Post Office Savings Bank, Walter was obsessed with the idea that his children did not thrive in London and needed country air, so he sent Lilian and later her younger brother Gordon for holidays at St Juliot, then Max Gate.[36] Both Hardys, we may be sure, were delighted with the children and virtually adopted them for the greater part of each year. Their education was arranged and paid for, following which Hardy at Emma's instigation taught Gordon the rudiments of architecture[37] and procured him an apprenticeship with his old firm, Sir Arthur Blomfield & Sons.

Yet neither Gordon nor Lilian is mentioned in the *Life*, Hardy's sole reference to them being a note scribbled on a letter from their father to Emma. The note describes Walter as 'a tiresome brother whose children Emma helped to educate'.[38] But since Emma had very little money of her own and Hardy's allowance barely covered the housekeeping at Max Gate, let alone the entertaining, it follows that he himself must have financed the children's education. As she grew up Lilian became something of a problem, but not to any extent until after Emma's death. Gordon on the other hand, although accused by Florence Hardy of believing he had a right to inherit Max Gate[39] – a charge strenuously refuted by his daughter and her husband[40] as being utterly out of character – grew up into a quiet, gentle and unassuming individual. Lilian seems to have been a robust enough child, but Gordon suffered from severe respiratory weakness, which gave his father some sort of justification for sending him out of London. It may also be that Walter, realising the Hardys' intense disappointment at their own childlessness, sought either to exploit or (according to one's judgement) alleviate the situation.

If this was his aim, he succeeded at first, but Hardy's solitary and curious comment on the situation suggests that as they grew older his enthusiasm for the young Giffords waned. Why, then, did he continue to accept them and further their prospects, yet write afterwards as if the responsibility had been entirely Emma's? The only plausible explanation is that he continued to shoulder the burden (which he could have made Walter resume) out of some deep-lying wish to please Emma. It is fully consistent with his nature to have subsequently denied his magnanimity, just as it is consistent with her attitude in the nineties to see only that he resented her relatives, her substitute-children. A word of clarification from either might have turned the young Giffords into a means of narrowing the breach between the Hardys, but the inability to communicate that dogged them beset them now and the chance was lost.

In the late 1880s Hardy was working up to his peak period of literary productivity. Seven months after he had finished *The Mayor of Casterbridge*, and before the serial had even begun to appear in the *Graphic*, he started on *The Woodlanders* for *Macmillan's Magazine*. Work on this took him until February 1887, and during the ensuing nine years novels, short stories, poems and articles came from his pen in unflagging succession. Apart from the now inevitable attendance at the London Season, 1886's only journeys from home were a visit to the

Portsmouths at Eggesford, and towards the close of the year a short excursion by Hardy to London, where he called on the Jeunes and other aristocratic friends. *The Mayor of Caster-bridge* came out in volume form in May, to be followed by on the whole excellent reviews but dismayingly poor sales. In consequence, despite payments for the spate of stories and articles that he was now turning out, his income was still modest – far too modest for his new mode of life. It must have seemed to both of them and – equally important, as we shall see – to his brother and sisters that writing would never make him rich.

In the spring of 1887 they took another longish holiday abroad, this time in Italy. Whatever the mounting tensions at home, they could still enjoy one another's company on the Continent, where the interests they continued to share could come to the fore. Nevertheless, perhaps the most noticeable feature of Emma's diary of the expedition is that, although it contains a number of references to 'Tom', it is almost devoid of really personal touches – no record of his reactions to any spectacle or experience, no word of any discussions or arguments or (with one exception) shared excitements, none of the little emotional touches that give *Some Recollections* its charm.[41] On one page she does disclose that Tom was 'vexed and dyeptic' (her spelling) after a meal, which may be compared with the allusion in an earlier diary to his being cross with her for feeling tired after the drag round Waterloo; but that is all. Of photographically vivid description, plenty; of her own reactions, a fair amount; but of what her husband said or felt or became involved in, nothing.

The one exception concerns her part in saving him from an attack by robbers; but let us turn to Hardy's story of this. He too covers the Italian journey at length, devoting a whole chapter of the *Life* to it. Once again, however, though it records meetings with a number of people (all British except an Italian countess to whom he was introduced by an Englishwoman; on their journeys abroad the Hardys never sought to get to know the natives), the account is completely impersonal. Except that he writes 'we' instead of 'I', one might be forgiven for not realising that Emma was with him. The only passage in which he brings her to life, that concerning the attempted robbery, does not appear in the printed *Life*, being among the passages flattering to Emma that Florence deleted.[42] The type-script says that while Hardy was carrying home a small paint-ing:

. . . three men prepared to close in on him as if to rob him, apparently mistaking him for a wealthy man owing to his wearing a fur-edged coat. They could see that both his hands were occupied in holding the picture [an old painting he had bought], but what they seemed not to be perceiving was that he was not alone, Mrs Hardy being on the opposite side of the narrow way. She cried out to her husband to be aware, and with her usual courage rushed across at the back of the men, who disappeared as if by magic.

In her own account Emma admits to 'dreadful fright', which makes her apparent fearlessness all the more praiseworthy. It is possible to belittle her action by saying that for a strong-minded woman who had always been something of a 'toughie' it was instinctive, or even that she knew it to be in her own in-terest to protect Hardy so far from home; but it can also be said that the instinctiveness sprang from a regard for him that be-neath her present indifference, her future fancied hatred, was never lost. It was the same deep-seated affection that nearly a quarter of a century later was to inspire her musical attempts at reconciliation and the secret writing of *Some Recollections*. Possibly in 1887, certainly ten or twenty years later, she would have denied its existence, and probably believed her denial. But the sentiment was there, and in those later years of bitter-ness, had a sudden peril or dangerous illness beset Hardy, it would have broken through exactly as it did in Rome.

Her reward for her prowess was a poor one, for before leav-ing Rome she caught malaria. Hardy thought this was due to lingering too long in the Colosseum, and in so far as it was pla-gued with anopheles mosquitoes he was probably right, though he does not appear to have been aware yet of the dis-covery a few years earlier of the malaria-carrying properties of the insect. Her illness is ignored in the *Life*, even the typescript.

The Woodlanders was published in volume form as the Ital-ian holiday was starting and, although the reviews were good, once again there were complaints of the story's 'immorality'. It also contains more explicit criticisms of marriage than any-thing Hardy had written hitherto. Yet still Emma showed no let-up in helping him – more than a hundred pages of the *Woodlanders* manuscript are in her hand. We know that as soon as she and Thomas had returned from London, where as usual they spent the Season, he began working on the background for *Tess*. In addition to bluffing her way into Wool Manor to report on the Turberville portraits and supplying him with the suggestion about the jewellery, it was she who drew his attention to the drunken man on the Dorchester pavement, whose mumblings about his aristocratic ancestors set Hardy off in quest of the Turbervilles. It is furthermore not impossible, since this had been their working-pattern in the past, that it was she who first went through the files of the *Dorset County Chronicle* picking out the minor items of news that he then carefully noted and used in the novel. From these activities, and her familiarity with Tess's earlier names, it is clear that she was as well acquainted as Hardy himself with the book's source-material and stages of construction. But if this means she was in a similar position regarding *The Woodlanders* it is especially interesting, for Gittings has brilliantly demonstrated the sources of that tale in Hardy's family history, that history which he had always been at such pains to hide from her.[43]

By a truly Hardyan irony, at the very time when she was giving him more help with *Tess* than with any book since *A Laodicean*, he embarked on the first of his literary dalliances with other women. Emma must by now have become used, if not reconciled, to his interest in pretty females, be they actresses, Society beauties, or girls seen in (and on) the streets or in trains and buses. But in 1889, while he was in the midst of writing *Tess*, he was sent a volume of verse, with a fulsome dedication to him on the flyleaf, by their composer, 'Graham R. Tomson'. The poet was in fact a lady, youthful and of great beauty, Rosamund Tomson. Hardy probably already knew this, and certainly knew it a year later, when he met her at Mrs Jeune's and seems to have lost no time in asking for her portrait. They began a literary correspondence and exchange of 'rhymes'.[44] She dedicated two later poems to him, and in his own poem 'An Old Likeness (Recalling R.T.)', composed long after her premature death, he looks back on a '. . . season/Of love and unreason' and kisses the faded painting 'As if I had wist it/

Herself of old'. Gittings suggests that a connection may exist between her poem 'The Bird Bride' and Tess's vision of the arctic birds.[45] Be this as it may, Hardy's interest in the attractive, socially acceptable, mildly gifted, and unashamedly admiring young woman, although it endured only two or three years, must have disturbed Emma.

Also in 1889, another matter arose that must surely have occasioned her distress, although nowhere is there a word to say so. Following Macmillan's collection and publication in book form in 1888 of some of Hardy's short stories under the collective title *Wessex Tales*, he was commissioned by the *Graphic* to contribute half a dozen new stories for publication together in a special issue of the magazine. This he did, using the general title *A Group of Noble Dames:* not without trouble, the directors of the *Graphic* rejecting the tales at first and forcing him to tone them down. But the trouble with the publishers was nothing to the trouble with a number of living members of the families to which the Noble Dames had belonged. There is some mystery about the extent of the upset, partly because Hardy disguised the names of people and places so well in most of the stories that to this day the disguise has not been penetrated.

On the one hand we have Rutland deriding the very notion of reality underlying 'such far-fetched tales',[46] and Millgate implicitly denying it by ignoring the question;[47] on the other we have Hardy claiming repeatedly, in letters to Edward Clodd and to *Harper's* and in the preface to the volume edition, that the majority of the stories are substantially true. In addition Emma told Rebekah Owen that only 'Barbara of the House of Grebe' was not factual.[48] In his preface Hardy even thanked certain living 'noble dames' for their comments on various of the tales that they had recognised as being about their own forebears. His implication is that the ladies were not displeased; but, if we can believe the somewhat sensational accounts by Sidney Heath, their menfolk were displeased to the point of banning Hardy's works from the local bookshops and threatening to dismiss any of their staff caught in possession of one of his books.[49]

Whether or not this is true, the extreme displeasure of one eminent family, that of the Earl of Ilchester, is beyond doubt, as must be its effect on Emma. During eight years in Dorchester the Hardys had made very little headway in Dorset society; against the many London engagements for 1891 listed in the *Life* a ball given by Mrs Sheridan is the only Dorset event. If Hardy was now alienating the local aristocracy, it was not only a blow to prospects of improving their status in the area, it could also have repercussions in London where the Hardys' standing was not yet invulnerable.

Simultaneously with the upset over *A Group of Noble Dames* came difficulties with *Tess*. In September 1889, Tillotson's, to whom Hardy had sent about half the novel, became alarmed at the contents and rejected it. So, a month later, did *Murray's Magazine*, the editor expressing his belief that it was both desirable and possible for women to pass through life in happy ignorance of the immoralities that went on. (What he thought they made of the prostitutes who thronged the West End streets, openly soliciting even in broad daylight, he forbore to state.) *Macmillan's Magazine* was Hardy's next target, only to find his work again rejected. At this stage the novel contained nothing of the Turberville element, the ancient-family-come-down-in-the-world theme, but opened with the ordinary, not to say hackneyed, picture of the working girl seduced by the boss's son. If this means that Emma had not yet overheard the drunken scion of the Turbervilles proclaiming his lineage, it also means that notwithstanding three rejections of *Tess* – each on account of its sexual impropriety – Emma was still prepared to give it her support. Nor was it she, but the editor, who insisted on its bowdlerisation as a condition of eventual acceptance for the *Graphic*.

The year 1890 was one of deaths among relatives and old friends of both Hardys. One death was that of Mary Antell, Jemima's sister and mother of Polly, of whom Hardy had probably seen more during his childhood than of any other relative outside his own home.[50] But of greater impact on him than even the decease of his favourite aunt was the premature death, two months earlier, of Tryphena. In the *Life* occurs this strange paragraph, quoted from his diary for 1890:

March 5. 'In the train on the way to London. Wrote the first four or six lines of "Not a line of her writing have I". It was a curious instance of sympathetic telepathy. The woman whom I was thinking of – a cousin – was dying at the time, and I quite in ignorance of it. She died six days later. The remainder of the piece was not written till after her death.'[51]

The title of the poem underwent a number of changes. The first must have occurred soon after the diary entry, for the manuscript is headed 'T——a/At news of her death'. When the poem was published in *Wessex Poems* it became 'Thoughts of P—a/At news of her death'. For the *Selected Poems* this was altered to 'At News of a Woman's Death', and finally in the *Collected Poems* to 'Thoughts of Phena/At News of Her Death'. Since *Wessex Poems* was published as early as 1898 it is of advantage to give the poem in full here, that readers may judge the likely effect on Emma – who may, indeed, have seen it earlier.

> Not a line of her writing have I,
>   Not a thread of her hair,
> No mark of her late time as dame in her dwelling, whereby
>   I may picture her there;
>   And in vain do I urge my unsight
>   To conceive my lost prize
> At her close, whom I knew when her dreams were upbrimming with
>   light,
>   And with laughter her eyes.
>
> What scenes spread around her last days,
>   Sad, shining, or dim?
> Did her gifts and compassions enray and enarch her sweet ways
>   With an aureate nimb?
>   Or did life-light decline from her years,
>   And mischances control
> Her full day-star; unease, or regret, or forebodings, or fears
>   Disennoble her soul?
>
> Thus do I but the phantom retain
>   Of the maiden of yore
> As my relic; yet haply the best of her – fined in my brain
>   It may be the more
>   That no line of her writing have I,
>   Nor a thread of her hair,

134

No mark of her late time as dame in her dwelling, whereby
    I may picture her there.

It is not necessary to maintain with Lois Deacon that the
poem proves Hardy's love for his cousin never to have waned:
death always released springs of tenderness in him. But did
Emma realise this? To her, the lines must have seemed yet
another witness to her small share in her husband's heart. An
interesting puzzle is what should have moved Hardy not
merely to think about Tryphena just before the news of her
death, but to start composing a poem about her. Bailey suggests that the references to writing (that is, letters) and a lock of
hair imply that Hardy had had both, but out of loyalty to
Emma had either returned or destroyed them – probably in
1870.[52] Yet something must have provoked the poem twenty
years later. It may have been a 'sympathetic telepathy', or
Hardy may have used that explanation to avoid stating in the
Life that news of Tryphena's illness (even if it contained no
hint that it might prove fatal) had come to him during one of
his visits to Bockhampton.

As we have seen, there are other poems believed to refer to
Tryphena – to those previously mentioned may be added 'Her
Immortality' – but Hardy's only other reference outside his
poetry is in the preface to *Jude the Obscure*, in which he states
that 'the scheme [of the novel] was jotted down in 1890, from
notes made in 1887 and onward, some of the circumstances
being suggested by the death of a woman in the former year'. If
Emma had seen the poem before its publication in *Wessex
Poems* and then recognised the Tryphena element in *Jude*, it
may have been a contributary factor in her dislike of the novel.

According to Gittings it was now that she began to keep her
series of 'black' diaries in which she denounced Hardy in the
harshest terms – or so we are told by Florence,[53] who herself
dates the denigrating notebooks from 'about 1891' and says
they continued to within 'a day or two' of Emma's death.[54] A
great deal of confusion has surrounded the diaries. Gittings
equates them with another derogatory creation of Emma's
called 'What I Think of My Husband', though this appears
rather to have been a single effusion unconnected with the diaries. Irene Cooper Willis, in her notes on the Hardys now in the

Dorset County Museum, further bedevils the issue by declaring that Hardy cut down *Some Recollections* for publication in the *Life* 'as it contained a great deal about their unhappy relationship and he said she would not have written that if her mind had not been affected'. But the manuscript of *Some Recollections* is written in a bound notebook and shows no trace of excision before its unmistakably original closing paragraph. What Hardy deleted for the *Life* was the *first* part of the *Recollections* about the early years in Plymouth. Presumably Miss Willis, having learned from Florence of the former existence of 'What I Think of My Husband', did not examine the *Some Recollections* notebook very closely and assumed the other work to have been part of it.

It is not easy at first to reconcile the keeping of hate-filled diaries with the writing of the love-inspired *Some Recollections*. Only Emma, Hardy and Florence ever saw the diaries or 'What I Think of My Husband' before Hardy burned them, and we have only Florence's word for their nature. But Hardy's extremely guarded references in one or two letters, and his allusions to his wife's latterday 'hatred' in some of the poems, justify a belief that the diaries were fairly scurrilous. The key to their reconciliation with *Some Recollections* lies, I think, in their purpose: to provide an outlet for Emma's growing misery and frustration, or in colloquial phrase to let off steam. It is unlikely that they were ever intended for any eyes but Emma's own, except possibly for Hardy's after her death to let him see just what she had endured at his hands. That this was a cruel and unjust intention, if it existed, is undeniable. But love is often cruel and unjust, and that at heart her love never perished is demonstrated by the writing of *Some Recollections*. It is seldom noticed that, whereas Hardy needed the dual shock of his wife's death and the discovery of her papers to set in being the flood of remorseful love-poems, Emma embarked on her recollections in the darkest time of estrangement and without any such stimulus. Is it too much to suppose that her desperate attempts at reconciliation towards the close of her life would have been followed, had they succeeded, by letting him read *Some Recollections* and destroying the black diaries?

It may be pointed out that Florence Hardy, too, had her need to 'let off steam', which with her took the form of writing letters. Their principal recipients were Edward Clodd and Rebekah Owen. To Clodd she wrote at the end of one letter in which she had unreservedly expressed her feelings on several topics: 'I ought not to write all this I know but it is a most tremendous relief to do so and I know you won't breathe a word to anyone.'[55] To Rebekah in similar circumstances she concluded: 'I write so freely to you because I know how safe everything is that I tell you. I would not tell that [a suggestion that after Mary Hardy's death her sister Kate was 'terrified' lest anyone else should inherit Mary's money] to my own sisters even.'[56] Other letters to both friends contain similar avowals.

The third death in 1890 was that of Emma's father at Compton Giffard, near Plymouth. She attended his funeral unaccompanied by Hardy. Sixteen years had elapsed since he and John Gifford had met, perhaps for the second time, perhaps only for the first, at Surbiton; eighteen years since he had met Mrs Gifford (who was to die in 1891) at Kirland, if at all. One wonders how Mr Gifford felt after the 'low-born churl' won renown (if not yet at its greatest) as an author and obtained the entrée to the best London society. But he never came to either Max Gate or London to see the swan into which the ugly duckling had turned.

Two members of Hardy's family had recently moved rather nearer Max Gate. Both Mary and Kate Hardy were now teaching in Dorchester, and in about 1890 Hardy bought them a house in Wollaston Road.[57] It does not appear that Emma ever visited them in their new home, or that they visited Max Gate from there. For this Emma is generally held to blame; but a possible alternative reason is that Hardy did not want them at Max Gate, where by this time distinguished guests were liable to appear not only when invited but also unheralded. Several of the contributors to the Toucan series of monographs testified, when interviewed by James Stevens Cox, to brother Henry's roughness and broad Dorset accent, and one said, of a family gathering that included Kate, 'They all talked like most Dorset people. Not too broad, like some I've heard.'[58] The homely accents, combined with the unsophisticated country clothes that photographs show the sisters to have worn, may well have made the sensitive Hardy anxious to avoid an embarrassing confrontation.

The year was also one of a good deal of travel for the Hardys, though apart from the annual excursion to London and a week in Weymouth their travels were separate. Hardy made three additional journeys, the first two with Henry. One was to Topsham, the small town near Exeter where Tryphena had lived with her husband Charles Gale, to offer him their condolences and lay a wreath on Tryphena's grave; the other to Paris, which Henry had not seen, purely for pleasure. Then in December, again without Emma, Hardy paid a second visit to London, where he stayed with the Jeunes. Emma's only journey on her own was to her father's funeral, but it meant that out of six expeditions only two were in one another's company. True, 'the autumn was passed in the country, visiting and entertaining neighbours, and attending garden parties', but these were activities in the company of other people.[59] Except for Emma's share in the preparation of *Tess*, it was not a good year for restoring a slipping relationship. On New Year's Eve, Hardy looked out across the snow at the pines he had planted, and they seemed to be saying ''Tis no better with us than with the rest of creation, you see!'[60] Certainly the fragment of creation within the house that they faced was in no promising condition at all.

The extent to which the *Graphic* required *Tess* to be bowdlerised made the firm's demands on *A Group of Noble Dames* seem like a quibble over punctuation. The serial ran in England from July to December 1891, and after Hardy had worked industriously to restore the watered-down features and recast the story as we know it today it appeared in book form in November of the same year. Like all the novels from *Under the Greenwood Tree* onwards it also appeared in America, but with one big advantage over its predecessors: in December 1890 the United States Copyright Act had been passed, enabling Hardy to reap the full financial benefit of sales there instead of seeing the authorised editions of his books sharing the market with pirated rivals.

Tess of the d'Urbervilles did four things for Hardy. It set the final cachet on his reputation as a novelist; it took him financially from modest success (thanks to *The Woodlanders*, which sold well) to wealth; it brought about the beginning of his resolve not to write further novels; and it caused him not merely to have the entrée to London society, but to be sought after by every hostess worthy of the name. These things were due less to the merits of the book than to the almighty tempest it had to weather at the start of its career. Some reviewers praised it, but others found it immoral, profane, and were especially outraged by the subtitle, 'A Pure Woman Faithfully Presented', and by the final reference to the President of the Immortals. No wonder Hardy wrote in his diary on Good Friday 1892: 'Well, if this sort of thing continues no more novel-writing for me. A man must be a fool to deliberately stand up to be shot at.'

But the controversy with its hint of fire and brimstone was precisely what Society looked for to relieve its perpetual round of pleasure and boredom, and the few doors previously barred were now opened wide to the bewildered Hardy and his much-shaken wife. Similarly the scandal surrounding the novel ensured its sales. Its true merits may or may not have won their deserts, but a whisper that a book is a piece of high-class pornography is a guarantee of profitability. With almost the suddenness of a modern pools winner Hardy found himself rich, and among the less expected results of his leap to wealth was apparently one for the clue to which we have to look ahead more than twenty years, to a time when Florence Hardy wrote two long letters to Rebekah Owen complaining of the 'plotting' by Hardy's near relatives to inherit his house and money. The essential passage for our present purpose appears in the second letter:

I see now that the dread was there always that some of the Hardy money should go to my family – or that I should have an undue share of even my husband's money. All this makes the quarrels between the first Mrs Hardy and her husband's people so easy to understand. It was not all the fault of one person or one side. There is that extreme family feeling – nobody but a 'Hardy *born*' – that is the phrase they are always using – must benefit by the money made or saved by Hardys. . . . But why they – or rather Kate Hardy – should imagine that I want to clutch more than just enough to keep me I don't know.[61]

This, then, would seem to hold the key to why and when the hitherto cordial relations between Emma and the Hardys changed. During Thomas's slow climb to moderate success his brother and sisters did not pay much attention to future prospects. The building of Max Gate should have been a pointer, but for some years afterwards, despite their London activities, Hardy and Emma probably did not impress even the Hardy relatives as being well off. Nor was the London Season handled without a struggle. As late as 1891, according to the *Life*,

Much as they disliked handling other people's furniture, taking on their breakages, cracks, and stains, and paying for them at the end of the season as if they had made them themselves, there was no help for it in their inability to afford a London house or flat all the year round. The dirty house-fronts, leaning gate-piers, rusty gates, broken bells, Doré monstrosities of women who showed us the rooms, left Em nearly fainting, and at one place she could not stay for the drawing-room floor to be exhibited.[62]

But a year later, after the wild success of *Tess* had revolutionised their position, the family realised not only that a rich man was in their midst, but that if he died before them all his riches would go to Emma and her nephew and niece. So from that time onwards Emma and the Giffords became their enemies. No doubt Emma reacted in kind, but after Florence's repeated denigrations of her, not least for her attitude to Thomas's sisters, the admission that she had a measure of justification is significant.[63]

Meanwhile, as soon as the book versions of *Tess* and *A Group of Noble Dames* were off his hands, Hardy had to supply Tillotson with a serial in place of the rejected *Tess*. It proved to be that strangest of all his full-length stories, *The Well-Beloved*, negligible as a piece of fiction but more intriguingly filled with half-heard autobiographical overtones than any prose work he had written since *A Pair of Blue Eyes*. In the same year that he was hurriedly writing this, Emma, too, saw herself in print, in the form of a long letter to the *Daily Chronicle* on the subject of the upbringing of children.[64] It is pithily expressed, and its views give the lie to those who have contended that she was incapable of intelligent or sustained thought. The following paragraph reveals her ideas on the treatment of the youngest group of all. Her pre supposition that they belong to the middle class, and that anyone of the 'uncultivated' class should be kept at a distance, is less an instance of her personal class-consciousness than of the customary Victorian middle-class outlook.

Regard attentively the position of infancy. Almost always the plastic minds and hearts are in ignorant hands. Even where a household is well looked after, a woman of the uncultivated class is chosen to attend the children in their early years. Listen to the talk of a nursery-maid, hear the reprimands given by her to a wondering little inmate of a baby-carriage, who wants to get out of it and see for itself what the world is. What is the child taught? Nothing, or worse, and it often returns home unhappy or dulled. That is a pitiable sight, and it is a most reckless way of saving the family funds and treating human material.

Hardy makes no allusion, either in the *Life* or in surviving correspondence, to the publication of this lengthy essay in a leading London newspaper, nor does he refer at any time to her other published letters and articles. By the early 1890s his attitude to her was becoming oddly ambivalent. While in London without her he could insert touches of affection into his letters that are not explained by saying that while the Hardys remained married a *modus vivendi* was necessary. He tells her that he is glad for her own sake she is not in London, 'though not for mine, everything being so dull'. He telegraphs that his return home will be postponed, then writes a letter in case the telegram is not delivered – 'otherwise you may be alarmed'. In the same letter he informs her that he has called at her dressmaker's about her new gown, and finding it already dispatched, has paid the bill. He writes one letter for no other reason than that 'it wants a few minutes to breakfast'. On the other hand he followed up the excursion to Topsham – itself a sharp reminder to Emma how much Tryphena had meant to him – by visiting the Stockwell Training College, not because he needed background for the training college adventures of Sue Bridehead – his own sisters had been to the very college in which he sets Sue – but obviously because Tryphena had been

at Stockwell. He dragged Emma round sordid London properties until she nearly fainted. He made no attempt to hide his interest in the glamorous Rosamund Tomson.

Both were inclined to hypochondria. Hardy carefully noted
every cold, bout of influenza, cough, attack of laryngitis or
indigestion, and similar ill that befell them. Now and then he
mentions his bladder trouble. Emma in her letters mentions
similar minor ills, but never her lameness, although it seems to
have been in one of its difficult phases, for in December 1890
Hardy conveyed a message from Mrs Jeune that Emma was to
stay with the Jeunes if she needed to see a London doctor
about it. Probably Hardy accepted the handicap as part of the
Emma he had always known, but in the orgy of self-
recrimination after her death the increasing infirmity of her
later years, and his indifference to it, were not forgotten.

> You did not walk with me
> Of late to the hill-top tree
>   By the gated ways,
>   As in earlier days;
>   You were weak and lame,
>   So you never came,
> And I went alone, and I did not mind,
> Not thinking of you as left behind.[65]

Inability to walk much, however, could be countered by
riding; inability to dance had no substitute. One can picture
her in the Society ballrooms, watching Hardy all a-gush over
some pretty partner, knowing the partner's place could never
be hers. As they became invited increasingly often into ever
more dazzling circles, the struggle of the undistinguished provincial woman to maintain her position would have been difficult without this gratuitous limitation, and not a little of her
jealous attitude towards Hardy's women friends surely sprang
from it.

At some time since leaving Tooting she had resumed riding,
for it was while travelling on horseback to the Sheridans' home
at Frampton Court, a month after their ball, that the sudden
thunder of a train crossing a railway bridge above the road
made her horse rear and nearly throw her. It did not succeed;

as Hardy, who never lost his wonder at her horsemanship, wrote in his diary, 'Very few horses could.' He states in the *Life* that this was the last time she rode, yet farther on he alludes to several later occasions.[66] His first reference to their bicycling is in the context of a Continental tour in 1895, but R. H. Tilley, who kept a cycle shop in South Street, Dorchester, says he taught both Hardys to ride about 1890; so the sad moment when Emma finally abandoned four legs for two wheels remains unknown.[67]

Apart from reporting his literary progress, Hardy's diary for 1891 reads more than ever like a Society column. Emma apparently accompanied him on at least half his activities during this, the last London Season before the storm over *Tess*, and probably on considerably more, since he frequently fails to make clear whether they were together or not. They also went to friends in Suffolk and Scotland, returning from the latter by way of a succession of cathedrals. The *Life* contains no reference to the death of Emma's mother – not because Hardy failed to record it, but because Florence once more cut the passage out.[68] If Emma attended the funeral, however, she did so alone.

CHAPTER SIX

From Tess *to the Century's End*

IN ADDITION TO BEING the year of the *Tess* phenomenon, 1892 beheld a phenomenon of another sort in the irruption into the Hardys' lives of the remarkable Owen sisters – Rebekah, an outstanding example of American womanhood at its brashest and most daunting, and Catharine, the elder of the two, a sweet and kindly being[1] of whom during her long years of inseparability from Rebekah not one independent action is recorded and only one utterance, which was that Florence Hardy could never visit her sister-in-law Kate 'without a gift in [her] paw'.[2] A fanatical disciple of Hardy from the age of thirteen, Rebekah was determined to meet her hero. In early summer the sisters and their maid left their home in Madison Square, New York, for England, where Rebekah, too shrewd rather than too timid to chance her luck on an unsupported assault on Max Gate, managed through a chain of intermediaries to gain an introduction.

In August the trio installed themselves on a four-month tenancy near Top o' Town, Dorchester, and the great encounter took place on 5 August, when both Owens appear to have formed an instant liking for both Hardys and vice versa. Rebekah was a good talker, a perceptive critic, and knew Hardy's work almost as well as he knew it himself. Moreover she was good-looking (unless she had changed radically from her appearance in the photograph taken thirteen years before), and she had a vivacious manner. Her success with Hardy was foregone. What impresses more is the degree of friendliness

144

that Emma showed her; for here, almost on the heels of Rosamund Tomson, was another woman younger and more attractive than herself, taking over her rôle of literary consultant. Yet within days she had invited the Owens to tea, within days more she took them on a picnic organised by Teresa Featherstonehaugh to visit Bindon Abbey and Wool Manor, before the month ended she requested them to drive with her to Upwey and they had asked the Hardys to tea at their lodgings.

Throughout September the hospitality continued on the same level. The effects of the new association on Hardy's work were small but significant. Within a month of meeting him Rebekah was taking him to task for omitting from the English volume edition of *The Mayor of Casterbridge* the episode of Henchard's return to Elizabeth-Jane with the goldfinch, which had appeared in the serial and American editions. In due course he restored the incident. She pointed out two mistakes in *Far from the Madding Crowd*, which he corrected. He used in *Jude* her observation that Oxford looked 'like the heavenly Jerusalem'. For the 1896 edition of *Wessex Tales* he changed the name of Susannah in 'Interlopers at the Knap' to Rebekah. In both *Jude* and the volume version of *The Well-Beloved*, the former written and the latter adapted from the serial version after the Owens had become known to him, he described a girl's sun-hat closely resembling one in a photograph of Rebekah taken when she was twenty-one, which she probably showed him in return for his showing her (according to her diary) one of himself at the same age. After her death the sun-hat photograph was found slipped into her copy of *Jude* at the page containing the description.[3]

In October, Rebekah's allusions to the Hardys rather perplexingly cease, but not from any deterioration in the new friendship, for it was resumed the next year and for many years to come. There are few instances in Hardy's life in which he reacted so warmly to an unsought intrusion into his home and private life, and none, until the advent of Florence Dugdale, in which Emma behaved with such persistent generosity towards one whom in some respects she must have recognised as a rival, and who repaid her kindness in such base coin. It is sometimes stated that Hardy's genius required the stimulus of his 'other'

women, including his Society belles, to counteract the steadily
increasing bleakness of his marriage. But seeing that his attentions to other women were one of the things that made his marriage bleaker this argument creates a vicious circle. However,
whatever view is taken, Emma's exceptional warmth towards
Rebekah – who showed no personal interest in her – is in-
explicable.

When the news reached Hardy in London from his sister
Mary that their father's days were drawing to a close, and
Thomas and Emma returned to Dorchester earlier than they
would otherwise have done, it is evident, if nowhere explicitly
stated, that Emma did not visit the dying man with him nor
afterwards attend the funeral. How different things might have
been if Jemima Hardy, instead of Mrs Gifford, had died the
previous year! It is difficult to imagine the kindly and easy-
going elder Thomas not having welcomed a reconciliation
with his daughter-in-law, nor the fundamentally kind-hearted
Emma having maintained any hostility towards this likeable
man, to the harmony of whose life-pattern Hardy paid tribute
in the memorial poem 'On One Who Lived and Died Where
He Was Born'.

During the year Hardy became a founder-member of the
Omar Khayyám Club, the creation of his friend Edward
Clodd, which may have added to Emma's gloom about his
beliefs. The philosophy of Omar Khayyám was not among
those she admired,[4] nor, for that matter, was Clodd's.[5] In
October, the month in which the serial version of *The Well-
Beloved* began to appear, Hardy paid a visit to Fawley in Berkshire, the future 'Marygreen' of *Jude* and a place filled with
family associations as keen as those of Dorset. 'Though I am
alive with the living I can see only the dead here,' he wrote,
'and am scarcely conscious of the happy children at play.'[6]
Emma was not with him, but the evocation of Fawley's dark
memories inevitably affected his mood when he returned.

The winter of 1892–3 was mainly occupied in writing the
first draft of *Jude* from notes made some six years earlier.[7]
Whether Emma saw this early 'rough' is to be doubted, despite
her association with all the stages of *Tess*. Her well-known
refusal to help Hardy with *Jude* does not appear to have been
made earlier than 1894, as we shall presently see. Certainly it

could not have been made before the summer of 1893, because what took place then was among its causes.

On 18 May 1893 the Hardys set out for Dublin in response to an invitation from Lord Houghton, the Viceroy of Ireland, to stay at the Viceregal Lodge. Houghton was a widower, and the place of hostess was taken by his sister Florence, Mrs Arthur Henniker. Their father had managed to be simultaneously a strict Unitarian, a famous and convivial host, and an even more famous collector of pornography, known in genteel circles as erotica. Florence, too, had literary tastes, but of a more respectable sort, and not confined to reading, for she had written three novels each of which had scored a moderate success. Add to this that she was thirty-eight years old, handsome rather than beautiful, slender and therefore appearing taller than she was, and possessed of a highly sophisticated vivacity, and inevitably Hardy became at once utterly enthralled. Indeed, although – as always – his passion simmered down in a very few years to the customary literary friendship, while it lasted its intensity justifies the assertion that during the whole of his life not more than half a dozen women, including his mother, elder sister, and both wives, affected him more deeply. Within days he was hoping to number her 'all my life among the most valued of my friends'. She was soon addressed as 'my dear fellow-scribbler' and 'a nearer friend – almost a sister', making her a sort of combination of Mary Hardy and Horace Moule. A brother-and-sister relationship, however, was scarcely that to which he must have struck Florence as aspiring. Of all his succession of pedestalled heroines between Tryphena Sparks and Florence Dugdale, Florence Henniker is the only one with whom it is possible to imagine him, had she been willing, committing adultery. But even with her willingness a number of factors would have stood in the way: his habitual diffidence, which would probably have been insurmountable if it is correct that since his illness at Tooting he had had problems with physical sex; a deep-seated loyalty to Emma when it came to the ultimate betrayal; and perhaps a tendency, not uncommon among notorious woman-chasers, to withdraw in terror from any woman prepared to allow fulfilment of their professed designs.

In any event, Florence was not prepared to allow anything.

For all her bonhomie, air of unshockability, and, one suspects, a certain come-hitherness of manner, she had two qualities for which Hardy was unprepared: strict fidelity to her husband, and a belief as unshakeable as Emma's in her religion. The latter, rather than the former, was the rock on which his exalted conception of her and of their incipient relationship was to be wrecked even sooner than most of his romances. But meanwhile the impact on Emma was almost catastrophic. Purdy, in his best meticulous but dry-as-dust manner, notes that 'Mrs Hardy's growing eccentricities were painfully manifest' in Dublin, but he fails to see or at least to name the reason. On top of so much that had transpired in the last four years – the Rosamund Tomson episode, the revival of Hardy's feeling for Tryphena, the phenomenon (due to reappear in a few months) of Rebekah Owen – the unashamed grovelling, which few can have failed to notice, at the feet of Mrs Henniker must have made Emma feel that her husband was not only slighting her but purposely turning her into a laughing-stock. Only one of her eccentricities in Dublin is named, her unsuitable style of dress – muslin and blue ribbons for a corpulent woman of fifty-two – which was precisely what no one could help observing, so that as she herself saw nothing amiss in her attire any covert smiles or comments surprised by her would be attributed to the situation she was being placed in by Hardy. At the end of the visit the Hardys went on by themselves to Killarney, where for a day or two they explored the countryside, he on foot, she riding a pony. The last time of which we have any record that they had journeyed in this way was on the cliffs near St Juliot, twenty years and more before.

> When living seemed a laugh, and love
> All it was said to be.[8]

As soon as Hardy was back home he began to assail Florence with letters, and within a fortnight they were both in London seeing Ibsen's *The Master Builder*, in which her sister had an important rôle. Further meetings followed. He gave her inscribed copies of three of his novels. She sent or handed over to him photographs of herself and 'many of the little pocket texts she liked to carry on walks'.[9] When Hardy and Emma saw Barrie's play *Walker, London* in June and afterwards went backstage he wrote Florence a long account. Barrie later observed that Florence Henniker 'took [Hardy] on holiday from himself' at a time of great strain at home. No one perceived that the holiday-resort might be contributing to the strain.

But strain was also beginning to creep into the ecstatic relationship. Hardy was finding out that notwithstanding Florence's enthusiasm for Ibsen nothing would shake her out of her respect for the Church and its teachings. Her obstinacy dismayed and infuriated him. At the beginning of August he sent her a letter (unfortunately lost) in which he set out all his basic views on life. Surely, if she really loved him, this would convert her; and when in reply she agreed to slip away from the Henniker country-residence at Southsea to meet him (similarly slipping away from Max Gate) for an expedition to Winchester he must have felt that victory was his. But alas, as they sat in the train taking them from their rendezvous at Eastleigh, the brief journey was long enough for her to make it fully clear that she could never accept the agnostic side of his views, nor offer him anything warmer than the regard of a sincere friend who shared much of his thinking on other subjects. Once again, as in so many of his romances, Hardy was brought down to earth, and if he fell harder this time than usual it was because the dreamer's wings had carried him higher. However, disillusion did not mean disengagement. He could capitalise on the relationship in verse, and better still, because it would bring them closer, they could collaborate on a short story. The story, which they called 'The Spectre of the Real', was written in October and published in *To-Day* a year later; the poems were spread over several years and include 'A Broken Appointment', 'A Thunderstorm in Town', 'At an Inn', and half a dozen more including, in part, the finest of all, 'Wessex Heights'.[10]

Weber picks out this period to introduce many of the anecdotes in disparagement of Emma already quoted. Few of the incidents are dated by him, but they may well belong to this dark season. In August 1893 the Owens appeared again in Dorchester just after the Hardys had left it to visit friends in Wenlock. Seeking out people who knew them, Rebekah wrote to Amy Williams, the daughter of Mr and Mrs Clapcott, who replied: 'I don't know Mrs Hardy and from what you told me feel the opposite of attracted.'[11] Meanwhile the Hardys had returned to Max Gate, and on being informed of the Owens' presence in the town the unattractive Mrs Hardy immediately wrote inviting them to lunch, adding: 'We shall be very glad to see you both again, and think you are very appreciative of Dorchester to return to us so kindly.'[12] After the lunch Hardy walked with Rebekah to the remains of Faringdon Winter-bourne Church, the 'Faringdon Ruin' of *The Trumpet-Major*, and while away from Emma told the American of his excursion to Winchester with Florence Henniker. He also gathered a big bunch of flowers for her, but apparently did not take any back to his wife. Perhaps he thought she had enough in the garden.

Later in the summer Amy Williams did see Emma at two garden parties, and reported to Rebekah that 'Mrs Hardy was got up just like "Charlie's [*sic*] Aunt", her hat and old-fashioned white lace veil being quite an amusement. Nor did she seem to know anyone but her hostesses.'[13] Nevertheless, Rebekah valued her contact with Hardy too highly not to con-tinue suffering the friendly hospitality of his wife. Host and guest went out for at least one other long walk together, dis-cussing *The Woodlanders*. But when Rebekah expressed a wish to revisit Bere Regis it was Emma who hired a carriage and took her not only to the village but to Woodbury Fair (the 'Greenhill Fair' of *Far from the Madding Crowd*) on the neighbouring height.[14]

Hardy now had relations with two literary ladies at once, although direct contact with Rebekah was limited to the time the Owens remained in England. (They left again, tem-porarily, in November 1893.) In addition to the hours spent with the ladies, he was preoccupied with *Jude*, with 'The Spectre of the Real', with collecting and preparing for book publication the stories in *Life's Little Ironies*, with drama-tising (at J. M. Barrie's request) his story 'The Three Stran-gers' for the stage, probably with preliminary plans for the dramatisation of *Tess*, with the first of the poems inspired by Florence Henniker, and with one or two that were not. There were also his London distractions and some in the

country, the two occasionally merging as when he and
Emma stayed with the Jeunes at Arlington Manor, near
Newbury, and picnicked in Savernake Forest.[15] Yet he could
find both the time and the mood to compose in this year, according to Weber, the poem 'A Two-Years' Idyll', harking
back to Sturminster Newton. It is a grim, grey poem, its theme
the folly that had prompted both Emma and himself to regard
their simple happiness as nought 'Save as a prelude to plays/
Soon to come – larger, life-fraught'; and the failure of those
larger things to materialise, so that looking back on the phase:

> What seems it now?
> Lost: such beginning was all;
> Nothing came after: romance straight forsook
> Quickly somehow
> Life when we sped from our nook,
> Primed for new scenes with designs smart and tall. . . .
> – A preface without any book,
> A trumpet uplipped, but no call;
> That seems it now.

Most critics take the poem to indicate Hardy's final disillusionment with his marriage. And so no doubt it was; but once
again, as with his other poems of disillusionment, its intensity
and bitterness betray the latent affection he still felt for his
wife. Long afterwards, in 1913, Florence Dugdale, telling
Edward Clodd in a letter that Hardy was on one of his pilgrim-
ages to St Juliot, wrote:[16] 'He says that he is going down for the
sake of the girl he married, and who died more than twenty
years ago.' That would fix her 'death' in about 1892. By 1913
he had read her 'black' diaries, but in 1893 he had probably
already persuaded himself that the high aspirations of the
Sturminster days had become a mockery – not because in material terms all but one of them had not been fulfilled, but because the love that alone could have given them meaning had
withered on the way. Emma's obsession with trying to change
his beliefs, her occasional remarks intended to humiliate him,
the absurd clothes with which she sometimes seemed to be
caricaturing their Society friends, her jealousy of his interest,
so natural to an author, in literary figures who just happened

151

to be women, and young, and handsome, and out of the top drawer: these were all proof, we can see him arguing, that her love for him was dead – for did he not always treat her with consideration, as his letters showed, did he not express pleasure in her company, at any rate when there was no other, was he not always loyal to the matrimonial vows even though he felt it his duty to proclaim ever more unequivocally his disbelief in the sanctity of marriage? If she still loved him, as he rose to prominence she would have made interest in that prominence increasingly her sole concern, sunk herself in his career to the exclusion of all else, as did the wives of all eminent men whose marriages were as successful as their careers. By 1893 he had convinced himself she no longer cared for him, and so in self-defence he must convince himself he no longer cared for her. But the depth of regret in 'A Two-Years' Idyll' betrays him, as other poems were to do at intervals, almost through to 1912. If his love had been dead he would have written of it cynically, sentimentally, or not at all, but never with the acerbity and strength of feeling that characterised his treatment of the subject during the two decades on either side of 1900.

Self-persuasion that Emma now meant nothing to him was unquestionably made much easier by his surge of affection for Mrs Henniker, which must have been nearly all that was needed to persuade Emma. She was finally convinced, as far as we can be precise, in 1894, when he is most likely to have shown her the full version of *Jude*. The outline draft, as already stated, was probably (despite Millgate's doubts[17]) completed by the spring of 1893.[18] Hardy then wrote the full version between August 1893 and some point in 1894. In the former year he had arranged for serialisation, on both sides of the Atlantic, in *Harper's New Monthly Magazine*; but by April 1894 the story that 'could not offend the most fastidious maiden was carrying him into unexpected fields', and he asked for the contract to be cancelled. This was refused, but after reading the first instalments the editor insisted on the all-too-familiar bowdlerisation. Hardy resignedly assented, and the serial, under its original title of 'The Simpletons' – changed after the first instalment to 'Hearts Insurgent' – ran from December 1894 to November 1895. Meanwhile Osgood, McIlvaine, who were to publish the book, received all but a few chapters of the unexpurgated version by the end of 1894 and the balance by March 1895. *Jude the Obscure* was published on 1 November 1895. It is probable, then, that it was the full version written during 1893–4 that was seen by Emma, the manuscript being presumably passed on for her customary comments and suggestions. If it is correct, as often stated, that one of her reasons for repudiating the work was that she saw in the character of Sue Bridehead more than a little of Florence Henniker, at a time when she knew Florence to be still occupying a major place in Hardy's affections, this is additional evidence that she did not repudiate the first draft, written before Hardy and Florence had met.

So we reach the most celebrated of all the tales against Emma put about by Carl Weber, that of her visit to Dr Richard Garnett, LLD, Keeper of Printed Books at the British Museum, to persuade him to use his influence towards preventing the publication of *Jude* on the grounds of its evil views. She is supposed to have first written Dr Garnett a letter, and on the failure of this to produce results to have gone up to London to see him, even shedding tears in his presence, all to no avail. One biographer after another has repeated the story, from Evelyn Hardy in 1954[19] to Harold Orel in 1976.[20] It remained for Robert Gittings to show the extremely dubious source from which Weber drew his material, and which he discreetly omitted to disclose. The anecdote comes from *Mightier than the Sword*, by Ford Madox Ford, a writer comparable in his generation only with Frank Harris for his unfortunate relationship with veracity. Gittings has quoted the gist of what Ford wrote, showing that he professed a disinclination to believe his own words. But so widely known is the Emma Hardy–Richard Garnett story that it may be of service to see in more detail exactly what Ford did write, and to examine the evidence for his statement.

In 1894 he was twenty, and still bore the surname of his German father, Hueffer, changing it to Ford only after the First World War. Already, in 1892, he had had a book, *The Brown Owl*, published by T. Fisher Unwin, a firm to which Dr Garnett was literary adviser, and he knew the Garnetts well. His account of the alleged incident is as follows (the dots are his and do not indicate omissions):

Then a storm burst on the British Museum. The young Garnetts went about with appalled, amused, incredulous, or delighted expressions, according as the particular young Garnett was a practising Anglican, an Agnostic, or a Nihilist . . . It began to be whispered by them that Mrs Hardy, a Dean's daughter, had taken a step . . . She had been *agonized* . . . she hadn't been able to *stand* it. The reception of *Tess* had been too *horrible* . . . for a Dean's daughter . . . All the Deans in Christendom had been driven to consternation about *Tess*. They had all arisen and menaced Max Gate with their croziers. (I know that Deans do not wear croziers. But that was the effect the young Garnetts had produced.)

It came out at last. Mrs Hardy had been calling on Dr Garnett as the Dean of Letters of the British Isles and Museum to beg, implore, command, threaten, anathematize her husband until he should be persuaded or coerced into burning the manuscript of his new novel – which was *Jude*. She had written letters; she had called. She had wept; like Niobe she had let down her blonde hair . . . The Agnostic and Nihilist young Garnetts rejoiced, the Anglicans were distraught. Doctor Garnett had obdurately refused . . . I don't believe I cared one way or the other. I didn't like the Church of England. On the other hand I didn't want any lady or a multitude of Deans to be distressed.

Ford goes on to claim that he had already met Hardy (he does not say if Emma was present) at a reception given by a Mrs Lynn Lynton (a name unmentioned by Hardy, mentioned once in a letter by Emma) and, finding that Hardy thought *The Brown Owl* was about birds, had written to him at Max Gate to explain its true nature. 'A long time afterwards', and following Emma's supposed visit to Dr Garnett, Hardy had written inviting Ford to 'drop in' at Max Gate, but when Ford did so he found only Emma 'in her Junonian blondeness' present. She read him her poems over 'a perfectly appointed tea-table', but he was more interested in discovering how false an image of Max Gate the young Garnetts had given him, in addition to substituting a 'Dean's daughter' for an archdeacon's niece. There is no suggestion that either *Jude* or Dr Garnett was discussed.

Everything turns on whether the young Garnetts really told Ford the story he professes to pass on, and whether, if they did, they were speaking the truth. There were six of them: May, the eldest, in 1894 aged thirty; Robert, twenty-eight, working with a firm of solicitors; Edward, twenty-six, a reader for T. Fisher Unwin and married; Olive, twenty-four; Lucy, nineteen; and Arthur, thirteen. Their parents probably did, as Ford states, already know the Hardys, for in Olive Garnett's vast diary covering the years 1892–1906 Dr and Mrs Garnett are mentioned as spending a fortnight's holiday at Max Gate in August 1901[21] – a lengthy sojourn suggesting a well-established friendship. The next question is why Emma should pick on Dr Garnett, a man distinguished for liberal rather than religious thinking, to whom to address herself. There are two possible reasons. A 'father-figure' to all his friends, he had a wide reputation for helpfulness and it was common knowledge in literary circles that he had recently shown immense patience in dealing with Lady Shelley, the poet's daughter-in-law, who had wanted him to write a biography of Shelley on extreme hagiological lines that in conscience he could never adopt. He had succeeded in declining the task while leaving Lady Shelley unoffended.

On the other hand the supreme tact that he had shown with Lady Shelley makes it highly unlikely that if Emma had made an approach he would let her confidential business become known to his household, let alone noised abroad by them in the manner asserted by Ford. Indeed, if either letter or interview ever had a basis in fact there is strong internal evidence that he kept them from his family; for surely Olive would have noted the meeting in her diary, and in addition there is still surviving a large scrap-album in which Dr Garnett's wife pasted letters from most of the literary figures who wrote to her husband.[22] Here, too, there is nothing from either of the Hardys.

A few years ago a number of letters to Dr Garnett from famous people were sold, but the present members of the family have no recollection of any from Emma. Nor are there any among the letters remaining with the family, nor in the Garnett correspondence in the British Library, nor listed in the British Museum Letter Books for the years 1892–5. The Visitors' Books for the same period have perished. The official records, however, are of secondary importance, since in 1894 the Garnetts were living in the Librarian's House in the Museum block itself,[23] so that Emma could have visited the Doctor without passing through official channels.

On balance, the negative evidence and the probabilities both seem to discount any truth in Ford's story. At the same time he must have had *some* source for the tale, however much he embroidered and garbled it. Against his bad reputation, summed up in Edward Garnett's description of Ford's biography of the artist Madox Brown as 'slovenly, vague, and full of generalisations about things of which he knew nothing',[24] there is the comment of Professor Tom Moser, Ford's principal biographer, that 'Certainly more often than not I have found apparently fabulous tales of his own life to be literally true'.[25]

Ford wrote a number of articles on Hardy, published in 'Literary Portraits' (*Daily Mail* Books Supplement No. 3, 6 July 1907), 'Literary Portraits' IX, *Outlook* XXXII, 8 November 1913, *American Mercury* XXXVIII, August 1936, and *Portraits from Life*, 1937. In November 1936 Carl J. Weber wrote a long letter to the editor of *American Mercury* pointing out several mistakes in Ford's August article. In the same issue Ford replied with a letter equally long that included the paragraph:

The fact is, sir, that as I sufficiently announced to you before writing this series of articles, I have been trying – to the measure of the light vouchsafed me – to preserve the memories of a body of men to whom I, as must be evident, was much attached – but to preserve them as I saw them, not as Mr Weber deduces from Official Biographies. The Carl J. Webers of this world are all most honourable men and I hope they may all die rectors of Heidelberg, Jena, or Gottingen Universities.

Neither Ford nor Weber mentioned Mrs Hardy.

Finally there is a piece of evidence that, if true, not only further discredits the Garnett story but also invalidates all speculation on the stage at which Emma read the *Jude* manuscript. In his memoirs entitled *Celebrities and Simple Souls* (London, 1933, page 58) the dramatist Alfred Sutro describes a luncheon at Max Gate to which he was invited soon after the publication of *Jude*:

I was loud in my praises of that work. Mrs Hardy was far from sharing my enthusiasm. It was the first novel of his, she told me, that he had published without first letting her read the manuscript: had she read it, she added firmly, it would *not* have been published, or at least, not without considerable emendations. The book had made a difference to them in the County. . . . Hardy said nothing, and did not lift his eyes from the plate.

As far as I am aware, no attention has been drawn to this statement by any of those who have discussed Emma and *Jude*. Can it be that Hardy did indeed make some excuse for not showing her the manuscript, precisely because he knew the objections she would raise? It is not impossible that she first read the story as a printed serial, and that what, according to Dr Fisher, she flung back at Hardy was not his manuscript but whichever instalment of the serial contained what she felt was the final straw. She could still have gone to Dr Garnett in an attempt to prevent book publication, but she had enough common sense to have more probably realised that by then it was already too late.

Whatever the truth of the Garnett affair, it seems to be a fact that Emma told Hardy she would have nothing to do with any further novels he wrote.[26] The immediate practical effect of her decision is obscured by the circumstance that, apart from the volume adaptation of *The Well-Beloved*, he wrote no more novels. It has been suggested that among the reasons for the 'end of prose' was the actual physical strain of virtually writing a book twice over in the absence of an amanuensis.[27] But a reference to Purdy shows that since *The Woodlanders* Emma had done very little fair-copying,[28] and in default of her it should have been no trouble for a man in Hardy's position to hire a reliable copyist. It was in realms other than the practical that Emma's withdrawal made a difference. Her reason may have been the profane tone of the new novel, coming on top of years of less and less acceptable attitudes in Hardy's earlier work, but the result was precisely the same as though, without specific disapproval of *Jude*, she had suddenly given up her losing fight to compete with Hardy's newer literary women. Their path was now open. He need not worry (not that he did) any longer about his wife's claims. For twenty-four years she had been his professional helpmeet, but now more intellectual companions were available, and her voluntary retirement was unexpectedly diplomatic, if somewhat violent in execution.

Possibly her failing control over the one remaining major bond between them was a factor in her decision to sever it, but unquestionably *Jude the Obscure* filled her with a distaste and indignation that none of her husband's previous books had provided. Many conjectures have been made as to exactly what in the novel outraged her most, conjectures not rendered any simpler by differences of opinion on how many real-life prototypes whom Emma knew or knew about were blended in the characters, and to what extent. It has been plausibly argued that in the development of Sue Bridehead Emma saw a mockery of her own religion. Since neither in letters nor in reported conversations did Hardy ever criticise Emma *personally* for her beliefs (as she criticised him for his), showing what happened to fictional characters of similar persuasion may be accepted as his method of demonstrating, to her and to the world, the measure of his disagreement. But Emma already knew Thomas's views, and he had been airing them in his novels with growing pungency for years past. Nor was he the first in the field to criticise marriage. As long ago as 1855 Harriet Grote, wife of the respected historian of Greece, had published a poem part of which ran:

> Full many a sorrowful and tragic tale
> Enfolded lies beneath the semblance frail
> Of wedded harmony and calm content!
> How oft the heart in aching bosom pent,
> And careworn thoughts, are borne abroad unseen,
> Veiled in the aspect of a cheerful mien,
> By the sad murmur of a home unblest,
> A faith dishonoured and a life opprest.
>
> Thus since the State direct that woman's fate
> Should hang upon the fiat of her mate,
> Slight hope that private feeling will assume
> A juster tone, or mitigate her doom.
> Bereft of rights, she learns to wear her chain;
> And seeks, by art, the mastery to gain,
> Unworthy study, which a juster code

Might turn aside, or turn to nobler good.
The want of will in men – not want of power,
Defers redemption to a distant hour.
Far distant! for what eye hath seen the strong
Relieve the weak because he did them wrong?

There were one or two other early pioneers, including such popular song-writers as T. H. Bayly; and, in a letter written in November 1895 to Edward Clodd, Hardy himself referred to the 'sheaf of purpose-made novels we have had lately on the marriage question'.[29]

So neither the attitude to religion and marriage in *Jude* nor the introduction of certain *innamorate* seems quite enough to explain the intensity of Emma's reaction, and it is possible that the additional, clinching cause was something more personal to her than even her faith, namely her sexuality – or lack of it. For, although she would almost certainly, one feels, have been mistaken, there is a strong possibility that she may have seen in the frigid yet teasing Sue a satire on herself during the first years of marriage. Narrow-minded she was not, but Sue's custom of tempting men while always too fastidious to have carnal relations with them – even with the student with whom she told Jude she had lived – may, if indeed Emma had found herself frigid during the early years of wedlock, have seemed like a cruel lampoon. Worse still, when Hardy and Emma were trying to produce a child at Sturminster Newton it was presumably with love, and certainly with a wish to become a mother, that she overcame her distaste, if she felt any, for the sexual act, all to no purpose. When Sue by contrast overcame her distaste and gave herself to Jude, it was only out of a cold, jealous desire to keep him from a re-entanglement with Arabella – yet she bore children, in whom her interest was negligible. 'Such a type of woman', wrote Hardy to Edmund Gosse, apropos of Sue, 'has always had an attraction for me.' It is unlikely that he had his wife in mind, but there could be just enough validity in the comparison for her to see more than was intended. Some such deeply intimate personal affront, however unintended, is needed to explain her actions.

Matters were not improved the following year – mid-1895,

two months before the book publication of *Jude* and while as 'Hearts Insurgent' it was in full run as a serial – by Hardy's becoming enamoured of yet another high-born beauty of literary pretensions, almost before his passion for Florence Henniker had simmered down. It chanced that in the course of the social round, which he and Emma kept up as usual, they were invited to stay for a week near Tollard Royal, on the Dorset fringe of Wiltshire, with General and Mrs A. H. Pitt-Rivers at their mansion, Rushmore. General Pitt-Rivers, distinguished archaeologist, authority on weapons, and eccentric philanthropist, had laid out part of his estate as a park for public recreation. This was the Larmer Gardens, so named from the presence in them of the Larmer Tree, an ancient wych-elm under which tradition has it that King John used to assemble his huntsmen prior to hunting in Cranborne Chase, and where later the Court Leet used to be held. Here, in beautiful woodlands around a vast and superb lawn, the General constructed an ornamental pool, a bandstand, theatre and 'temple', and a number of picnic-houses, in various styles of Indian architecture, which he supplied with furniture and even crockery. The whole fairyland was approached by a broad avenue of trees festooned with lamps. At the peak of the venture 24,000 people visited the Gardens on a single Sunday.[30]

Among the attractions was a Sports Day, and this occurred during the Hardys' visit. Events were not limited to sports, and included a concert and, finally, dancing; and when the ballroom dancing gave way to country dancing the first dance was led off by Thomas Hardy and the General's stately and beautiful daughter Agnes, Mrs (later Lady) Grove. Once more, as in Dublin only a little over two years earlier, Emma saw her husband pass instantly under the spell of a woman, this time little more than half his age – or her own. Emma was, in fact, distantly connected with Agnes Grove, Mrs Jeune being by her first marriage Agnes's aunt; but although they were destined to become reasonably friendly, Agnes being more than once a guest at Max Gate and at the Hardy tea parties during the London Season – where she took over the rôle of hostess on occasions when Emma felt too unwell – at this first encounter Emma appears to have been quietly ignored. Agnes Grove's diary entry for the day reads: 'Went to Larmer Tree sports.

Met and talked to Thomas Hardy, found him interesting. Dined there.' One is left to wonder whether she was introduced to Mrs Hardy at all. More than thirty years later Thomas, then eighty-six, was moved by news of Lady Grove's death to compose the poem 'Concerning Agnes', recalling their first encounter and including the lines:

> I could not, though I should wish, have over again
> > That old romance,
> And sit apart in the shade as we sat then
> > After the dance
> The while I held her hand. . . .

A stranger seeing the two figures hand in hand in the shadows, and who knew that Hardy had arrived for the evening escorting his wife, might have pardonably supposed that Agnes was she. Mrs Grove had to leave for London the following day, but Hardy had already discovered that she was interested in journalism. Pausing only to tell Florence Henniker that he had just experienced 'the most romantic time I have had since I visited you in Dublin', he proceeded to initiate his usual routine of fervent correspondence, and in next to no time Agnes was established as his journalistic trainee, soon to be praised as 'my good little pupil'. Unlike Florence and himself, they had to wait more than six months before they could meet again, but meanwhile *Jude* had been published and he immediately sent her a copy, confident that it would meet with her approval although she was happily married and the mother of three children. Fiery and dominating, a militant champion of women's suffrage, anti-vivisection (both equally dear to Emma), anti-vaccination, political Liberalism, and various other 'advanced' causes, Agnes was in many ways a woman after Hardy's own heart, though he never, it seems, felt the stirrings of sexual passion for her that he had felt for Mrs Henniker, and the relationship sobered down into the post-infatuation phase more rapidly. Fortunately, too, Walter Grove, the husband, was an amiable man content to stand, as it were, placidly chewing the cud two paces behind his flamboyant wife, whom he called 'my little pepper-pot'.

Desmond Hawkins, to whose article in *Encounter* magazine

I am indebted for much of the foregoing information, reiterates the view that Hardy needed the stimulus of these new women friends for his work.[31] If Emma had been the type of wife content to sink her own personality in the furtherance of her husband's career, this might have been so, but since his turning to other women served merely to worsen considerably his home atmosphere the net effect on his work is debatable. The combined inspiration of Mrs Henniker and Mrs Grove did not inspire any new novels after *Jude* – which would have been written, probably no less brilliantly, had there been no Mrs Henniker – and, apart from those poems addressed (in effect) directly to them, it is difficult to believe that Hardy's verse would have remained unborn without the two ladies. It was not they, but his gloom over Emma, that inspired most of his best poetry during the 1890s and 1900s.

Even Emma could not have anticipated the critical virulence that greeted *Jude*. Screams of 'Jude the Obscene', 'dirt, drivel, and damnation' and 'Hardy the Degenerate', news of one copy burned by a bishop and the ashes of another sent from Australia, a critical rebuke even from Edmund Gosse, meant that the distressed Emma, who must have felt that all these strictures were personally directed by God, found herself, in Gittings's words, 'marked down as the wife of a notorious blasphemer and pornographer'.[32]

Yet life had to be carried on, and Society, having decided that in *Tess* Hardy had qualified for lionisation, not ostracism, was indisposed to reverse its judgement for the sake of the same sins grown blacker. Only in Dorset did the press condemnation of the novel produce what Hardy somewhat darkly refers to as 'phenomena among his country friends which were extensive and peculiar'.[33] He was not so alienated from his wife as not to be distressed by this. Despite his interest in Mesdames Henniker and Grove his depression had, ever since the death of his father, been steadily deepening; and it found its expression at about this time in three linked poems which he at first called 'De Profundis' but later (after Oscar Wilde had used that title) 'In Tenebris'. In essence they summarise and expand the old sense of personal victimisation that he had felt from the time of the *Spectator*'s blistering review of *Desperate Remedies*. Thus victimised, he is spiritually dead, and it would have been better had he died altogether. Blow after blow has smitten him, until he has become immune to further thrusts. So the first poem; the second exchanges the despair of the first for a righteous anger at those who in their smug all's-right-with-the-world philosophy dare to revile him for pointing out (in *Tess* and *Jude*) that all is *not* well. It is this poem that contains the line often cited as the key to Hardy's 'pessimistic' philosophy: 'Who holds that if way to a Better there be, it exacts a full look at the Worst'. It is also the poem that, by asserting (in ironic terms) his duty to be true to his own experience at whatever cost, moves Bailey to suggest that part of that cost may have been the pain he knew he was causing Emma by overriding her (supposed) pleas for the abandonment of *Jude*.[34]

The third 'In Tenebris' poem returns to the resigned and gloomy mood of the first, recalling three moments at Higher Bockhampton during his childhood when it would have been better for him to have died than have lived on to suffer disillusion. Although the critical reception of *Jude* was obviously a major motive of these poems, it is impossible not to connect their mood also with the state of his marriage. His behaviour towards his wife continued to be a paradox. On the one hand he humiliated her by holding Agnes Grove's hand in public, upset her beyond measure by going ahead with the publication of *Jude*, considered her love for him to be dead (as revealed in the letter by Florence Hardy quoted on page 151), and virtually read the burial service over it in framing 'In Tenebris'. On the other hand only in April 1895, barely a month after completing the book version of *Jude* and not long, one must judge, after she had thrown it back in his face, he wrote to her during a stay in London: 'I was afraid you might think by my advising you not to come till Tuesday that I do not want you here. Of course I do, as it is very lonely and dismal. I meant solely on your own account.'[35] Less than a fortnight after *Jude* had appeared he told Florence Henniker he was 'acting as head nurse to Em', who had neuralgia.[36] The following January she fell ill again, with what Mrs Jeune believed to be shingles, and went to Brighton to recuperate. Early in February, after reporting from London that he was just getting over a 'fearful depression', he wrote to her in Brighton: 'If I take a house soon you must promise to come straight up into it, and not go out of doors while this sort of weather lasts.'[37] In a letter to Mrs Henniker some two years earlier, on learning that she was going to a ball, he had adjured her: 'Don't fag yourself out. Promise you won't.'[38] Critics have quoted this as an example of his tender consideration for her, but no such comment is made about the similar solicitude in the letter to Emma.

Two days later, after his letter to Brighton, apparently following the expression by her of a doubt about her rooms, he ordered her not to have a cheap lodging, and offered 'willingly [to] pay the difference between the prices'.[39] Soon afterwards he developed a chill, followed by rheumatism, as a result of which he decided to join her in Brighton. They must have been there together, cut off from friends both provincial and metropolitan, while the rage over *Jude* was seething at its most effervescent. Perhaps the consciousness of being fellow-victims of the abuse drew them together in spite of themselves. Unquestionably Hardy was to blame, but the very Christianity that had made Emma feel it her sacred duty utterly to try to reject the book may have acted on her basic affection to make her also feel a wife's obligation to stand by her husband in adversity.

Yet it is later in the year that we can discern a gleam of fleeting reconciliation, a kind of *lux in tenebris*, like the one spring day that never fails to grace the most wintry of Februarys. After a mainly unremarkable London Season, prolonged until the beginning of August, they returned briefly to Max Gate, then went on holiday to the West Midlands, where they climbed the Worcestershire Beacon, he on foot, she on a mule (once again that ghost of Beeny!), penetrated as far as Coventry, then moved south-eastward through Reading to Dover. Here they dallied a fortnight during which Hardy, who either bought or already had with him a volume of Matthew Arnold's poems, wrote against 'Dover Beach': 'Sept. 1896 – T. H./E. L. H.' Some believe he was drawing attention in particular to the words 'Ah, love, let us be true/To one another!' and see in this the main hint of reconciliation. I do not dispute the hint of reconciliation, but to understand the poem's bearing on it we must read the whole stanza:

> Ah, love, let us be true
> To one another! for the world, which seems

To lie before us like a land of dreams,
So various, so beautiful, so new,
Hath really neither joy, nor love, nor light,
Nor certitude, nor peace, nor help for pain;
And we are here as on a darkling plain
Swept with confused alarms of struggle and flight,
Where ignorant armies clash by night.

The poem was probably already familiar to Emma, who found
'comfort' in Matthew Arnold's verse.[40] Knowing this, Hardy
may have felt she would share his reading of its message that,
following their own belief in a land of dreams, they, too, in
their clash of 'certitudes' over what was wrong with the world
and what would be right for it, had reached a point where there
was no certitude, nor peace, nor help for pain. The last three
lines could well describe the turmoil roused by *Tess* and *Jude*,
leaving the author and his wife as on a darkling plain. In such a
context, the exhortation 'Ah, love, let us be true/To one
another!' presents itself as a tentative invitation to Emma not
to hate him too much in a situation in which the happiness of
both had been mislaid. That by now he seriously believed she
hated him, probably as the result of *Jude*, is demonstrated by
another poem composed by him at about this time, 'The Dead
Man Walking'. It opens:

They hail me as one living,
    But don't they know
That I have died of late years,
    Untombed although?

– then describes the stages of his dying, until we reach the
stanza:

And when my Love's heart kindled
    In hate of me,
Whereof I know not, died I
    One more degree.

'Whereof I know not', though at first impression disingenuous, may in fact have been true. The remaining words are
without ambiguity, and once again prove Hardy's underlying

affection, or his wife's 'hatred' would not have caused him to 'die' a little more. His obvious distress at it is another reason for believing he made an attempt in this year to mend matters.

Douglas Brown also believed in a temporary reconciliation at this time, but from a different cause. Hardy, reasons Brown, sought in travel with Emma a means of forgetting the notoriety occasioned by *Jude*, and with his thoughts turning more and more (as shown in his notebooks) towards *The Dynasts*, that prospect and the vision of devoting his remaining years to poetry were such that 'he recovered his composure and he and Emma experienced a brief return to happiness'.[41]

Weber, as might be expected, will have none of this, rebuking Brown and falling back on the commencement of 'In Tenebris' in 1895 and the letters of that year, 'eloquent in what they do not say', as his authority.[42] But I have quoted some of the things the letters *do* say; furthermore, whereas Weber in his editing of *'Dearest Emmie'* attaches great significance to the cooling of affection evidenced by Hardy's change in 1893 from the superscription 'My dearest Em' to 'My dear Em', several 1895 letters revert to 'My dearest Em', and at the close of one of them the habitual 'Yours affectionately' is replaced with 'Yours very affectionately' – the only letter in the collection to bear this warm valediction.

Whether by prearrangement or on impulse – possibly as the outcome of warmer relations – from Dover they crossed the Channel for a tour of the Low Countries. For a year or more now they had both been addicts of the fashionable cycling craze, doing most of their riding together, sometimes unaccompanied, sometimes with Gordon and Lilian Gifford, Hermann Lea, or the Wood Homers.[43] Now Emma's bicycle, presumably summoned from Max Gate for the purpose, went with them to the Continent. Her bicycles, like her attire, tended towards the spectacular, and were usually of a colour to match her costume, which for cycling was always of velvet. Her present machine, painted a splendid green and called The Grasshopper, lived up to its name by frequently disappearing, generally while in transit on the railway, only to reappear triumphantly just when given up for lost. The pair spent a month abroad, and Gittings suggests that perhaps they were trying to recapture the spirit of their honeymoon travels.[44] In so far as Hardy had told his brother that his honeymoon trip was for purposes of research, and he was now much interested in the scenes that would figure in *The Dynasts*, this is undoubtedly correct. But on this occasion, though he again visited the field of Waterloo, he did not walk Emma off her feet there, which is perhaps as good a reason as any for considering the journey one of reconciliation. Yet there were shadows even now. Staying deliberately in the same hotel in Brussels that they had occupied more than twenty years before, Hardy found the experience melancholy enough for him to write to his 'dear little friend' Florence Henniker (who was holding her own gallantly against Agnes Grove) that he wondered why he was in Brussels again instead of 'underground'. And he counselled her, if she replied, to put 'Mr' on the envelope.[45] Reconciliation did not extend to the discouragement of his lady friends' correspondence, only to making sure it did not fall into his wife's hands.

After the return to England he had one more prose task to accomplish, the preparation of *The Well-Beloved* for book-publication. But before the end of the year he also composed the poem 'Wessex Heights', with its enigmatic references. One must infer that Emma, having repudiated her husband's prose, was not at this period reading his poetry either. It is all but impossible to believe that she was privy to 'In Tenebris' or to 'The Dead Man Walking', with its direct reference to her 'hate'; and of 'Wessex Heights' it has been said that its appearance in print was deliberately postponed to spare her feelings.[46] However, if she returned to his prose to read *The Well-Beloved*, published in March 1897, she can have derived little solace from it. Perhaps she had read the serial version six years earlier; her only recorded comment on the story was made in a letter to Rebekah Owen in 1901, when she remarked that she did 'not like "The Well-Beloved" as some people do'.[47] There was plenty in it to displease her, if she chose to see it there: the ageing Pierston on his perpetual quest when other men had matured and become fathers of families; the three Avices, with their reminder of the three Sparks sisters who had successively attracted the young Hardy; the parade of London Society figures, some recognisably modelled on women she knew and regarded collectively as having lured him away from her; most wounding of all, the similarity between the ravaged Marcia in the last section of the book, 'the image and superscription of Age', and Emma herself to whom he was shortly to refer, if he had not composed the poem already, in the lines:

> 'O memory, where is now my love,
> That rayed me as a god above?'

> 'I saw her in an ageing shape
>   Where beauty used to be. . . .'[48]

Perhaps it was also with her in mind, or perhaps merely she so read it, that he made Pierston utter the following words to Somers:

'To see the creature who has hitherto been perfect, divine, lose under your very gaze the divinity which has informed her, grow common-place, turn from flame to ashes, from a radiant vitality to a relic, is anything but a pleasure for any man, and has been nothing less than a racking spectacle to my sight. . . . I have been absolutely miserable when I have looked in a face for her I used to see there, and could see her there no more.'[49]

Alma Priestley, in a long article in the *Thomas Hardy Society Review*, argues convincingly that in his pursuit of the unattainable Jocelyn Pierston is very much a projection of Hardy himself.[50] The above passage is quoted in the article, on another page of which the author also quotes the first part of the following extract from *Desperate Remedies*, written at the opposite end of Hardy's prose career:

With all, the beautiful things of the earth become more dear as they elude pursuit; but with some natures utter elusion is the one special event which will make a passing love permanent for ever. . . . Few knew that Gaye's unmanageable heart could never be weaned from useless repining at the loss of its first idol.[51]

The two passages are not directly associated by Alma Priestley, but if we do associate them and relate them to Emma they provide still further evidence that Hardy never entirely lost his love for her. In so far as he idealised and sublimated the woman he met on his visits to St Juliot, his sisters (as quoted by Florence Hardy) were right in maintaining that she had never existed. From the outset she was the Unattainable; and, as the realities of married life and the corrosion of Time sent the Unattainable farther and farther out of reach, the approach to 'utter elusion' did render Hardy's love 'permanent for ever', and his unmanageable heart, as the poems of his years of disillusion show, never unweaned from useless repining. He fancied, or persuaded himself that he fancied, that the Unattainable had transferred itself to Rosamund Tomson, Florence Henniker, Agnes Grove; but when Emma died he realised that the idol to which he had clung had been, all along, his pristine vision of *her*, and the truth came out in the flood of love-poems.

Perhaps it was the London scenes in *The Well-Beloved* that most perturbed her in 1897, with their reminder of what she believed Society, by elevating her husband to the summit of its esteem, had done to their marriage; for this year, to judge from the dates on the letters Irene Cooper Willis allowed to survive, began the correspondence in which she was to lay bare her inmost thoughts to Alfred Pretor, the wise and kindly Cambridge don. She must have commented to Pretor on the difficulties of being married to a celebrity, since he replies to her (in a note that is evidently no more than a postscript to his main letter, now missing):

Regarding my letter of yesterday, I think anyone who married a celebrity (i.e. *public* property) can rarely expect much private happiness or individual recognition. It sounds hard; but I should have been prepared for it if I had married (say *Patti*!) which I should have been proud to do.[52]

She was to raise the subject again more than once, and not only to Pretor, during the coming years. However, the tentative *rapprochement* of 1896 seems to have continued through 1897. With the Queen's Diamond Jubilee looming, Emma was reluctant to face the London Season this year, and Hardy effected a compromise by arranging for them to stay in Basingstoke, from which it was an easy train-journey into the metropolis each day. One of their regular practices for some years past had been to attend the popular concerts at the Imperial Institute in South Kensington, and unlike the exchanges of hospitality with their friends, or even the visits to the annual Academy Exhibition at which it was *de rigueur* to be seen, patronage of the concerts 'mostly neglected by Londoners'[53] can have had no motive but pleasure. The music was provided by Continental light bands or orchestras, such as the Viennese musicians conducted by Edward Strauss,[54] and generally the Hardys went together. One wonders whether it touched a chord in either when a melody came up, as in the nature of things it must sometimes have done, that they had known at St Juliot. Hardy's diary for 1898 provides what may be a pointer. In that year he attended some of the concerts by himself, and he notes that on one occasion the band (Italian this time) 'played a "Contemplazione" by Luzzi'. One possible explanation for his singling out this item by a composer whose vogue was extremely modest even in his lifetime (1828–76) is that Hardy had heard this or another piece of Luzzi's played by Emma at the Rectory. Perhaps it was his reaction to similar experiences when Emma was with him that afterwards prompted her to play the old melodies as her final attempt at reconciliation.

They also saw in 1897 one or two plays by Ibsen, a dramatist the liking for whom is cited as testimony to an *avant-garde* outlook when the enthusiast is Florence Henniker but is passed over without comment when she is Emma.[55]

As the Diamond Jubilee junketings drew near they slipped away to Switzerland, where, everyone of note having travelled in the opposite direction to crowd into London, 'the charm of a lonely Continent impressed the twain much'.[56] Once more Emma kept a diary, a good deal less detailed than its predecessors and lacking her former enthusiasm. Norman Page has noted 'a tendency for them to go their separate ways' in references to Emma having breakfasted and gone out before Hardy was up, or to his walking far behind.[57] This may be true, but it is possible to read too much into it: couples who have been married much more happily than the Hardys for nearly a quarter of a century do not always perform every action in unison as they did when on honeymoon. He may have walked behind because, as he told Florence Henniker, the heat 'pulled him

down' during part of the trip, whereas Emma remained 'in excellent health and vigour',[58] or because for part of the time she
saved her energies by riding a pony (having been dissuaded
from tackling the Alps on a hired bicycle!) whereas he journeyed throughout on foot. Similarly too much can be made of
her alluding to him in the diary as 'TH' instead of the previous
'Tom'. Florence Hardy, once she had passed the 'Mr Hardy'
stage, always referred to him in correspondence as 'TH'. Brevity in these matters springs more often than not from simple
convenience.

In August they visited Wells, Frome, Longleat and Salisbury, where they attended service together in the Cathedral,
and in the autumn they cycled to 'many places' before the pastime was brought to a temporary halt by Emma suffering an
accident. Not yet, it would seem, the next rupture; and so
through almost all of 1898 until December, when *Wessex
Poems* was published. Identification of some of the protagon-
ists who inspired the personal poems in this heterogeneous collection is uncertain, but from Emma's point of view all that
mattered was that they were about young women towards
whom Hardy had had romantic leanings. Nearly a dozen
poems fall into this category, against only one – 'Ditty', composed way back in the earliest St Juliot days – dedicated to herself, and one, 'The Ivy-Wife', which she took (whether rightly
or not) to be a direct and cruel attack on her.[59] There was also
'Thoughts of P—a', the 'lost prize' beside whom, as the world
would read it, she was only second-best.

What explanation can be found for the wanton bring-
ing-down of this jackboot on the tender seedling of better
matrimonial relations? Some critics, among them Gittings[60]
and Zietlow,[61] believe that Hardy's extraordinarily cryptic
preface statement that the poems are 'dramatic or personative
in conception; and this even when they are not obviously so' is
a disclaimer of any personal involvement – though Zietlow
points out that Hardy justifies his assertion with the words 'in
large degree'. Perhaps so, but the tenor of the whole preface is
a defence addressed to the critics and the public, not to Emma.
It seems more likely that the key lies at the other end of the
volume, in the poem he significantly placed last, 'I Look Into
My Glass'. In this he laments that within his worn-out frame

he remains only too distressed 'by hearts grown cold to me'. Notwithstanding the tentative *rapprochement*, he was convinced that the coldness which had frozen Emma's heart had not yet melted. What should she care, then, if he looked back on happier romances? After all, by including 'Ditty' he had allowed her a place in the company, and lest he push matters too far he had omitted 'Wessex Heights'. True, he may have omitted it simply because he felt it unsuitable for a first collection; but other omitted poems, such as the 'In Tenebris' trilogy, appeared in the next volume, whereas 'Wessex Heights' was held back until after Emma's death.

Those who believe that the breach between the Hardys in the 1890s was complete, and that their association was entirely limited to what was necessary to preserve appearances, maintain that Hardy published his wounding poems because he no longer cared what effect they had on his wife. Against this I have tried to show not only that much that they continued to do together was not required by 'appearances', but also that a succession of poems composed during the period reveal his deep hurt at the barrier that had risen between them. 'I Look Into My Glass' demonstrates that the hurt continued, but that he believed there was no corresponding hurt in Emma. What should she, in her unlovingness, care about these other loves!

But she did care. Deeply wounded, she turned to her counsellor, Alfred Pretor, for whom she was currently correcting the proofs of his first volume of short stories, written at her prompting. He had now retired from Cambridge and was living at Wyke Regis, close to Weymouth. They visited one another sometimes; in his reply to her appeal he deplores her 'nasty ride home' and names his free days for coming to Max Gate, for he was Hardy's friend as well as hers, which made it easier for him to understand their differences. Since *Wessex Poems* appeared with less than three weeks of the year left, his letter, dated 1898, implies that Emma had read the poems before publication, perhaps in proof. He concludes:

If we want romance for a poem or a story we all naturally hunt up and exaggerate details from the days of our youth – simply because *there* we find the romance and sparkle that have ended in sterling, sober happiness of quite another kind.

The following April, still indignant, she clearly had the poems in mind when she wrote to Rebekah Owen, who with her sister Catharine and the maid had now left the United States for good and acquired a house in the Lake District,

I hope you do not like all TH's [poems] because I dislike some: his delicate irony is too often taken for tenderness I suspect. He should be the last man to disparage marriage. I have been a devoted wife for at least twenty years or more – but the last four or five alas! Fancy it is our silver wedding this year! The *thorn* is in my side still.

Irrelevant to the sore question of the poems, but shedding further interesting light on Emma's standard of literary education, another part of the letter reads:

By the bye! Was it not Mirabeau who said, Let me die with flowers and was their true lover? *not* Robespierre. Yet Irving in the new play carries a bouquet. I cannot refer to Lamartine or a Biography because I have so few books of my own.... I mean to have a small library soon – pocket editions.

Evidently access to Thomas's library was forbidden.[62] Still in the same letter, Emma confesses she does not carry books to read on cycling expeditions, as she can no longer see to read out of doors. She had been having trouble with her sight since at latest 1894, when Lady Jeune, as she had then become, advised her to see an oculist.[63] Whether her failing eyesight had anything to do with the succession of minor cycle accidents she suffered it is impossible to say. In May 1899 she experienced another, this time spraining her ankle; and once more Hardy, who chanced to be in London, wrote with seemingly genuine concern.[64]

At some point she wrote again to Pretor on the theme of marriage to a celebrity, eliciting this reply:

Thanks for your very kind letter. It has interested me though at the same time troubled me deeply more especially as it throws new light on a character that I have always admired, and also because I can give so little advice or help.

All I can do is to express my own feelings on the subject. In the first place such an ideal union as the Brownings' is (I venture to think) unique, at any rate between two such gifted people, although I know it often occurs among the unheard-of 'many'. At any rate, no one in the lottery of life has a right to expect or reckon on it.

In the next place (and I say it at the risk of offending you) a person who elects to marry such surpassing [word illegible] – literally at the head in the particular line – seems to me to *have* her reward. I think I could merge myself completely in such success and be proud of it without expecting anything for myself but the smallest crumbs either from the person in question or from the world. No one could hope to *emulate*, and (except in the case of the Brownings where the talent was nearly equal) I should be content not to try.

But remember this does not excuse the character and actions of the partner. Were I he, I should recognise in every way (by dedications and all other means) the help and happiness which I had greatly owed to another. This may make a *private* grief, but it is certainly not a public one. The public (including myself) know nothing of the details. On the contrary, there is a general and most widespread belief not only that you copy out and labour at another's [word illegible] (which is actually admitted in the Laodicean) but that you help, and can compose passages, in the writing of the books. Consequently you *are* duly recognised in public, and with the private life the public has nothing to do and certainly knows nothing. I *do* wish T.H. would dedicate a book to you: shall I some day suggest it? Better *not*, perhaps. Meantime to aid and befriend others (as in my case) is a better and higher duty. You shall see any fresh services. . . .

I will gladly read any story of yours.[65]

From this answer we can almost read Emma's missing letter word by word. But it happens that at about the same time she revealed many of her feelings in a letter that has survived. The recipient was Elspeth, the recently married wife of the author Kenneth Grahame.[66] Grahame was now forty, and set in bachelor ways like a fly in amber. Elspeth, a woman of forceful disposition, was also set in her ways, which were those of a dreamer occupying a totally different dream-world from Kenneth's. It did not take her long to become disillusioned with, not to say dismayed by, her husband's notion of married life.[67] It chanced that her sister had lately painted Hardy's portrait, she herself had composed some verses which a mutual friend had shown him, and she had followed this up with a valentine to which Hardy responded. Presumably Elspeth had heard a thing or two about the Hardys, and now she was inspired to appeal to Emma for counsel.

She can hardly have anticipated what she was letting herself in for. Emma's reply has been quoted in part in many works on Hardy, but never *in toto*. Yet it forms as full and valuable a statement of her current estimate of her own marriage as we possess, and to reproduce only extracts is like inviting judgement on a painting on the strength of one or two details. The disclosure of Emma's feelings and attitudes is complementary to that revealed by the letter, just reproduced, from Pretor.

Dear Mrs Graham [*sic*]

It is really too 'early days' with you to be benefited by advice from one who has just come to the twenty-fifth year of matrimony. (I knew T.H. in 1870 (April) married Sep. 1874.) You are *both* at present in a 'Benedict' state. (Women can be anything in these days.)

Do I know your choice, perhaps I have met him, perhaps not. However it is impossible to give 'directions for all' – besides characters change so greatly with time, and circumstances. I can scarcely think that love proper, and enduring, is in the nature of Man – as a rule – perhaps there is no woman 'whom custom will not stale'. There is ever a desire to give but little in return for our devotion, and affection – their's being akin to children's, a sort of easy affectionateness, and at fifty a man's feelings too often take a new course altogether. Eastern ideas of matrimony secretly pervade his thoughts, and he wearies of the most perfect, and suitable wife chosen in his earlier life. Of course he gets over it usually somehow, or hides it, or is lucky!

Interference from others is greatly to be feared – members of either family too often are the cause of estrangement. A woman does not object to be ruled by her husband, so much as she does by a relative at his back – a man seldom cares to control such matters when in his power, and lets things glide or throws his balance on the wrong side which is simply a terrible state of affairs, and may affect unfavourably himself in the end.

Keeping separate a good deal is a wise plan in crises – and being both free – and expecting little neither gratitude, nor attentions, love, nor *justice*, nor anything you may set your heart on. Love interest, adoration, and all that kind of thing is usually a failure – complete – someone comes by and upsets your pail of milk in the end. If he belongs to the public in any way, years of devotion count for nothing. Influence can seldom be retained as years go by, and *hundreds* of wives go through a phase of disillusion, – it is really a pity to have any

175

ideals in the first place. This is gruesome, horrid, you will say – and mayhap Mr Graham is looking over the bride's shoulder as bridegrooms often do – but you have asked me. Ah some day we may talk further of these matters. There is so much to say – and to compare. Everyone's experience is different – *very*. The Spartan style was wise doubtless.

Yet I must qualify all this by saying that occasionally marriage is undoubtedly the happy state (with Christians always if *both* are) which it was intended to be. There must, of necessity, be great purity in the mind of the *man*, joined with magnanimity, and justice, and where, or rather, how often are these qualities to be found combined? Similarity of taste is not to be depended on, though it goes some way, but rivalry, fear, jealousy, steps in often.

A love-match has failed completely over, and over again. Christian philosophy is the only oil certain to work the complication. I see that continually.

However let me now give you my congratulations in due form dear Mrs Graham (though I rather congratulate a man in these cases.) If you come into my neighbourhood both, or either, I shall be delighted to see you, do drop into our roadside cottage.

Believe me
Yours very sincerely
Emma L. Hardy.

You must enjoy Fowey, what a lovely spot to choose, but best in the winter. I know North Corn. a little.

Most of the comments by Hardy writers on this outburst are what one might expect. What is *un*expected is what many of them miss. Gittings pointed out[68] the clear reference to Jemima in Emma's objection to being ruled by a relative at her husband's back – and this is a key factor in the estrangement. A number of writers, noting the advice to keep separate a good deal, fail to observe that Emma adds *in crises* – not all the time. Nor is there much appreciation of the real *cri de cœur* in the ensuing lines in which she warns Elspeth to expect little in the way of love, attentions, gratitude or adoration. Emma may have exaggerated, but some points we can check for ourselves. For example – as Pretor realised – despite her years of literary help, Hardy never dedicated a book to her. The only known works even inscribed to her on the flyleaf are a copy of *Desperate Remedies*, in which he wrote distantly 'The Author to E. L.

Gifford', and *The Hand of Ethelberta*, marked 'E. L. Hardy from the Author'.[69] Twelve years after her death her initials figured with those of five others in a multiple dedication of *The Famous Tragedy of the Queen of Cornwall*. After Elfride in *A Pair of Blue Eyes* the only times he may perhaps have used her in creating fictional characters are in some of the less agreeable aspects of Sue Bridehead, and as the ravaged Marcia at the end of *The Well-Beloved*.

In spite of her fulminations against the male (that is, Hardy's) interpretation of marriage, as extensive and strongly worded as any of her utterances that have come down to us, it will be observed that at no point even in this letter does Emma admit to having ceased to love her husband, nor does she warn Elspeth against ceasing to love hers. It is the man whose love wanes, and the implication behind the letter is that it is the worse for the woman because hers does not.

In the same year that she wrote this proclamation she gave Hardy a new Bible for his birthday. On her own birthday she too received a book – from Alfred Pretor, his *Ronald and I* with its printed dedication to her. If Hardy behaved true to form, he did not even remember the date.

To some extent the Hardys were distracted from too much brooding over one another while at Max Gate by the two young Giffords. In February, Emma, now working in oils, painted Gordon's portrait – unhappily lost. During the spring Hardy sent him to complete his education with a period at a school in Paris, on his return from which Emma chatted with him in French, read to him, and taught him to paint, while Hardy at her persuasion began to instruct him in the rudiments of architecture. Emma also 'got up a little music occasionally' for Gordon's enjoyment, 'singing hymns in as grand a style as I can accomplish' and varying them with the 'Marseillaise' for which he had a great liking. In appearance Gordon showed the youthful beauty that sometimes goes with frail health; in manner he was garrulous but gentle, a quality accompanied, rather incongruously, by a great interest in firearms.[70] He was at Hardy's side, despite the state of his lungs and the drenching rain, to watch the departure of troops from Dorchester for the Boer War, 2 November 1899, as commemorated in the poem 'The Going of the Battery'.[71]

177

Lilian displayed neither her brother's good looks nor his charm. Rebekah Owen, whose comments on other people (except, naturally, Thomas Hardy) seldom err on the side of charity, is nevertheless confirmed by Lilian's niece, Mrs Ethel Skinner, when she describes Lilian as 'fat as butter and the image of a china doll, with bushy frizzy dark hair, and red cheeks between which the tiny nose is scarcely visible'.[72] To atone for these physical shortcomings she was much addicted to spectacular clothes: when her aunt, Helen Holder, died and Max Gate went into mourning, Lilian continued to wear bright colours.[73] She was also addicted to parties, and in September 1899 Emma observed to Catharine Owen that 'we have therefore been somewhat lively in that way, at home and elsewhere'. What with the activities occasioned by Gordon and Lilian, in addition to housekeeping which, though 'a bore, has to be attended to often', millinery work, caring for two sick cats 'strayed in from neighbours' and instructing the patients 'in morals as regards Birds', cycling expeditions, at-homes, supervision of the laying-out of a croquet and tennis lawn, no wonder Emma, with her lameness, eye trouble, sprained ankle, 'terrible' cough the winter through, and any aftermath of shingles or malaria, found one head and pair of hands insufficient. 'Perhaps', she wrote to Rebekah, '*freaks* with two heads or two prs hands do a double amount when not on exhibition, though one does not hear of any increased mental powers under such conditions.'[74]

At the beginning of 1900 Gordon began his employment with Sir Arthur Blomfield & Sons. For Lilian, however, affairs were not so well arranged. A touch of the old Gifford snobbishness dissuaded Emma from having her niece trained for any occupation beyond housekeeping, a mistake that in later years was to cost Lilian dear, less because she could not have learned a skill even then than because she had been taught to deem it beneath her dignity.[75] The young Giffords spent all the autumn of 1899 at Max Gate, and in March 1900 Lilian was there again. In the same month Hardy, who was in London, took Gordon to the South Kensington Art Library to show him how to borrow books, and made plans to go through *Architecture in the Academy* with him.[76] Hardy's conception of non-involvement with the 'children whom Emma helped to

178

educate' is curious indeed.

In the letter that tells of his activities he commiserates with Emma over a sprained ankle, though whether this indicates a new sprain or residual trouble from the sprain incurred the previous May is not clear. Two months later (May 1900) she complained to Rebekah that she was still handicapped.[77] She also confessed that she was beginning to weary of the London Season, which had already daunted her in 1897, and to lament her growing shyness. Nor was she the only one to lose spiritual momentum. The *Life* opens its chronicle of 1900 with the passage: 'His personal ambition in a worldly sense, which had always been weak, dwindled to nothing, and for some years after 1895 or 1896 he requested that no record of his life should be made.'[78] It was the nearest the reticent Hardy came to admitting, in prose, how deeply the reception of *Jude* and the apparent loss of his wife's love had eaten into his spirit. His only consolation seemed to lie in furthering the career of Gordon Gifford and in the composition of poetry, most of it elicited by the Boer War but including, at the very end of the year, one of the most moving and memorable of all his poems, 'By the Century's Deathbed', better known as 'The Darkling Thrush'.

It was a cheerless close to the century for both. For one thing, they were both profoundly upset by the war. To us, still reeling from the effects of two subsequent wars of such immeasurably greater magnitude, the impact made by the South African conflict seems almost unreal. But it was real enough in its day, and it differed from the impact of the later wars in that feelings about it were far more mixed. Emma was not alone in her characteristically 'progressive' opinion that 'the Boers fight for homes and liberties – we fight for the Transvaal Funds, diamonds, and gold'.[79] Yet it was personal affairs that threw the deepest shadows over Max Gate.

In October, Helen Holder, now exiled from both Devon and Cornwall at Lee-on-Solent in Hampshire, was stricken with what was to prove – although she was only sixty-three – her last illness. Emma immediately departed for Lee to look after her, leaving Lilian in charge at Max Gate, to which during the next two months she was able to return only for fleeting visits. While she was in Lee a letter reached her announcing that Rebekah Owen contemplated descending on Dorchester again, alone this time; Catharine, too, was nursing a dying woman, their faithful old servant. Despite her preoccupation and anxiety, Emma sent a welcoming reply:

Pray forgive my delay in replying to your kind letter of Oct: 31. I should indeed very much like to see you again – and do not forget that we are quite old friends by this time. You will see many other old friends too, if you come to Dorchester – where we have not at all forgotten you and your sister. But at present I am wholly occupied with the affairs, and the care, of a relative who is seriously ill, and have only been able to return home for a few days. With kind regards to you both.[80]

The note could have suggested to Rebekah that it would be more considerate to remain at home and help her sister. But she persisted with the Dorchester visit and, with Lilian conveniently at Max Gate to save propriety, soon got herself invited there. Hardy seemed delighted, persuading her to cycle with Lilian and himself up to the Ridgeway, entertaining her to tea, autographing books and carrying them home for her, and finally arranging to escort her by night on a tour of the Mill Street slums, the 'Mixen Lane' of *The Mayor of Casterbridge*. Just after this expedition Emma made one of her periodical reappearances, and Rebekah, who was staying with the Moule family, wrote to sister Catharine:

No action of Emma Lavinia's ever surprises me and probably does not her husband; but niece, just gone, says 'Auntie took us by surprise and returned last night'. . . . I haven't a doubt it was niece's letters telling of my being here that brought Madam home. Mrs Sheridan says 'she leads him [Hardy] a hell of a life', so I expect he caught it if she arrived while he was traipsing through the slums with me. . . . We all think it so rude in Mrs TH not to invite Margie [Moule] and me out. Margie says for me to go tomorrow if I don't go to Frampton. If I do, she will go with me to Max Gate on Saturday, and between us we can quell her from any open hatefulness. She is so uncertain, she may be quite gushing.[81]

There follow some of the remarks about Emma by the Moules and Mrs Sheridan quoted in a previous chapter. But before the Saturday expedition to ascertain whether Emma would be hateful or gushing could take place she had once more gone to her sister's bedside. Helen died on 10 December. Emma stayed on a few days, presumably for the funeral, and Hardy wrote that he was 'rather anxious lest you should be broken down under your exertions'.[82] Rebekah meanwhile left Dorchester for home, and her friend Mrs Clapcott wrote hoping that Emma had only amused and not annoyed her.[83] Nothing if not punctilious, Rebekah wrote to thank Lilian for the hospitality, and Lilian replied without mentioning either Emma (now finally returned) or Hardy. 'Word got around later', reports Weber, 'that Hardy returned home one day to find that the lively niece had been banished from the premises.'[84] However, since Emma wrote to Rebekah shortly after returning home that Lilian was 'a bright little soul and we do not like to part with her to her parents',[85] this may be another Weber myth. Rebekah also sent Emma a calendar for Christmas and promised some flowers from the Wordsworth country, but offered no condolences on Helen's death. On New Year's Eve, Emma wrote to thank her for the calendar – 'all the year I shall be able to remember you by it' – and to regret having missed her at Dorchester. She confessed to being 'not at all in a bright, and seasonable mood – everything has a heavy, too sober effect on my thoughts'.[86]

So the century passed, and the spiritual rift between husband and wife remained unbridged. Some time during the year, according to a note (later crossed out) on the manuscript, Hardy had composed the poem 'A Second Attempt'. The first and last stanzas read:

> Thirty years after
> I began again
> An old-time passion:
> And it seemed as fresh as when
> The first day ventured on. . . .
>
> Firm the whole fabric stood,
> Or seemed to stand, and sound
> As it had stood before.
> But nothing backward climbs,
> And when I looked around
> As at the former times,

There was Life – pale and hoar;
And slow it said to me,
'Twice-over cannot be!'

How much literal truth the lines contain cannot be known,
but evidently he had made an effort of some sort to re-arouse
his wife's love: an effort either unperceived or disbelieved,
possibly because the birthday Bible that had marked her own
tentative approach already lay ignored and unannotated. Perhaps he should have pressed harder, persisted longer. Instead
he turned his mind to collecting together, and supplementing
by further composition, the verses that were to form his second
collection, *Poems of the Past and the Present*, and were once
more to affront his wife.

CHAPTER SEVEN

The Twentieth Century

IN MARCH 1900, Miss Bertha Newcombe, who knew the Hardys well enough to be invited to spend a night at Max Gate and have the invitation repeated a week later, wrote to the wife of Edmund Gosse a letter containing her impressions of Emma on the first visit.[1] After remarking that her fellow-guests included 'a very eligible bachelor, who is designed for me by Mrs Hardy but he fails to charm me' – so Emma's disillusion with the married state did not preclude her from match-making – Miss Newcombe goes on:

I felt a great sympathy and pity for Emma this time. It is pathetic to see how she is struggling against her woes. She asserts herself as much as possible and is a great bore, but at the same time is so kind and goodhearted, and one cannot help realising what she must have been to her husband. She showed us a photograph of herself as a young girl, and it was very attractive. I always thought she must have had a certain 'beauté de diable'.... She says it was she who encouraged him to go on writing and to give up the architect's profession. I don't wonder that she resents being slighted by everyone, now that her ugly duckling has grown into such a charming swan. It is so silly of her though isn't it not to rejoice in the privilege of being wife to so great a man?

The last question could have been asked by Alfred Pretor. It goes to the heart of Emma's inability to live in contentment with Hardy: her failure to realise that, like many geniuses in many fields, he was incapable of not putting his work first, his

183

human relationships, even that with his wife, afterwards, and that the only way to coexist successfully with such a man was to sink all considerations of self and identify with him. Given that where this is the temperament of genius the possessor of it can scarcely help himself, Hardy's periodical awareness that it might be for him rather than Emma to take the lead in seeking a better understanding is both exceptional and creditable. But Emma was convinced that the only way to return to the proper rôle of a husband was for him to recover his Christian faith and standards and renounce the world that had led him from her side and filled his mind with wickedness. Time and again the idea that the 'world' had stolen him from her is manifest in her letters or in the replies to them. It was to crop up again in a letter to Rebekah Owen the following year: 'I can scarcely keep a "mere" cat to say nothing of a "mere man" whom all the world claims, which would not so much matter if his later writings were of a more faithful, truthful, and helpful kind.'[2] In the same letter she expressed, somewhat spasmodically even for her, her feelings on *Poems of the Past and the Present*:

Do not read, or at least accept, as anything but fiction some of the poems of the second part – the kind which Goethe denounced as "mimic" that is personal – moans and fancies etc. – Written "to please" . . . others! or himself – but not *me*, far otherwise.

The reference to the 'second part' is illuminating. The poems to which Emma might have been expected to take most exception – the graceful, lightheartedly nostalgic 'To Lizbie Browne', recalling his boyhood love for Elizabeth Bishop, the redhaired daughter of the Yellowham Wood gamekeeper, 'I Need Not Go', 'A Spot'[3] and 'The Inconsistent', all probably associated with Tryphena Sparks, and several poems about troops setting off for the Boer War that Emma surely knew were composed with Florence Henniker (whose husband was among those departing) in mind, together with 'A Broken Appointment', also addressed to Florence – all come within approximately the first half of the volume. The second half contains little or nothing involving Hardy's 'other women', but does contain several poems likely to offend Emma on religious grounds, or more precisely for their evidence of unrepentant lack of belief: 'The Respectable Burgher', a satire on the excesses of the authors of *Essays and Reviews* (but Emma may have failed to grasp that satire was intended); the three 'In Tenebris' poems, with their 'moans and fancies' (Emma always maintained that life should not be treated as if it were all gloom); and 'The Church-Builder', the soliloquy of a master-builder who, having given his all to pay for the church, finds the gesture unappreciated, his life a wreck, and in his disillusionment is about to hang himself near the Crucifix.

The collection also includes 'Memory and I', the theme of which is the gradual removal of youth, love, religious faith, and joy in labour, hope or ambition, leaving them as the ghosts of Memory. The well-known final stanza, in which Memory tells the poet that it saw his once goddess-like beloved as 'an ageing shape/Where beauty used to be' is almost universally taken as a proclamation that Hardy's love, like his youth, faith, etc., was dead. As Pinion points out, Emma's letter of March 1902 to Rebekah Owen, quoted above, certainly implies that this was her view; though there is nothing in her words to prove that she was criticising anything but Hardy's pessimism and irreligion.[4] But it is not necessary to take the poem so negatively, nor for that matter to treat it as a true statement: Hardy may have abandoned his prose ambitions, but his mind at this time was filled with his most ambitious project of all, *The Dynasts*, and it is difficult to believe that he took no joy in the labour of its shaping. Again, he may have lost his faith, but some find evidence that nothing would have pleased him better than to regain it.[5] So with his beloved. Of course the years had changed beauty into an 'ageing shape', as it does for all of us who have had any beauty to start with; but we know it does not follow that love dies, though it may change its nature. The final two lines read:

> 'That her fond phantom lingers there
>   Is only known to me.'

Surely that means that the poet's eye still sees, beneath the disfiguration of age, the beauty he once learned to love, but only he – not she – knows that he sees it still. This interpretation accords exactly with the postulate that at the bottom of the chasm separating Hardy and Emma the waters of love still flowed, and it is borne out by one other poem in the volume, 'Wives in the Sere'.

> Never a careworn wife but shows,
>   If a joy suffuse her,
> Something beautiful to those
>   Patient to peruse her,
> Some one charm the world unknows
>   Precious to a muser,
> Haply what, ere years were foes,
>   Moved her mate to choose her.
>
> But, be it a hint of rose
>   That an instant hues her,
> Or some early light or pose
>   Wherewith thought renews her –
> Seen by him at full, ere woes
>   Practised to abuse her –
> Sparely comes it, swiftly goes,
>   Time again subdues her.

What is this but an expression of the poet's belief that, however aged the shape, the man who loves can still see in it fleeting glimpses of the woman who first won him? And that Hardy had Emma in mind is indicated by the 'hint of rose/That an instant hues her'. Quick, short-lived blushes were a well-attested characteristic of her earlier years.

But in her indignation at the poems that did not please her she failed to notice, or to read correctly, the few verses that might have brought pleasure. The depression from which she suffered in 1901, however, was not caused by *Poems of the Past and the Present*, which did not appear until November, and would not have been available in proof before autumn. It was caused by many happenings: the death of Helen, the growing difficulties with the expensively disposed and spiteful Lilian, the slow withering of the latest *rapprochement* with Thomas, and, not least, her health. In addition to her lameness – not helped by the sprains – and eyesight difficulties, a general lassitude seems to have overcome her. In February,

Hardy reported to Florence Henniker that Emma was averse to the effort of taking a London flat that year.[6] In April she confessed to Rebekah Owen that she was afraid now to cross London streets, in which 'I have had narrow escapes now I am old'.[7] The previous year she had 'quite hated it' when she had to go up to London on business connected with her sister's death.[8] Nevertheless, they did take a flat, in the familiar Paddington area, and in June Florence was told that, although they had been to a concert, 'Emma is very languid and goes practically nowhere'.[9] Yet they went to other concerts, apparently with enjoyment.

The letter also speaks of a visit by Hardy to an all-male gathering at Edward Clodd's home in Aldeburgh, and it may have been on this occasion that there occurred – if it did occur – a curious incident related by Ford Madox Ford.[10] According to him, Clodd had summoned a representative group of friends to ascertain, from their various professions of belief, the current state of English religion. It turned out that there were five Roman Catholics, two spiritualists, and two agnostics, including Clodd. But when it came to Hardy's turn he astonished them all by declaring that he was 'a practising and believing communicant of the Church of England.' Ford offers no explanation of this phenomenon, confining himself to saying that Hardy confessed his faith only with great diffidence for fear of wounding his agnostic host and friend.

Emma found greater energy at Max Gate. The usual garden parties took place, the lawns now including a tennis court and croquet layout, to be joined in later years by facilities for archery. At the end of June a great army of journalists and *literati* from the Whitefriars Club was entertained in a marquee, arriving in a fleet of open carriages which, as they passed the end of Higher Bockhampton Lane, were watched by 'a little bright-eyed lady in a shady hat' seated in a bath chair and accompanied by two younger women. Only afterwards did the company learn that the little old lady was the great Hardy's nearly nonagenarian mother escorted by his two sisters.[11] Emma's old foe, it seemed, still had more energy than her daughter-in-law, despite Emma's capacity (which she retained to her pain-racked end) to continue playing the grand hostess.

Other guests, about this time or a year or two earlier, included a party of Spaniards (introduced by a local friend), who sat on the drawing-room floor and sang to guitars, affording both Thomas and Emma 'evident pleasure'. The friend who had brought the Spaniards, Benita Thornton (afterwards Mrs Weber – but not Mrs Carl Weber) later observed that both Hardys 'showed a remarkable knowledge of Spain and its history'. Miss Thornton was also fascinated by Emma's 'uncanny power' over birds, which she would call to her as she and her guest sat on a garden bench, and the birds would fly down from trees and bushes and alight on the bench beside them.[12] One of Dr Fisher's daughters recalled her amusing some young guests at a garden party by trying, or pretending to try, to establish friendlier relations between the birds and the cats. For Miss Fisher the memory of Emma, nearly three-quarters of a century later, was of a jolly lady who would meet the four little Fisher girls out for a walk and roar with laughter at things they said. Mrs Fisher, too, sometimes gave garden parties, and at first debated whether the Hardys were suitable guests because of Thomas's irreligious attitude, but decided that Emma's well-known piety outweighed it.[13]

Both Mrs Weber and Miss Fisher have testified that, whatever fame Hardy may have earned elsewhere, whatever gatherings of the illustrious may have assembled at Max Gate, by the great majority of Dorchester people the Hardys were thought very little of. Many considered Hardy slightly potty, and most were sure Emma was potty without qualification. The knowledge that she disseminated religious tracts, the rumour that she had begun to compose poetry, and the sight of her careering down High West and High East Streets in her green velvet dress on her green bicycle were more than enough to convince the average strictly conventional, class-conscious country-townsman and townswoman that here was a lunatic, if a harmless and rather amiable one. Later the green velvet gave place to sky blue, matching a new bicycle.[14]

Christine Wood Homer has left a record of some of Emma's eccentricities in the years around the turn of the century. During the picnics that went with their cycling expeditions she would never sit on the grass with the others for fear of being bitten by the tiny red 'harvest bugs', but preferred to install herself on the roadway. Any visitor to Max Gate whom she suspected of having come only to see Hardy and not herself was apt to find that Hardy was not informed of the visit until it was over. Having asked once to see Christine's pet animals, she was taken to where they were, but spent the time admiring the way the flies on the window 'washed their faces' with their antennae. On another occasion she took the girl to see a friend's aviary, then deserted her while she and the friend retired to another room and read poetry. During a rail journey home from Parkstone (between Poole and Bournemouth) she travelled first class while Christine travelled third.[15]

Christine Wood Homer, as already remarked, was a discerning friend. She soon detected that to remain in Emma's good graces one had to play up to her sense of personal dignity, admire her verses, and never ignore her in favour of Thomas. She also perceived the rift between husband and wife, for which she was inclined to blame Emma more than Thomas – though again, there is her remark that pity rather than censure seemed to be demanded. But even Miss Wood Homer's insight could not penetrate the full circumstances that had led to the situation at Max Gate, or the full subtleties of the situation itself, and when, speaking of Hardy just after Emma's death, she says 'one felt he had forgotten and forgiven the many unbridgeable differences and insuperable difficulties which had spoilt so many years of their married life' one realises that his share of the responsibility remained unsuspected by her. The point, however, is that in spite of her overestimate of Emma's part in the breakdown, in spite of her recognition of Emma's failings, she confesses that she and her family 'rather liked' Mrs Hardy. Mrs Weber 'liked them both, Hardy and his wife, very much'.[16]

Emma had begun writing poetry before the turn of the century. In a letter of 24 April 1899 to Rebekah Owen she offers to send along some of her verses, adding with rather calculated diffidence: 'I write at sudden moments a line or two sometimes – and perhaps everyone does. I find many of my friends privately poetize.' But the fact that she seems to have embarked on her poetic career immediately after Hardy had published his *Wessex Poems* offers strong reason for concluding that her purpose was to show him that if he could write verses so could she. Her motive is customarily said to have been plain vanity *ad absurdum*; vanity pretty certainly played a major part, but there was also pretty certainly an admixture of yet another attempt to reattract Hardy's interest. It was unfortunate for her that one of her worst poems was the first to be published – out of deference to Hardy – in the *Sphere* for May 1900. For her verses, though feeble, are not so ludicrously appalling as generally was made out; with an output no matter how large, she would still never have achieved the outrageous status of an English McGonagall. Many poems would be just acceptable but for one lamentable line or stanza. The technique of most critics, led by Carl Weber, is to quote the worst passage and ignore the rest; and invariably, or nearly so, Emma's poems are judged without any reference to the taste of the time. Not all the verse-reading public was attuned to Tennyson, the Brownings, or Meredith. There were many whose simple tastes derived greater pleasure from, say, Martin Tupper or Frederick Locker-Lampson:

> I hope I'm fond of much that's good
> As well as much that's gay;
> I'd love the country if I could;
> I like the Park in May:
> And when I ride in Rotten Row
> I wonder why they call'd it so.[17]

Popular, too, was 'A Rhyming Letter: the Aunt's Apology' by the poetess 'B.H.':

> Every stitch of the frock I am sending
> I worked at by mornings and eves,
> 'Twas I did the darning and mending,
> 'Twas I made those sweet little sleeves,
> And if I've done some of it badly,
> And put in my stitches aslant,
> Just say, when you glance at it sadly,
> ' 'Twas made by my well-meaning Aunt.'

To readers who enjoyed poetry of this sort Emma's poems may well have seemed almost too intellectual. Indeed, she sometimes modelled her efforts on classical prototypes. Her

190

best-known poem, 'The Dancing Maidens', despite its absurdities, shows strong evidence of being inspired by William Blake's 'Long John Brown & Little Mary Bell', a comparison the more credible because, as we shall see, Emma's religious prose-writings in the last year or two of her life bear a similar affinity with some of Blake's prose. As an average example of her versifying, here is a poem never before printed. It was copied by the painter's wife on to the back of a photograph of a landscape painting – possibly showing the Frome near Dorchester – executed by one Fred Whitehead, who dated it 1901. The poem is untitled, but subscribed 'Mrs Thomas Hardy'.[18]

> Where the river stilled its depths by the weir,
>   The Painter sat apart,
> In a place of peace, and they passed unaware
>   Of his glowing heart,
>   And his burnished brush,
>   Catching the gleam
>   Of the evening's flush,
> Poised in the edge of the shining stream,
>   The glories gathering in.
>
> Only the people of the cottage knew,
> None from the outer world, how
> Cunningly the path's slight clue
> Led on behind to the slippery bough
> Where his canvas hung above yellowing leaves.
> The kettle sings and bubbles and heaves
> In his van a yard or two away
>   At the end of October's day.

The Edwardian years were so alike for the Hardys that few features stand out. The black diaries evidently continued to be compiled, yet one or two phrases in Emma's letters let slip her yearning for a return to conjugal love. Following her advice to Rebekah Owen about *Poems of the Past and the Present* she added: 'Nature's beauties console, but not altogether. Love and sympathy we still pine for, also we want affinities.' It would be surprising indeed if the poetising were not in part an attempt to establish an 'affinity'. Nor were relations at Max Gate so uniformly grim as they are sometimes painted. Not only must they, as Hawkins has properly pointed out, have had their good and bad phases, but also the good phases were not necessarily simply formal or with conversation limited to essentials. Emma's contention that life was not all gloom and should not be treated as if it were was not a pose. When she felt the atmosphere was too heavy she would sometimes, in default of other expedients, rouse the household by playing loud marches on the piano. But she and Thomas could still sometimes talk as of old. In March 1903 he wrote to Florence Henniker that he and Emma had both read Henry James's *The Wings of the Dove* and had been arguing ever since about what became of the people in it, finishing up with wholly conflicting opinions.[19] Yet some visitors to the house, like H. R. Harraway a few years later, remembered only the 'lengthy gaps between eating and conversation' and felt 'very uncomfortable'.[20]

Apart from natural ups and downs in the temperature, it is possible that the Hardys talked more when alone than in front of others. But it should be borne in mind that Thomas was now fully engrossed with *The Dynasts*, and Emma had been accustomed ever since the Sturminster days to the long periods of withdrawal that preoccupation with a new work involved. He began the actual writing of *The Dynasts* in 1902 and virtually did not desist until mid-1907, the intensiveness of his activity being not a little due to a growing obsession that he would never live to finish the work. To us who know that he lived, a reasonably healthy old man, until 1928, this fascination with death seems just a manifestation of his chronic morbidity, but in fact during Edward's reign Hardy did suffer from an endless succession of colds, bouts of influenza, headaches, rheumatism and other 'routine' ailments which, added to his chronic bladder trouble, made him look ill enough to a number of his friends for them to have had some justification if they had judged him in truth the 'dead man walking' of his poem.

Yet he still found time – and energy – for verse-making unconnected with *The Dynasts*, for keeping up his correspondence with Mrs Henniker and his literary sponsorship of Agnes Grove, and for devoting time to the young Giffords. September found the pair at Max Gate for the whole month, and the following summer he took Lilian to the Royal Academy Summer Exhibition – 'she never saw anything like it, poor child'.[21] In a letter reporting this to Emma at Max Gate he makes the observation that weeks have elapsed since he had any letters from Higher Bockhampton. This is noteworthy, not for what it says, but for his taking it for granted that Emma will be interested. Bockhampton cannot have been expunged altogether yet from her map.

In the spring of the same year, 1903, she had made the effort to face another London Season, and while they were away H. J. Moule, brother of Horace and the artist to whom more than twenty years earlier she had broached the idea of collaborating with Hardy on a book about Dorset, was accorded the rare privilege of being given the loan of Max Gate in which to recuperate from a severe illness.[22] While Moule and his wife were in residence Emma was kept supplied with news (mainly of cats) by a series of letters from Bessie Churchill, the parlourmaid, whose style, respectful but relaxed, is a testimony to Emma's good relations with her staff.[23] The exchanges were renewed in November, when she took Lilian first to Dover and then to Paris and Calais. The *Life* does not mention either of these absences, but there are as many as seven letters dated November in '*Dearest Emmie*', most of them acknowledging a letter or a card received and therefore showing correspondence to have been fairly energetic. Yet none of the letters ends with sending Emma love, although it is regularly sent to Lilian. In reciprocity, Bessie Churchill thinks it unnecessary to make more than a very occasional mention of Hardy; and when, at the close of the year, Emma spent yet another week in Dover and Calais, a rare card[24] written by her *to* Max Gate instructs Churchill to take great care of the cats but gives no such injunction about Hardy, possibly because he had just reversed an intention to join her.[25]

After 1903 there is a gap in the '*Dearest Emmie*' letters until May 1908, nothing from Emma to Rebekah Owen until November 1906, and nothing of moment in Hardy's correspondence with Florence Henniker again until May 1908. To the year 1904 every writer prior to Gittings attributed the first appearance at Max Gate of Florence Emily Dugdale, the future second Mrs Hardy. The error, initiated by Carl Weber, was due to confusion of different bearers of the name 'Florence': Florence Dugdale herself, Florence Henniker who is supposed to have already been her friend and effected the 1904 introduction (in fact they first met in 1910), and Florence Griffin, the Max Gate housekeeper.[26] It is references to 'Florence' in certain of Hardy's letters, now known to mean Florence Griffin, that were taken by Weber and all his successors to mean Florence Dugdale.

The significant events of 1904 for the Hardys were several deaths and the composition of one much undervalued poem. Even the appearance of the first part of *The Dynasts* was, after the sensations of the nineties, nothing like the earth-shaking event its years of back-breaking creation had foreshadowed. The deaths were: in February, that of Hardy's early mentor and long-standing friend Leslie Stephen; in March, that of H. J. Moule, despite the improvement his health seemed to have undergone at Max Gate the previous year; in April, that of the indomitable Jemima Hardy; in October, that of Walter Gifford, father of Gordon and Lilian; and, in November, that of Richard, Emma's eldest brother, the former sufferer from 'angina pectoris' as Emma was to term it in *Some Recollections*. For some years Richard had been in an asylum for the insane, a fact of which Florence Hardy was to make use in persuading Hardy of Emma's 'madness'. Emma had not seen him for several decades, but – her other brother Willie having died two years before Walter – his death meant that of the Plymouth household of seven in which she had been brought up she was now the only survivor.

The poem whose true significance is seldom perceived is 'Shut Out That Moon'. Although the first half apparently harks back to childhood days at Bockhampton, the second stanza in particular being inspired by the death of the much revered Jemima, the tenor of the poem as a whole, and the similar pattern of other poems, indicate that these stanzas are but a prelude leading into the real purpose of the composition, the poet's utter despondency at the metamorphosis of his loved one's devotion into hatred. It is more revealing than any of the exquisite laments inspired by her death, because no sudden event *involving her* had occurred to release Hardy's feelings. The only shock – and it can scarcely have

been unforeseen – probably just preceding the date of composition, was his mother's death, and if we accept that as
having set the poem in train we are still left with the evidence
that the first effect of his grief at this loss was to bring home to
him with renewed anguish the greater loss of his wife's love.
The indications that the real substance of the poem lies in its
second half are made sharper by the fact that the third stanza is
arguably the most beautiful and poignant that Hardy ever
penned.

> Close up the casement, draw the blind,
>   Shut out that stealing moon,
> She wears too much the guise she wore
>   Before our lutes were strewn
> With years-deep dust, and names we read
>   On a white stone were hewn.
>
> Step not forth on the dew-dashed lawn
>   To view the Lady's Chair,
> Immense Orion's glittering form,
>   The Less and Greater Bear:
> Stay in; to such sights we were drawn
>   When faded ones were fair.
>
> Brush not the bough for midnight scents
>   That come forth lingeringly,
> And wake the same sweet sentiments
>   They breathed on you and me
> When living seemed a laugh, and love
>   All it was said to be.
>
> Within the common lamp-lit room
>   Prison my eyes and thought;
> Let dingy details crudely loom,
>   Mechanic speech be wrought:
> Too fragrant was Life's early bloom,
>   Too tart the fruit it brought!

Possibly it was Hardy's conviction that he was on the threshold of death that turned what may well have been intended
only as a threnody for his mother into a more haunting lament
for lost love than any he had written before. It is especially to
be noted that the poem was composed within months of the

chilly relations evinced in the correspondence of both Emma and himself at the end of 1903. 'Shut Out That Moon' was not published until it appeared in *Time's Laughingstocks* in 1909. Emma may have read it earlier in manuscript, but even if she did her belief expressed to Rebekah Owen in 1899 that 'his delicate irony is too often taken for tenderness' would have made her take his tenderness here for delicate irony, such was the lack of communication between them. A legitimate if unconfirmable conjecture is that in 1909, when she herself felt (with better reason than Thomas) that death was drawing near, she read the volume containing this poem and that, his sincerity being at last perceived, 'Shut Out That Moon' was among the influences that urged her attempts to penetrate the emotional barrier with the emotive music of their past.

The strained atmosphere at Max Gate can hardly have been alleviated by the monotonous run of casualities to the household cats. Three had been killed on the railway in 1901, doubtless another reason for Emma's depression in that year; now in 1904 yet another suffered the same fate, prompting Hardy to the composition of one of the finest animal poems in the English language, 'Last Words to a Dumb Friend'. At about this time Alfred Pretor also lost a favourite cat.[27] For the first time the *Life*'s record of the year contains no mention of Emma, even when touching on Hardy's seasonal visit to London or his now equally regular autumn cycling. Perhaps remembrance of the emotions engendered by 'Shut Out That Moon' precluded the autobiographer from recording more mundane recollections of that time. A letter to Edward Clodd in November declines an invitation for them both to go to Aldeburgh on the ground that Emma was contemplating visiting her uncle, Archdeacon Gifford, in Oxford, but it is not known whether the visit took place.[28] Its interest lies in the evidence that relations between the Archdeacon and his niece had not declined from their cordial level of earlier years, thus helping to compound the unlikeliness of what is already one of the least easily swallowed of Florence Hardy's anecdotes in denigration of her predecessor.

According to Florence, Lady Jeune once asked the Archdeacon to escort Emma in to dinner, adding 'I think she is a relative of yours'; to which the distinguished divine is supposed to have replied: 'Mrs Thomas Hardy is my niece and the most horrible woman in the world.'[29] Two possible explanations of this astonishing incident occur. One is that the whole affair was a joke. Lady Jeune, of whom it was a necessary qualification as a successful hostess to remember as much as possible about each of her guests, is surely unlikely to have forgotten that her own connection with Emma had come about because Emma was the niece of this clergyman who had married into the Jeune family; nor would Emma have spared her from frequent reminders, as guests at the 'crushes' were given the inevitable information that Emma was an Archdeacon's niece. It is not beyond belief that, only too aware of this foible, Lady Jeune made her remark in mild jest, and that the Archdeacon, taking the point, replied with a quip of his own. The very formality of his reported phrasing supports this reading. We do not know the date of the episode, but if he was still on his former good terms with Emma as late as 1904 he is hardly likely to have changed his attitude later: he died in 1905.

The other possible explanation is that, amid the hubbub of conversation, Lady Jeune misheard the operative word in the old man's answer. He may not have said 'horrible' at all, but something similar in sound, like 'honourable'. Whatever the solution, it is difficult to take the story at face value, especially as 1915, when Florence launched it in a letter to Rebekah Owen, was the year that saw her most embittered denunciations of Emma and all the Giffords; she was not the one to cast doubts on an anecdote so well suited to her mood.

April 1905 saw Hardy off to Aberdeen, where the University had offered him an honorary LLD. Emma did not accompany him, but shortly after his return she did agree to taking a flat once again for the London Season. They went to the usual concerts and art exhibitions, and presumably dinners and 'crushes'; but not surprisingly he visited his old idol Swinburne without her. In September there was another mammoth entertainment in the grounds of Max Gate, the guests being two hundred members of the Institute of Journalists. In October, Part Two of *The Dynasts* was finished, and was published in February 1906. That spring Emma faced yet another London

Season in a flat; they 'entertained many friends' and went to 'various meetings and dinners'.[30] But the strain told, and in May she felt obliged to return for at least a day or two to Max Gate. There she gardened a little, but then experienced 'a strange fainting-fit. . . . My heart seemed to stop.'[31] It was the first of several during her remaining years. Coupled with the increasing pain from gallstones, it is small wonder that this new affliction, added to those with which she was already familiar, made her look ill. The fashionable French portrait-painter, Jacques-Émile Blanche, who had a studio in Knights-bridge and was as familiar a figure in London as in Paris, came to know the Hardys well and was commissioned in the summer of 1906 to paint Hardy's portrait. Of Emma he afterwards wrote:

In 1905 nothing remained to her of the full-blooded, rosy, jovial freshness attested by those who had seen her while still young. Instead, shrunken as if age had made her smaller, she adopted a defensive shield, retaining in stereotyped form the smile of former days as if fixed for all time by a photographer.[32]

Blanche, too, gives a rather different view of the Hardys during the Season from that conveyed by the *Life*. According to the French artist, who seems to have possessed the same ca-pacity for comprehensive and dispassionate observation as Goya, during their seasonal sojourns in their 'provincially fur-nished' flat their only contacts with metropolitan social life apart from official conferences and visits to publishers were re-ligious 'meetings', or occasions when Thomas would attend a royal levée or Emma a garden party at Windsor Castle. Few Londoners would have recognised them. 'Leur vie ordinaire restait très limitée.' It was Blanche, too, who noticed that during the small tea parties given in the flat, and to which he and his wife were invited, Emma let Agnes Grove 'make the small-talk with the scribblers' while she herself seemed to be saying 'she is of less good birth than I, without natural gaiety or worldly affability'.[33]

Finally, it was from Blanche's memories that Weber took one of the best-known of all the stories against Emma, that of the drive in open carriages from Windsor railway station to the

Castle on 2 June 1907 for a garden party. In the carriages there proved to be fewer places than there were guests, and as it was an excessively hot day Mme Blanche, noting how frail and fragile Hardy looked, invited him to take the seat she was about to occupy beside Emma. But Emma intervened, saying something like 'the walk will do Hardy good'; and off went the carriage with the two ladies in it, while their husbands walked behind up the sunbaked hill.

It is not a pleasant anecdote, however much we may try to excuse Emma on grounds of possibly being in great pain. But it is noticeable that Blanche appears a good deal less scandalised by it than Weber or those who echo Weber. The Frenchman merely observes drily: 'Such were the etiquette and pattern of domestic life in this illustrious household.'[34] The elderly poet's air of frailty that so smote the hearts of other witnesses to the incident may have left the painter less impressed because he would recall that for the preliminary portrait-sketch only the previous year the supposedly brittle figure (who was now, after all, sixty-seven, not eighty-seven) had climbed four flights of stairs – also on a broiling hot day – immediately after which he had suggested that he and Blanche make a tour of the Royal Academy.[35] True, he had finished the ascent covered in perspiration, as would anyone else in such weather, so that Blanche had had to revive him with an iced drink; but after that feat of stair-climbing the slow ascent of the Windsor hill must have seemed to both a minor ordeal. The real unpleasantness of the affair lies not in any hardship imposed on Hardy, but in Emma's disregard of the embarrassment her apparent callousness must cause him.

His first reaction on seeing Blanche's preliminary sketch had been to wonder what Emma would think of it – 'and also, I guessed,' Blanche adds, 'what that connoisseur of painting, Lady Grove, would think'. What Emma thought was summed up in her injunction 'Don't make Mr Hardy look miserable' – on which Blanche commented subsequently: 'It would be so unfitting for a gentleman.'[36] After her fainting-fit she returned to finish the Season with Thomas, but later that summer remained at home while he went off on a tour of some English cathedrals accompanied by his brother Henry. To what extent these severances were due to deliberate mutual avoidance – her 'wise plan in crises', as she had told Elspeth Grahame – or to sheer physical exhaustion on her part it is impossible to determine. In 1906 the Reverend Richard Bartelot became Vicar of Fordington – the parish in which Max Gate lies – and Emma made her request to him to start coming to tea once a week 'to try to make Tom more religious'. Bartelot complied, taking tea at Max Gate every Thursday; but, although Hardy always came down from his study, every time the Vicar tried to elicit a comment on the subject of God 'he would draw back into his shell like a snail', despite attempts to cajole him with the loan of the old manuscript choir-books used at the church in 1805, and a manuscript carol-book used at Swanage in 1813.[37]

Emma was a regular witness to these attempts and their failure. For her own part, like many another sufferer from frustration in human relationships, she turned more and more to religion. Always, like her paternal grandmother in the Plymouth days, sternly anti-Catholic, her Protestantism took a more active turn during her last years. Since 1902[38] she had been distributing Protestant papers, and was to be doing so still in 1911.[39] In the former year a friend wrote to say that, since she was incorrigibly Roman Catholic, would Emma kindly desist.[40] Nine years later the papers had become 'beautiful little booklets'.[41] In 1905 she is seen praying for as many Protestants as possible to be returned in the forthcoming parliamentary election.[42] At Max Gate guests found an open Bible placed in their bedrooms.[43] These anti-Papist activities may have been a little old-fashioned in the Edwardian era, but it is too easily forgotten that during the nineteenth century the Established and Nonconformist Churches, assailed on one side by the Evolutionists and on the other by Catholic emancipation, felt a very real fear lest the Catholics, on the plea that only they could counteract the Secularists, should effect a 'take-over' of the country. The activities of Wiseman, Newman, Manning and other Catholic prelates were looked on with at least as much apprehension as those of the anti-religionists, if only on the well-known principle that a rival brand of Christian is a far worse enemy than an unbeliever. One has only to study the life of that noteworthy rescuer of children, Dr Barnardo, to realise the resentment, at times nearly fatal, felt by his Nonconformist helpers towards the

Catholics working in the same field – who for their part seem at times far more interested in saving souls than bodies.

Yet another story concerning Emma that is almost certainly without foundation is that she was so deeply apprehensive of a Catholic 'invasion' from France that she kept a suitcase ready-packed for flight.[44] In December 1906, in the course of a letter to Rebekah Owen, after referring to the 'engrossing' political (not religious) situation in England, she wrote: 'I am concerned about France, too, the country I love most after our own, and the one I shall want to fly to, perhaps, someday or other when fighting comes on here, or our beautiful free land changes its character.'[45] It was *to* France, Catholic but beloved, that she contemplated possible flight. In December 1908 the *Dorset County Chronicle* published a long article by her (the preparation of which naturally had no assistance whatever from Hardy) entitled 'In Praise of Calais'.[46] Predominantly a detailed, well-observed and strongly 'visual' essay in the best style of her early travel diaries, it is not limited to descriptions of buildings and scenery, but pays considerable attention to the townspeople and their ways, yet with only a touch here and there of anti-Catholic bias, and those touches never offensive. Emma seems to have been more tolerantly disposed towards French Catholics than English; for her own country she went so far in 1911 as to advocate that all nunneries (though not, apparently, monasteries) should be placed under government supervision.[47] Yet apart, perhaps, from this last, none of her activities suggests the 'religious mania' – let alone symptoms of insanity – with which they are often associated. The pamphleteering was essentially no different from the doorstep canvassing by today's Jehovah's Witnesses. The open Bibles merely foreshadow the placing of a Bible in nearly every hotel bedroom by the Gideon Society.

But Emma did develop a form of religious mysticism that found expression in four or five apocalyptic essays which she caused to be published together in 1911 under the title *Spaces* but were probably written at various dates. It as been suggested that they were inspired by Marie Corelli,[48] but Emma did not like 'Corelliism'.[49] As we have seen, one source of inspiration was most probably Colonel Serjeant's *Spirit Revealed*; others seem to have been Blake, Dante and St John the Divine. But they do not indicate mania: rather, the spiritual gropings of a deeply religious woman who felt that all she held to be of value in life had crumbled to dust, and that the time before she must crumble to dust herself was growing very short.

The year 1906 closed with Emma nursing Thomas through a chill. Her account of this – in her usual picturesque language – to Rebekah Owen gives a glimpse of the health of both Hardys at this time:

I had managed to keep well through fogs and rainy weather, but at 4.30 the next afternoon I descended to the drawing-room for tea from my eerie, and doors and windows had been left open all over the house, for it was one of those strange warm days occurring at that time, then a house-breeze caught me, and a draught swept down to my lungs and vitals and laid me up for nearly 3 weeks, I have had a relapse too and now have another and a barking cough and a husband to nurse he has a chill, but not a serious one his colds are short usually but the effects linger in liability to get fresh ones and consequent weakness. I shall, I expect keep my cough till summer weather comes, and it is hindering me much and so is Christmas I am overpowered with its business, and these complaints, only one eye to see, and a shake-cough.[50]

After commiserating with Rebekah over what was to prove the final illness of the Owens' ancient servant, and expressing her own dread of the difficulties of getting over an illness in advanced old age, Emma observes: 'I have no really sweet attentive relatives to sympathize.'

On the eve of Good Friday 1907 Hardy completed the third part of *The Dynasts*, and finding that he had neither died prematurely nor appeared likely to crown his undertaking with a dramatic demise immediately afterwards, he induced Emma to face yet another Season at the Hyde Park Mansions flat, where she was forced to leave even more of the duties of hostess to Agnes Grove.

As it happened, she had already visited the capital once that year; on 9 February, in such shocking weather that the event became known as the Mud March, between three and four thousand Suffragettes and sympathisers marched from Hyde Park to Exeter Hall, in the Strand, and according to a laconic note in the *Life* Emma travelled up to London on the previous day to march with them.[51] The following year, on 21 June, there was a far larger rally when seven columns of marchers, in all some fifty thousand people, with forty bands, converged on Hyde Park from every part of London. This time Emma, possibly worried by the effect of the 1907 march on her lameness, contented herself with being one of a number of distinguished ladies who headed the marching columns in open carriages.[52] Hardy does not mention this episode.

Agnes Grove had by this time sufficiently benefited from Hardy's tutelage to publish books, and she now acknowledged the fact by dedicating her latest, *The Social Fetish*, to him. If this can scarcely have pleased Emma, the book's contents must have pleased her even less, since they consist of a collection of witty essays in the vein of Nancy Mitford's celebrated *Noblesse Oblige* of thirty years later, satirising middle-class notions of gentility, that could have been aimed expressly at Emma's foibles. But any significance held by Lady Grove for Emma's dwindling hope of rescuing her marriage was nothing to the significance of the woman who was to enter Hardy's life that summer, for it was then, although neither the precise date nor the circumstances nor the place (save that it was in London) is known, that he met Florence Emily Dugdale.[53] Her father was the headmaster of St Andrew's Church School at Enfield, on the northern fringe of London, and she herself, born in January 1879 as the second of his five daughters, also became a teacher in the school, uncertificated at first, then from 1905 certificated with a special credit in English literature and kindred subjects. The classes were large and unruly, the conditions imposed by the church authorities humiliating, the pay miserable. Even the environment, once that of a pleasant small market-town, was now a huge dreary wilderness of suburban brick. Florence became a radical-romantic atheist, as class-conscious as Hardy or Emma, and a prey to painful ill-health that lasted throughout her life, which it cut off at the age of fifty-seven.

The only aspect of her upbringing against which she did not rebel was its stern sexual code. She had had her romantic affairs before she met Hardy, but almost certainly on a strictly decorous basis. All her life she remained much more of a prude than Emma. Her remedy for escape from her humdrum world was not by becoming a man's mistress, nor yet a lady's companion, though she did attempt this last, but through creative literature, humble as it was – at first, small stories for small children, published in the local paper, then elementary schoolbooks and readers. The most fortunate outcome of this, as it chanced, was that one of her elderly admirers gave her a typewriter, with which she was able to lend a semblance of justification to her early association with Hardy by offering her services as a typist.

When he met her she conformed to nearly all his requirements for succumbing to a new infatuation: half his years, dark hair, huge doe eyes worthy of a creature in her own *Book of Baby Beasts*, and a willowy stance that could have served to illustrate the Grecian Bend. She had won a toehold in literary achievement that she aspired to making into a firm footing. Only the absence of a high-society background differentiated her from his other literary passion-flowers, and this she atoned for by having something of his own self-made beginnings. Gittings adds to these attractions her total absence of religious belief, but it is by no means certain that in the early stages she let Hardy know of this; her surviving letters to Emma, none written before 1910, contain several allusions to co-operation in Emma's anti-Catholic work, which Emma would surely not have accepted from a known atheist.[54] Florence could be as two-faced as Janus when it suited her, but that she should jeopardise her entrée into the Hardy home – already made hazardous enough by the secret association that had preceded it – by presenting a totally different religious face to Emma from that which she had been presenting for two years to Hardy, does not seem very likely. All the letters to Rebekah Owen in which she reveals her unbelief were written after Emma's death; it is more credible that she kept her counsel with Hardy until after that event as well so that he should not witness the measure of her hypocrisy.[55]

He lost no time in presenting signed books to her: *Wessex Poems* and a copy of the *Rubáiyát* are both dated 1907. Nor, it seems, did he lose much time before venturing to crown their London meetings by kissing her goodbye at the station, if the poem 'On the Departure Platform' is based on fact. Perceiving the delicacy of her health, he wrote her letters filled with a tender care he had not shown since the first delirious months of imagined love for Florence Henniker (the imperious Agnes Grove did not invite tender care), except in rare passages in letters to Emma; and, whereas the phrases addressed to Emma were seldom backed up by conduct when face to face, those addressed to Miss Dugdale fairly certainly were. Florence's literary interests were immediately taken in hand on a scale without precedent, beginning with massive letter-writing to likely editors and ending with actual material written by himself for Florence to publish under her own name.

All this activity had the same rejuvenating effect on him as had been produced by the other Florence and by Agnes. Fortunately, perhaps, for him, Emma and their friends must have put it down to relief at having completed *The Dynasts*, particularly since with the publication of the whole work the reviews became unexpectedly gratifying. Fired with fresh zeal, he undertook a tedious commission to prepare a new edition of his old friend William Barnes's works; fired with fresh love, as he supposed it, he began to assemble another volume of verse, including further rediscovered poems to early loves. This was the volume published in 1909 as *Time's Laughingstocks*. Nor was new poetry limited to 'On the Departure Platform', and there was quite a spate of letters to the press. Meanwhile Emma was indulging another of her life-long interests, her delight in children. In August 1907 the Owen sisters, paying their annual visit to Dorchester, were invited to watch sixty children 'at their games' in the Max Gate grounds.[56] In November of the following year, one of the now frequent performances in Dorchester of plays adapted from Hardy's novels – in this case *The Trumpet-Major* – was delayed by a violent storm. Emma, but not Hardy, was at the theatre (the Corn Exchange), and so was Maurice Evans, the small son of the play's adapter, A. H. Evans. It was the little boy's first visit to a play, but as the delay lengthened it was deemed that the end of the performance would come much too late for him to be still up. So it was Emma who offered to take him home, which she did, clinging to her ample cape with one hand and his own small hand with the other while they battled through the rain and wind. Half a century later, when he was a distinguished Shakespearian actor, Evans still recalled this kindly deed by old Mrs Hardy.[57]

In May she pursued the subject of Women's Suffrage and

kindred matters in a long and well-expressed letter published in the *Nation*.[58] She demanded not only the vote, but also that women be allowed a place in government, 'not to supersede men's rule, but to share it, standing on the same platform with equal rights'. Farther on she observes: 'The truth of the matter is that a man who has something of the feminine nature in him is a more perfectly *rational* being than one who is without it . . . and the reverse holds good, but in a less degree.' Nevertheless, despite the sentiments here revealed she deplored that anyone should regard her as a militant. In a letter of 22 June 1910 the Secretary of the London Society for Women's Suffrage apologises if an impression had been given that the Society believed Emma to be a supporter of the 'militant Societies', as they knew how much she objected to the militants' methods.[59] Hardy, therefore, whose attitude to the movement was somewhat equivocal, need have no fear that his wife would start chaining herself to railings or breaking shop windows.

Also in May 1908, in a letter addressed to both Owen sisters, Emma was moved to declare: 'My Eminent partner will have a softening of the brain if he goes on as he does and the rest of the world does.'[60] Had she had any opportunity to know of her Eminent partner's clandestine meetings with his latest girlfriend in London, one might have thought this a wife's bitter comment on the fruits of infidelity; but it is extremely unlikely she had any inkling yet of Florence's existence. One is left to assume that the philosophy embodied in *The Dynasts*, that of the Unconscious Will of the Universe and its tiny but growing measure of freedom granted to Man's own will, provoked the stricture. She was not to foresee that, by a truly Hardyan twist, within a few years a war even vaster than that involving Napoleon would bring the philosophy of *The Dynasts* down about the poet's ears and for many people doom her revered Christianity to a similar débâcle.

The *Life* tells us that in the autumn of 1907 they 'still kept up a little bicycling' together,[61] but early the following year Emma seems to have been trying to reconcile herself to cycling alone; in a February letter to Rebekah she wrote of her pleasure in taking 'odd meals in remote cottages on country roads with my bicycle waiting outside'.[62] To combat her loneliness she tried having a companion at Max Gate, but the experiment did not work.[63] Nor was her isolation improved by the loss at this time of the man who for ten years had been her most valued friend, Alfred Pretor. With Roman stoicism he had written to announce his coming death to Hardy and to ask him for an epitaph, which Hardy sent. A man of great learning, unlimited kindness, much wisdom, and a passion for cats that matched the Hardys' own, his letters and spoken counsel to Emma probably gave her more comfort during years of intense difficulty and sadness than she derived from any other source.

Another friendship of far more dubious worth also nearly ended in 1909. In June, Rebekah Owen wrote from Paris to say she had become a Roman Catholic, a disclosure that inevitably provoked a long, severe and predictably useless lecture from Emma on the evils of the Roman Church, including the implied charge, hardly likely to please the Lake District's American immigrant, that had she been English she would have known better than to be converted.[64] Only Rebekah's fanatical determination not to lose contact with Hardy, and Emma's generous continuance of hospitality, prevented Max Gate from being rid of this unattractive visitor.

This year, after a desultory search for a flat for the Season, Emma for once pleaded that she was not strong enough to run one, and Hardy ensconced himself in a small hotel alone. After a gap of several years previously referred to, the *'Dearest Emmie'* letters resume; and Weber gravely notes that, with the resumption, Hardy's superscription and signature lapsed into a cold 'Dear E.' and 'Yours, T.' or 'Yours, T.H.' respectively.[65] Yet the suggestion that by now the couple could hardly bear one another's presence is not borne out by a careful study of the evidence, and is largely due to a misleading statement by Newman Flower, often made worse by a wrong reading of what he wrote. Thus Evelyn Hardy, giving Flower as her source, informs us: 'Hardy had an outside staircase built at Max Gate so that he might ascend to his study without going through the house.' In the context this clearly means 'so that he might avoid meeting Emma while going through the house'.[66]

There never was such a staircase, and even the proposal for it had a totally different aim. What Flower wrote was that Hardy 'consulted a builder' – surely brother Henry – 'as to the best way of building a staircase to his study from the garden so that he should not have to go through the house. . . . He would have all his meals in this room. He would live there.'[67] As it happens, the rough plans that Hardy sketched for the project involving this staircase have been preserved for us in the Dorset County Museum. The main purpose of the enterprise was to provide Emma with a new boudoir (despite the fact that he was already having a dormer window put into her present boudoir) on the second floor, immediately above the manservant's room which in turn was above the applestore. Access to the manservant's room was by a door from the garden and a staircase. Immediately alongside the man-servant's room, but without access from the staircase and entered only from the opposite side, was Hardy's study, to gain which it was necessary to go through the entrance hall and up the main stairs. Hardy's plan was to build a second staircase from the garden door, at right-angles to the manservant's stairs, to a landing from which a new door would give access to his study and a further flight would continue up to the new second-floor boudoir. Thus to reach her new room Emma could choose between using the two new flights of stairs, passing Hardy's new study door on the way, or going through his study to the landing, from the centre of the house. Far from keeping Emma and Thomas apart, the alterations would greatly have increased the chances of their meeting. Hardy's object in giving himself direct access from the garden was not to avoid his wife, but to dodge the constant stream of visitors.

There is a direct reference to the project in a letter he sent her later in the year while she was staying in Calais to escape the chaos caused by the insertion of the dormer. After announcing the completion of this, he adds: 'I think you will like the room now, and you can retain it until a room is made for you over the man's room, which will be a matter of time.'[68] If the aim had been to get away from her, surely it would have been a matter of urgency. But in fact the project never came to anything.

Earlier in the year there had been another, if slighter, piece of evidence that they could still endure one another's proximity. When Emma did decide to visit London in June, Hardy wrote to say that his hotel had offered them the choice between a twin-bedded room or an extra single room, and he asked her which she preferred.[69] She must have chosen the twin-bedded room, for in a follow-up letter he told her that was what he had secured.[70] This proof that they were prepared to share a bedroom, even when an alternative was available, is not made any less real by the campaign he suddenly launched to prevent her from coming to London at all just then. A third letter, posted the day after the second, unexpectedly warns her of the great heat in London.[71] Should she not feel fit enough to come up, he will get over the difficulty of having engaged the room. She ought not to attend the function that was the object of her trip unless she would really *like* to. . . .

But she did like, for three days afterwards yet another letter acknowledged a card from her and expressed his anxiety at the thought of her 'venturing up here'.[72] Again he stressed the heat, adding belatedly that the hotel was very noisy – he feared she would be 'prostrated'. Perhaps she ought to wait until she had found out how much good her new spectacles would do for her sight? And he added a PS that he would rather take her to Cornwall than about London.

She took the hint at last and stayed at home, without any doubt greatly to her husband's relief; for, in the light of what we now know, this sudden zeal to dissuade her from her journey immediately after notifying her that he had booked her a room suggests only one thing: that he had been apprised of an unexpected visit to the West End by Florence Dugdale. The *Life* notes that 'in July Hardy was again in London with Mrs Hardy', and that he went on to the Milton Tercentenary celebrations at Cambridge.[73] This, however, was later in the month: in any case, the exact tercentenary of Milton's birth was not until 9 December. Possibly Hardy was thinking of his situation between Florence and Emma when in August he wrote in his diary: 'If all hearts were open and all desires known – as they would be if people shared their souls – how many gapings, sighings, clenched fists, knotted brows, broad grins, and red eyes should we see in the market-place!'[74]

In the autumn Hardy went to visit one of his sisters, who was taking a holiday at Swanage. They could scarcely fail to be reminded of the day, thirty-three years earlier, when Mary and Kate had gone to Swanage for their first – and so successful –

meeting with Emma. In September, after Hardy had agreed to the insertion of the dormer window in her room, Emma's decision to avoid the discomforts entailed by betaking herself to Calais was determined with such abruptness that a party due to be held at Max Gate had to be cancelled.[75] In the flurry two of the invited guests were not notified of the cancellation, a blunder uncharacteristic of Emma, whose accomplishments as a hostess are seldom denied.

While she was in Calais, Hardy was free to see Florence when he pleased, but he was now eager to introduce her to his home. Before he could think how to do so, however, he became involved in a situation straight out of French farce. He had begun by bringing her into touch with the dependable Clodd, who in the summer of 1909 invited them both to Aldeburgh. That same summer was to see the first night at Covent Garden of Baron Frédéric d'Erlanger's opera *Tess*, which, with an Italian libretto, had made its début in the illustrious San Carlo Opera House at Naples as long as three years before. Counting on the disinclination of Emma, who was again far from well, to leave Dorchester for London, Hardy invited Florence to the London first night. But to his dismay Emma said she would very much like to see the opera. Here were all the farce-writer's standard ingredients – the elderly married lover, the inamorata half his age, the stern wife threatening discovery, the faithful and conniving friend. Frantically Hardy wrote to warn Emma of the noisy hotel room they would have to occupy, the difficulty of getting her club to provide her with an alternative room at such short notice, the fatigue of the journey, even the fact that his hotel was full of Americans.[76] She brushed aside his objections, and he must have been at his wits' end when Clodd offered to take Florence out to dinner and on to the opera, leaving Hardy free to escort Emma.

And thus, presumably, it happened. His first reaction afterwards was to succumb to one of his fits of depression. Within a week he has writing to his 'dear friend' Florence Henniker that he was 'very much depressed with London, and, alas, with life, which I should not be particularly sorry to take my leave of'.[77] This was after returning to Max Gate. Can it be that following the manœuvres which only just avoided disaster over the opera visit he panicked? Perhaps, having committed himself to introducing Florence into the Max Gate *ménage*, he went through a period of guilt. Mrs Henniker and Lady Grove had both visited his country home and were familiar guests at the London flats, and there was always Rebekah Owen, but never before had he tried to integrate into his household a woman whom he had been meeting for two years without Emma's knowledge. At any rate, almost a whole year was to elapse before he achieved his aim, and then it may have been achieved only by chance.

The first encounter between Florence and Emma took place, so Florence long afterwards told Irene Cooper Willis,[78] at the club of which she and Emma were both members, the Lyceum.[79] Whether it was accidental or engineered by Hardy remains uncertain, but Emma 'took a fancy' to the younger woman and in due course – in June 1910[80] – invited her down to Max Gate. Strictly, therefore, Florence's début at Dorchester was made as Emma's friend,[81] which paved the way for the legend that she met Hardy only when she arrived there: a legend also, of course, believed by the writers who followed Weber in supposing she was introduced there by Florence Henniker in 1904. Emma's immediate liking for Florence must have exceeded Hardy's highest hopes, and the fact that the newcomer, being versed in research, secretarial duties, and typing, could help him with his work – as indeed, again unknown to Emma, she had apparently offered to do as far back as 1907 – ensured that her visits quickly became a regular occurrence.

Inevitably the question arises, what would have been the consequences if Emma had not 'taken to' Miss Dugdale in London. Possibly no worse than they proved as it was, for now that we know Florence to have made her début at Max Gate not in 1904 but in 1910 it can be seen that Emma quickly caught an inkling of this secretary's true rôle in Hardy's life, because Florence's arrival coincides with Emma's last and most desperate campaign to win him back. The fainting-fits and heart pains, the increasing agony from her gallstones, her failing sight, all convinced her that she had not much time. In May 1910 she forced herself to go to London again for the Season, allowing Hardy to take what proved to be their last apartment. As a demonstration of her continuing ability to share in his life it must have fallen rather flat, since for once the

Life fails to record any activities or persons met other than their 'usual friends', though among unrecorded happenings must have been the meeting with Florence. In June all their engagements had to be cancelled because, ironically, Hardy, not Emma, fell ill. In the Birthday Honours he had just been awarded the Order of Merit, and fortunately he recovered in time to present himself at Buckingham Palace in July. But now it was Emma who, probably through the strain of nursing him, had become so unwell again with a cough and a chill that she had to return to Dorset one week before the ceremony. Two of Hardy's letters to her make this perfectly clear, and in the context of her renewed exertions to please him the suggestion that she boycotted the Order of Merit ceremony to show her indifference is manifestly unsound. Only four months later she was present to see him awarded the Freedom of Dorchester.[82]

Hardy mentioned quite openly that 'Miss Dugdale' would be visiting the flat to type letters and 'see if I am all right' after Emma's departure. What he did not mention now or at any time was that since the spring of 1909 she had been once or perhaps twice to Clodd's home at Aldeburgh with him and once to Ventnor, Isle of Wight,[83] and had now borrowed a friend's flat in central London to which he could come and see her whenever and for as long as he liked. It would have been out of character – the character of either – for adultery to have taken place during these excursions and London meetings; yet Florence, like Hardy, must have felt some guilt about the deception of Emma. Florence's attitude to Emma throughout 1910 was one of excessive deference and simulated enthusiasm for everything that interested her. Either Emma, while perceiving that here was the latest in Hardy's chain of literary protégées, did not at first realise the full threat to herself that Florence represented, or she decided that the best way to meet it was by continuing her initial friendliness as though nothing were amiss. From whatever motive, she lost no time in disclosing her own literary ambitions, even disinterring her thirty-five-year-old story 'The Maid on the Shore', and Florence diplomatically lost no time in return with attempts to use such publishing contacts as she had to try to place some of Emma's work. Thus, while Hardy, who had done nothing to further his wife's efforts, was straining all his resources to promote those of his latest spiritual mistress, that lady was prudently exerting herself to realise the literary aspirations of Mrs Hardy.

How Florence conducted herself while under the Hardy roof we again do not know, but her letters to Emma combine a degree of false encouragement amounting almost to cruelty with an obsequiousness worthy of an old-fashioned Italian waiter. So, after saying that all seemed to be going well for publication of 'The Maid on the Shore' (when in fact its now dated style virtually ruled out its chances from the start), Florence is 'glad to know you are getting on well with the writing. We *must* accomplish something.' Another story, now lost, is 'distinctly good and original'. A third, or perhaps it was an essay, is 'touching, and comforting, and exquisitely written. . . . You have put it so clearly and so beautifully. Could you not write some of your sweet verses to go with this.' A poem, 'A Ballad of a Boy', which Emma had sent her and then asked her to withdraw, is 'so good and full of life and originality'. (One wonders what else it was full of, for Florence tantalisingly adds: 'Personally I cannot see one line in it that would identify the boy with Mr Hardy.')

True, she occasionally sounds a note of caution: 'Perhaps the stories of yours I have read are hardly modern enough, though exquisitely written'; 'I am afraid there will be no *financial* gain in publishing this – because the highest forms of literature seem rarely to have any great commercial value'. Florence also suggests that the description of clothing in 'The Maid on the Shore' might be modernised. But these criticisms are lost under the billowing froth of flatteries: 'A privilege to be allowed to help you'; 'It will be a delight to be in your dear little room again'; 'The days I spend at Max Gate are all so happy that I sometimes feel I shall be spoiled for the sterner realities of life'; 'It will be a very great pleasure and an honour to do anything for you'. When one of the cats (Markie) died, Emma was exhorted to 'write one of your delightful poems to her memory'. Allusions to Florence's enthusiastic collaboration in Emma's anti-Catholic activities are several, for example, (apropos of a letter in *The Times*), 'With teaching like that within the Church of England how can we resist the deadly attacks of Rome?'[84]

Clearly Florence had either quickly perceived for herself or

213

been notified by Hardy that the best way of making sure she remained *persona grata* at Max Gate (from which, she had doubtless been warned, unceremonious expulsions were not unknown) was to play on Emma's vanity. Yet how much of all this soft soap adhered to Emma is another matter. In November 1910 Florence wrote to Clodd a letter in which, after observing that 'Mrs Hardy seems to be queerer than ever' – a rather different tone from that adopted to Mrs Hardy herself – she says that Emma has just asked her whether she has noticed the great resemblance between Hardy and Dr Crippen (the recent notorious wife-murderer who had decamped with his secretary, Miss Le Neve).[85] Emma had speculated on the likelihood of being found, like Mrs Crippen, dead in the cellar one day, and Florence had hastily departed before she was asked if she didn't think she resembled Miss Le Neve. 'All this', she assured Clodd, was in 'deadly seriousness'. It may have been, but there is another possible explanation. Florence's letters show that she had very little sense of humour. Emma, on the other hand, had, whether it expressed itself in teasing Hardy,[86] making such observations in letters as 'even biographies are fiction, I find',[87] sketching humorously in her travel diaries,[88] or telling Gosse that she always beat Hardy in the mornings – but only with a rolled-up copy of *The Times*.[89] It would not be beyond her, having noted the humourlessness of the new 'secretary', to play deliberately on it and give her a scare – especially if she had just assessed the 'secretary' as her latest rival.[90]

There are several pointers that both the opening of Emma's eyes and the Dr Crippen episode occurred in the same week, between 11 and 19 November 1910. In a letter to Clodd on the earlier date Florence senses nothing amiss: 'Mrs Hardy is good to me beyond words, and instead of cooling towards me she grows more and more affectionate. I am *intensely* sorry for her, sorry indeed for them both.' So the 'cooling' that Florence was guiltily awaiting had not yet developed, because Emma still suspected nothing. But a week later the letter relating the Dr Crippen episode goes on to reveal that Emma had just proposed 'to go abroad for some months because that would "have a good effect on T.H." I thought it might be an experiment worth trying, until she told me she wanted me to go with her.'

Something had revealed the truth to Emma, and in her distress her first thought was to get Florence away from Hardy for as long as she could. But Florence, forgetting alike Emma's inexpressible goodness, her own intense sympathy, and the great pleasure and honour it would be to do anything for Emma, declined point-blank to be got away, at least until the middle of 1911, when yet another passage neatly deleted by her from the typescript of the *Later Years* tells us that 'in July Mrs Hardy accompanied by her friend Miss Florence Dugdale went to stay at Worthing'. This curious excursion, however, did not indicate any real change in the new position. Emma succeeded in reducing the number of Florence's sojourns at Max Gate from the end of 1910 until she herself died, and there were no more letters, sycophantic or otherwise, from Florence to the woman who was now just 'queerer than ever', no more expressions of compassion to Clodd.

If Hardy had lost his head to some extent over Florence Henniker, he lost it completely over Florence Dugdale. Already, by the time of her introduction to Max Gate, he had taken her to Aldeburgh and Ventnor. Between introducing her and Emma's death he was to take Florence to Aldeburgh at least twice more and once to Worthing; and once he visited her while she was staying at Weymouth. No one knows how often they met in her London flat, where she introduced him progressively to the members of her family.[91] Nearer home, he had no qualms about taking her to visit his sisters and brother, on whom, in the absence of all danger that she might feel any consideration for Emma, the visitor made a good impression. His letters to editors on her behalf were written with no regard for the gossip he might be stirring up. He composed verses that she inserted into her books as her own, and a 3,000-word story published in February 1911 in the *Cornhill* was in reality written entirely by him.[92] Florence's literary pride was as abject as the personal pride displayed in her letters to Emma.

When he was not gallivanting with Florence, Hardy's absences from home were mainly with his relatives. In February 1911 he and Henry went on another cathedral tour, in June they visited the Lake District (but not the Owens' house there); in July after Emma and Florence had returned from Worthing he took Kate to Somerset and north Devon. It was the second time in three years that they had been to Devon together, but although according to his poem 'The West-of-Wessex Girl' Emma had wanted all her married life to visit Plymouth with him, he had never taken her to Devon.

> And she would laud her native town,
>   And hope and hope that we
> Might sometime study up and down
>   Its charms in company.
>
> But never I squired my Wessex girl
>   In jaunts to Hoe or street. . . .

In 1908, trying to keep her away from London, he had written with more agitation than sincerity that he would rather take her to Cornwall. But he never did this either, though in 'The Going', one of his earliest compositions following her death, he realises that even in her last years the trip would not have been impossible.

> Why, then, latterly did we not speak,
> Did we not think of those days long dead,
> And ere your vanishing strive to seek
> That time's renewal? We might have said,
>   'In this bright spring weather
>   We'll visit together
> Those places that once we visited.'

But she did think of those days long dead, as throughout 1910 she relived, in the writing of *Some Recollections*, her youth and her predestined love for him. Had he given her the chance, the probabilities are that she would have risen above her ailments and made the most of the excursion. Even in the cold of December she accompanied him, in 1910, on one of their now rare expeditions together out of Dorchester, to a dance aboard the flagship of the United States fleet, then on a visit to Portland Roads.[93]

She must have realised how few were her weapons against not only Florence, but also his general indifference. We have no clue whether she intended, at the right moment, to invite him to read *Some Recollections*; whether, when death overtook her, she was reserving it as her last resource after the power of music had failed; or whether, like the black diaries that since the death of Alfred Pretor were her only outlet for relieving the miseries that beset her spirit, *Some Recollections* was always intended for no eyes but hers. If death caught her, against intention, with the diaries undestroyed, it may equally have caught her with the memoirs unintentionally undisclosed. The 'theme' of the little book, that the whole of her early life had been a divine preparation for her meeting with the man destined for her, accords with her deepened religious feeling and onset of mysticism at the time when she wrote; and her style, perhaps because of the profound sincerity inspiring her task, is an improvement on that of 'The Maid on the Shore', even if here and there one is reminded of Daisy Ashford's *The Young Visiters*.[94]

Nevertheless, the nostalgia and escapism of *Some Recollections* did not inhibit her from expressing herself, when she could find anyone to listen, in her old forthright manner on the subject of men in general and Hardy in particular. In 1910 she acquired a new friend and correspondent, Lady (Alda) Hoare, wife of the hereditary owner of the beautiful Stourhead mansion and gardens in Wiltshire. Alda Hoare, in some respects an archetypal bluff, tweedy and doggy upper-class countrywoman, was no Alfred Pretor, but she was sympathetic and not unintelligent, and certainly did not justify Irene Cooper Willis's surprisingly acid description of her as a 'rich, would-be cultured, large country-house lady, genial, gracious, and adulatory to a nauseating degree, dipping her pen literally, one would think, in syrup'.[95] To Lady Hoare, Emma wrote:

I am ensconsing myself in the study in *his* big chair foraging – he keeps me out usually – as *never* formerly – ah well, I have my private opinion of men in general and of him in particular – grand brains – much power – but too often lacking in judgment of ordinary matters – opposed to unselfishness, as regards themselves – utterly useless and dangerous as magistrates! and such offices – and to be put up with until a new order of the universe arrives (*it will*).[96]

For once we have both a letter from Emma and the reply or most of it. In answer Lady Hoare wrote:

There is one part of your letter that is *not* quite clear to me . . . about 'men'; do you know, I think we women expect from them, *sometimes*, rather too much? Now, *I* was brought up to expect *O*! And I never do expect anything. . . . I mean, that is, in *one* sense – I admire their sex infinitely more than our own. . . . But what I mean is, I think we often attach too great importance to what, in their eyes, is of none; and then the sexes quarrel thereover! I think we don't try, *sometimes*, to forsake our own selves for theirs. . . . It does so widen our outlook! – for, the better the woman, the more [last sheet of letter missing][97]

Not very profound, perhaps, but better than nothing for the lonely Emma. It says something for the friendship between them that it persisted after Lady Hoare had filled one letter with unstinted praise of *Jude the Obscure*. Mainly the pair exchanged views on French literature, which at least provided Emma with a distraction from her personal affairs. In May she made a final effort to mingle in her husband's London activities by asking him to take her to a reception at the Foreign Office, which he apparently did. But as an attempt to please him the request was another failure, for his only mention of it is in a letter to Florence Henniker in which he asks if she will be in town during a certain week, when he will be there on account of Emma's demand that he take her to the reception, 'so I suppose I must'.[98] It was her last London visit.

The writing of *Some Recollections* during 1910 and Florence Dugdale's change of attitude towards the end of the year point to this being also the time when Emma launched her final effort to get through to the inner Hardy by means of his susceptibility to evocative music. Indeed, the tenderness that moved the penning of *Some Recollections*, and must in turn have been accentuated by the process of reminiscence, can hardly have failed also to incline her towards the medium in which she had always felt most confidence. Except for mention of her last long piano performance,[99] Hardy does not allude in the *Life* to her efforts; but the poems that followed her death contain several allusions. Strictly, of course, the poems are not historical records, lacking even the dubious standing of the *Life*. But the 'Poems of 1912–13', particularly the poems of 1913, were composed at a time when Hardy was so engrossed with the remembrance of facts that there is little reason to doubt their veracity.

The first stanza of 'Lost Love' depicts Emma playing the old familiar airs on the piano, as she was to do in 'The Last Performance'. He passes the door, but his step does not falter and he goes on up the stairs. In the second stanza she tries singing the airs, and this time she hears his footstep 'near/As if it would stay', but it does not stay, and presently she hears a distant door shut. She sings again in 'The Singing Woman', but there is none to heed her lonely 'crooning'. The impression is that these recitals were repeated many times. But if he was outside the room he did not enter, and if he was inside he went out, as at the start of 'That Last Performance'. In 'Penance' he describes her playing in wistful solitude, for 'I would not join, I would not stay/But drew away . . .'. The poem states that she played thus at evenfall 'from year to year'. His phrase 'I would not join' perhaps means that he too might have sung, as he had been wont to do in the past. 'An Upbraiding' repeats the picture of her tempting him to sing:

> Now I am dead you sing to me
> The songs we used to know,
> But while I lived you had no wish
> Or care for doing so.[100]

Finally, the most important of the poems revealing her musical peace-attempts, 'The Last Performance,' is important less because he confirms its authenticity than because of its indication that she knew she was defeated, yet, as if reluctant even now to give up hope, went on and on with her playing until his return, just in case God, who had once guided this man to her as her Destiny, should remember and perform a miracle.

> 'I am playing my oldest tunes,' declared she,
>   'All the old tunes I know, –
> Those I learnt ever so long ago.'
> – Why she should think just then she'd play them
>   Silence cloaks like snow.
>
> When I returned from the town at nightfall
>   Notes continued to pour
> As when I had left two hours before:

'It's the very last time,' she said in closing;
   'From now on I play no more.'

A few morns onward found her fading,
   And, as her life outflew,
I thought of her playing her tunes right through;
And I felt she had known of what was coming,
   And wondered how she knew.

   1912

But it was all in vain. His love was there, as her death was
dramatically to prove, and it may even have been less deeply
and hopelessly interred beneath his obsession with Florence
than at first sight appears. Why, if he were utterly unmoved,
should he always leave the room when she started to play the
familiar airs?[101] The all but incredible *volte-face* in his attitude
from the hour when she slipped out of his reach is less incredible if we realise that his poems show there had been moments
when she nearly broke through to him, that it was not total
absence of emotional response but total powerlessness to untie
the bonds of shyness, shame, doubt, ingrained reticence, that
inhibited him. Each failure to respond, each flight from home
with or without Florence, each day passed at Max Gate with
them siting alone in their respective 'eeries', made communication more difficult.

   She tried other ploys besides music and (if he was ever
intended to see them) the recording of her memories, such as
arranging for Longmans of Dorchester to publish a 'volume' –
it was no more than a pamphlet – of her poems, in a ludicrous
yet pathetic attempt to show him that in this field too they
had a common interest. By an unintended irony, Albert
Bankes, to whom she sent a copy, promised in his letter of
thanks to bring both her collection and Hardy's *Wessex Poems*
to Max Gate for autographing.[102] She also made small over-
tures whose nature we do not know, as indicated by the poem
'The Peace-Offering'. These too, Hardy understood yet rejected: 'It was but a little thing. . . . But I would not welcome
it. . . .'[103] But she could not bring herself to appeal to him
directly in speech. Twice she had written to Rebekah Owen
that with the advancing years she was growing shyer. Now

there was always the fear of a rebuff to restrain her. And although her letters and diaries are fluent enough, she had never found it easy to express herself orally. Carl Weber, in one of his grosser misconceptions, holds up the poem 'You Were the Sort That Men Forget' as the outstanding example of the patient Hardy turning on his insufferable wife and striking back at her tactlessness and 'lack of social art'.[104] In reality, as most critics have perceived, in 'You Were the Sort That Men Forget' Hardy laments compassionately Emma's inability 'to make men see how sweet your meaning' by uttering 'words inept' that offend them, whereas with better power of expression she would have 'charmed them glad'. The failing included an incapacity to understand friends who were in the same predicament, even when the meaning behind their crude ways of conveying it 'outprized the courtesies of the bland'. Because of the woman's handicap, the poet imagines himself the only person, perhaps, who remembers her, and concludes 'What a waste that Nature/Grudged soul so dear the art its due!'[105]

Another poem, 'Without Ceremony', though specifically directed to her disconcerting habit of suddenly disappearing while he was showing guests to the door, or even leaving home for a protracted absence before he had so much as noticed that her trunks had been brought downstairs, is also an extension of the same theme. 'Goodbye is not worthwhile!' was her philosophy, he accuses, even when departing into death; but the implication is that she found the saying of goodbye beyond her powers of adequate expression.

'Had You Wept' is variously held to be addressed to Emma, Florence, Tryphena, and no one at all. The last suggestion is advanced by K. G. Wilson in an essay that sets out convincing reasons for supposing Hardy to have derived the notion of the poem from one translated from the Spanish by Florence Henniker.[106] But because this was its source it does not follow that he necessarily composed 'Had You Wept' with no specific woman in mind. Those who, like Evelyn Hardy, believe the subject to be Florence Hardy, point to the reference in the second line to 'your large and luminous eye', which is certainly not applicable to Emma. Yet, as Zietlow points out, the behaviour of the woman is 'consistent with Hardy's presentation of

Emma in the poems about division'.[107] In truth the whole portrait of the woman in the poem tallies remarkably closely with
what we know of Emma, and very little with what we know of
Florence:

Had you wept; had you but neared me with a hazed uncertain ray,
Dewy as the face of the dawn, in your large and luminous eye,
Then would have come back all the joys the tiding had slain that day
And a new beginning, a fresh fair heaven, have smoothed the things
    awry.
But you were less feebly human, and no passionate need for clinging
Possessed your soul to overthrow reserve when I came near;
Ay, though you suffer as much as I from storms the hours are bring-
    ing
Upon your heart and mine, I never see you shed a tear.

The deep strong woman is weakest, the weak one is the strong;
The weapon of all weapons best for winning, you have not used;
Have you never been able, or would you not, through the evil times
    and long?
Has not the gift been given you, or such gift have you refused?
When I bade me not absolve you on that evening or the morrow,
Why did you not make war on me with those who weep like rain?
You felt too much, so gained no balm for all your torrid sorrow,
And hence our deep division, and our dark undying pain.

Since there was no deep division or dark undying pain
involving him and Florence, the last line alone would seem to
rule out her candidature as the woman addressed. On the other
hand Emma is *par excellence* the deep strong woman who
scorned tears. Throughout the plentiful source-material about
her there is, I believe, no reference to her weeping.[108] But Florence on her own admission once burst into tears even while
taking tea with a friend.[109]

The records of Emma's day-to-day activities become fewer
and fewer towards the end. She continued to tend the garden
when she was well enough: one of the sights Hardy recalled
most vividly after her death was of her 'as usual coming in
from the flower-beds with a little trowel in her hand'.[110] Every
morning she used to walk along one of the paths, assisting herself no doubt with her black stick, 'the cat trotting faithfully

behind her';[111] and on Sundays the woman who had once as-
tounded the Cornish country people with her daring horsemanship was sometimes able to cycle to Fordington church,
but on other occasions had to be drawn in a Bath chair. The
note still survives in which, just before Christmas 1911, she
asked the Reverend Richard Bartelot whether he would object
to her leaving the Bath chair in the vicarage garden, as it was
'bran new'.[112]

The most detailed picture of the Max Gate regime at this
time was given to James Stevens Cox in 1972 by Mrs Alice
Harvey, who as a fourteen-year-old girl known as 'Dolly' Gale
was taken on by Emma late in 1911 to be her personal maid.[113]
The girl found Mr and Mrs Hardy leading entirely separate
lives, meeting only at dinner. She never heard them speak to
one another, nor did Emma ever talk about her husband. He
addressed Dolly only when obliged to, and never thanked her
for any errands she ran. There is no mistaking whose side she
was on, in this divided household. Hardy was 'a miserable old
thing' who, it was her impression, 'irritated most people and
certainly all those who worked in the house'. Indeed, because
of the many stories that his 'morals were not of the best', it
being 'common knowledge in Dorchester that he had a mistress in London named Florence Dugdale', Dolly's parents
only grudgingly allowed her to work at Max Gate herself.
Hardy's manner was supercilious, and throughout her term of
employment Dolly feared and despised him. Emma, on the
contrary, although repellent in that her scalp was covered with
eczema (one of the girl's duties was to brush her 'thin, long
grey hair'), was 'a most considerate and kindly employer'
whom the girl 'liked very much'. She was also generous, on one
occasion giving her young maid a present of a chain purse.

The account is biased, not always accurate (there are two
references to St Peter's Church instead of St George's), and
spiced with some silly gossip, but the description of the utter
collapse of communication between the Hardys rings true,
although one has to remember that many people refrained
from talking in front of their servants or discussing members
of the family with them. Moreover Dolly Gale says nothing of
the times when there were visitors at Max Gate. In November
1911, for example (though possibly just before Dolly moved

in), Florence Henniker was there, for she, Emma and Hardy attended a stage adaptation of 'The Three Strangers' and 'The Distracted Preacher'.[114] During October, Sidney Cockerell, Director of the Fitzwilliam Museum at Cambridge, called in quest of manuscripts of Hardy's works, and the following June, Henry Newbolt and W. B. Yeats paid 'a pleasant week-end visit' to present Hardy with the Royal Society of Literature's Gold Medal,[115] the week-end activities including the picnic on the Ridgeway (with Emma) commemorated in the poem 'Where the Picnic Was'.[116]

Hardy in fact was moving around as usual. Between spring 1911 and midsummer 1912 he made, in addition to the journeys with his relatives already noted and his trips to London to see Florence, excursions to Bath and Bristol, Gloucester, and London to stay with Lady St Helier – the former Lady Jeune. And if, as Dolly Gale noted, he spent most of the days at Max Gate in his study, it was because he was once more hard at work writing new prefaces and correcting proofs for Macmillan's Wessex edition of his works. He was also composing poems, including the superb and haunting 'The Bird-Catcher's Boy'. On the face of it his failure to notice Emma's deteriorating health and frequent periods of pain seems inexcusably callous; Gittings links it with his repeated protests, after Emma's death, at the utter unexpectedness of that event, as evidence of an acute feeling of guilt.[117] Dolly Gale recounts that in 1911 her new mistress 'permanently suffered from a pain in her back and constantly asked me to pat her back to give her relief'.[118] But apart from this, the eczema, and the intermittent need for a Bath chair, the maid does not mention heart attacks or any other signs of distress. Nor have those friends who met Emma during the last two years of her life, including such frequent associates as the Homers and the Bartelots, recorded seeing any signs of undue discomfort. There was not a little of the stoic in her, and the very nature of the events in which she continued to take part suggests that whenever an attack came on during one of them she masked her pain, so that her husband saw no more than the symptoms to which he had been accustomed since she first pleaded inability to face running a flat for the London Season. To a mind as preoccupied as his with human decay, even the advent of the

Bath chair would seem but another step in life's inevitable decline.

Irene Cooper Willis has recorded a remark by Kate Hardy that in mid-1912 Thomas contemplated moving out of Max Gate and into Talbothays.[119] Kate's assertion should be treated with reserve. In a mood of despair, perhaps after a quarrel with Emma, Hardy may well have said something like 'How I wish I could move into your happy household!' – which Kate, in her dislike of Emma, would have seized upon and tried to develop. One must remember too her anxiety – as Florence found – to acquire as large a slice as possible of Hardy's fortune. The transfer of his home to Talbothays would greatly enhance her prospects.

At some time during July 1912 Lilian Gifford descended on Max Gate 'to help'. Dolly Gale, who reveals this, also reveals that Lilian appeared to her to irritate Mrs Hardy, although she 'tried hard to please' her.[120] Having failed, however, to come up to her aunt's 'standards or expectations' Lilian left, though seemingly not for very long. Such records of her 'attempting to please' are rare indeed. On 16 July Emma steeled herself, despite a heat-wave, to preside over her last garden party – steeled herself so well that Hardy considered her 'apparently in her customary health and vigour', an opinion shared by the 'numerous guests'.[121] Early in August both Hardys took Lilian (evidently in favour again) to Weymouth to see a new stage comedy, although Hardy had already seen it in London with Lady St Helier.

Between the two events, both chronicled in the *Life*, occurred one unmentioned there, although in its combination of work for the church, giving pleasure to children, and physical courage, it was as fitting an *envoi* to Emma's public actions as one could seek. In 1907 the Reverend Richard Bartelot had married, and in due course his wife had given birth to a daughter, Evie, whom from the first Emma cherished like a beloved granddaughter, giving her many presents and, as soon as she was old enough, planning tea-parties and trips to the seaside. Now, at the end of July, the old sick woman organised, with the Vicar and his wife, a seaside outing for the girls of Mrs Bartelot's Needlework Guild, with the three-year-old Evie included in the party. Emma travelled with them in the 'two-horse brake' (which cannot have helped her back pains) to Osmington Mills, near Weymouth, where they had a 'most enjoyable time', a 'sumptuous tea', and stayed quite late, afterwards going back to Max Gate for more refreshments and the gift to each girl of a cup and saucer.[122] Lilian also took part in the expedition.[123]

As summer moved into autumn, Emma tried one more experiment to attract Hardy's notice. Having somewhere acquired the idea that love can never endure where there is a garden without a rose growing, she obtained a rose-bush and, according to the poem 'The Spell of the Rose', planted it secretly – the poem says, at dead of night.[124] But in order to grow, the rose had to await the following spring, and by then it was too late. Meanwhile autumn slid into winter, and Hardy finally conceded that his wife 'was noticed to be weaker.... though not ill, and complained of her heart at times'.[125] Now, towards the very end, they must have conversed a little, for he records an occasion when she consulted him on whether to go downstairs and see some visitors, a second when she agreed to see a doctor, and a third on which he asked whether she would mind his attending a rehearsal of *The Trumpet-Major*, adapted some years before for the stage. *He* asked *her* permission! The ice that all her stratagems had failed to break must have been very thin by then.

This occurred on 25 November, one day after her seventy-second birthday. Three days earlier, despite poor weather, she had driven over to visit the Homers, now no longer at Athelhampton but in a new house, Bardolf Manor, a mile or two to the north. Hardy conjures up her drive home in the poem 'Your Last Drive'; and if the two final lines of the first stanza are based on reality, when she reached home it was yet another time that they spoke, she telling him of the charm of the town lights seen like a halo as she approached. The following day she was 'distinctly unwell', and on her birthday she 'seemed depressed'. On the twenty-fifth, states the *Life*, 'two ladies' called.[126] In fact they were Catharine and Rebekah Owen, who were in Dorchester to see *The Trumpet-Major*. Though told Emma was unwell, Rebekah with crass and characteristic insensitiveness wrote on a card, 'Would you not see *us*?' and bade the maid take it upstairs.[127] After an interval they were let in, only to have to wait again while, unknown to them, Emma consulted Hardy on whether she should go down. He advised her not to, but she went nevertheless, entering the room very slowly with tears in her eyes. Mastering her obvious distress, she told the intruders they were welcome, and when even Rebekah made a show of leaving she insisted that they stay to tea. They learned that she had not eaten for several days and felt great pain in her back, but formed the opinion that nerves and melancholia were the real cause of her trouble, and that she actually seemed the better for talking with them. She held out no hope that Hardy would descend, and bade them return the day after seeing the play, to discuss it. But Rebekah was not going to be denied her hero, and herself dispatched the maid to tell him that Catharine and she would be 'very hurt' if he did not see 'such old friends'.

So Hardy too was forced to appear, with polite expressions of joy at seeing them again, and talked 'in the old delightful way' to Rebekah while Catharine chatted a little with Emma. At this point Rebekah repeats that Emma 'was no worse for seeing us, but better, I think. Only the pain came on now and then.' At last Catharine made the excuse that she fancied their chauffeur was outside in the darkness and rain (actually he was in the kitchen) and dragged her sister away. Both Hardys accompanied them to the door, but while Hardy stayed to watch the car-lamps lit, Emma went back. Rebekah states that both sisters implored Emma again and again to call a doctor, but she merely declared that she 'did not want to be cut up'. For some reason they did not appeal to Hardy to support them.

Nevertheless, on the twenty-sixth she did consent at last to be seen by a doctor. This was Dr Gowring, who had succeeded Dr Fisher on Fisher's retirement in 1910, and if Florence Hardy is to be believed, was scarcely a pillar of his profession. His verdict on Emma was that she was not seriously ill, merely weak from want of nourishment because of indigestion.[128] However, since she would not allow herself to be examined he cannot altogether be blamed for his diagnosis. In the evening Hardy went, as she had bidden him, to his rehearsal, and because everyone was in bed when he got back he did not disturb her.

On what happened next the accounts differ. According to

Hardy he enquired the following morning how his wife was, to be told by the maid that Emma had said she was better and would probably get up later, but that she now seemed worse.[129] Hastening to her room, he found her much worse, and unconscious. Gowring was again sent for, but she died before he could arrive. According to the maid, Dolly Gale, sixty years later, she entered Emma's room to find her moaning and very ill.[130] A great change had come over her since the previous evening.' She was not unconscious, but asked the frightened young girl to fetch Hardy. Despite the early hour he was already at his desk, from which on receiving her message he looked at her 'disdainfully' and after a few moments told her her collar was crooked, then carefully arranged the things on the desk before following her into Emma's room. As soon as he saw Emma, however, his composure vanished, and hurrying to the bedside he asked her, 'Em, Em, don't you know me? It's Tom', or something similar. Either because Mrs Harvey's – Dolly Gale's – account became unclear at this point, or because Stevens Cox did not note it down clearly, it remains obscure whether Emma was by this time still conscious; what is certain is that she was unable to answer Hardy. Within less than five minutes her life flickered to a close; during those minutes the servant remained at the foot of the bed, and would have heard if Hardy had spoken again. If Emma was conscious, therefore, any tender words she might have hoped to take into eternity with her stayed unuttered. She broke the stubborn ice in the end, but she never knew it, for the means by which she finally succeeded was death.

In due course Dr Gowring arrived, and eventually gave the cause of death as heart-failure due to impacted gall-stones. The extent to which Hardy is to blame for not having perceived the seriousness of his wife's illness while there was still time to do something about it will, now that Gittings has given the matter the attention it ought to have had years ago, undoubtedly be a subject of discussion for as long as Hardy remains a focus of attention. Gittings is unstinting in his condemnation. I have already set out some of the factors that deserve taking into account in mitigation. The first recorded reaction by Hardy himself to the implications of Emma's sudden end are in a letter to Florence

Henniker written just under three weeks later – before, one may suppose, he had decided on the campaign of guilt-concealing self-justification of which Gittings accuses him. Hardy wrote: 'I have reproached myself for not having guessed there might be some internal mischief at work, instead of blindly supposing her robust and sound and likely to live to quite old age.'[131] This is certainly what he felt at the time; and it is worth noting that Rebekah Owen wrote to a certain Mrs Fauty: 'There was no reason why she should not die first, and she certainly looked awfully [*sic*], yet one had always the feeling that she would survive him.'[132]

When Hardy observed in the *Life* that no one at Emma's last garden party suspected anything amiss with their hostess, this is plainly true and not a disingenuous afterthought. Ten days later the Bartelots were equally unsuspecting, or Richard would without doubt have entered a comment in the diary that he quotes in his memoirs. Another point to be noted is Hardy's difficulty, during the latter part of the estrangement, in bringing himself to broach any intimate personal subject to Emma, especially when he knew from long experience her strong dislike of medical attention. Her resistance to the Owens' attempts to make her see a doctor within two days of her death and her refusal to let Gowring examine her when he was finally allowed to come emphasise the hopeless task that would have faced Hardy even had he overcome his diffidence.

With Emma dead, he needed someone to run Max Gate, particularly on the social side: the efficient housemaid-housekeeper Florence Griffin was capable of handling the administration of the house. As it happened, Florence Dugdale was on her way to Dorset to see *The Trumpet-Major*. Hardy sent a telegram to Weymouth, where she was to stay for the sea air, and with what Dolly Gale considered 'inordinate haste' (in fact less than a month) Florence moved into Max Gate. Lilian Gifford also lost no time in appearing there, almost her first action on arrival being to hasten up to London to sell Emma's clothes. With typical deviousness Hardy told Mrs Henniker in the letter just quoted that Lilian had come to manage the household affairs, Florence merely to help him with some proof-correcting.[133]

Emma was buried in Stinsford churchyard on 30 November.

Her death had quickly become known throughout Dorchester, having been announced at the performance of the play, yet few people attended the funeral: Thomas, Mary, Kate, and Henry Hardy, the Owens, the Leslies from Came Vicarage (but seemingly no Moules apart from 'Margie', now Mrs Leslie), a deputation from an unspecified Dorchester society, and a handful more.[134] On the card accompanying Hardy's wreath was inscribed simply 'From her lonely husband – with the old affection'. He could have added 'twenty years too late'.

CHAPTER EIGHT

Assessment

EMMA'S PLACE in Hardy's life and career is fraught with as much irony as he ever put into a piece of fiction. On the one hand they were not so much temperamentally unsuited to marry one another as too old and therefore too set in character when they met for their temperaments to undergo the reciprocal adaptation possible for those of younger people. On the other hand if they had not married, and their marriage had not gone awry, we should have been deprived not only of the great blossoming of love-poems that followed Emma's death, and such poems composed during her lifetime as 'Shut Out That Moon', but also of Hardy's two finest novels, built as they were on the attitude to marriage inculcated in him by his own. Again, the picture of Emma handed down to posterity and virtually unchallenged for more than half a century is that of a scatterbrained woman, shallow, weak and incapable of exerting influence; yet the truth is that her character was stronger than Hardy's. Her inconsequential style of speech and (when she felt it did not matter) careless manner of letter-writing, her proneness to 'words inept' and periodical lack of perception, deceived many in her lifetime and have deceived many since into underestimating the power of thought that she could command when she wished: yet it is there on display for any unprejudiced student, in her surviving letters to the press, her newspaper articles, and the best of her private correspondence.

She failed as the wife of a great writer not because she was intellectually unable to keep abreast of his thoughts, but because

she strongly disagreed with many of them and was too forceful
a character, as well as, at heart, too fond of him, to stand aside
and see him praised for what she regarded as the dissemination
of wickedness. The common idea, though shared in her lifetime by some of her best friends such as Christine Wood
Homer, that she had no conception of Hardy's genius is belied
by Alfred Pretor's letters to her. These show that her problem
was not incapacity to realise her husband's stature, but inability to cope with it. Her fears that her own share in his
labours was not fully appreciated did not stem entirely from
vanity, but also from her belief – specifically stated to Rebekah
Owen, and almost certainly to Pretor – that the public was
stealing him from her. The ideal literary marriage for her was
that of the Brownings. If only she could be recognised as
having contributed *something* to Hardy's work, she might be
bracketed with him, not perhaps quite as Elizabeth Barrett
Browning, but sufficiently to halt the public obliviousness to
her existence that she sensed he was beginning to share.

But her desire to hold on to him by sharing in his recognition
had to be balanced against her duty, as a Christian, to oppose
his unchristian views. Too often her opposition is dismissed as
mere religious narrow-mindedness. She may have been narrow
in her anti-Catholicism, though she would not have been
thought so had she shown her zeal a few decades earlier, but
she made more efforts to understand Hardy's thinking than is
generally realised, even to the extent of attending lectures on
Positivism with him in the 1880s[1] and being invited, *as a sym-
pathiser*, to a Positivist 'presentation' ceremony (the equivalent of baptism).[2] Indeed, in many matters her thinking was as
progressive as his: on the need for a more humane attitude to
animals, on women's rights and the desirability of their
sharing in government, on the upbringing of children, on prostitution, concerning which she thought the clients should be
blamed rather than the women. In none of her letters is there a
single adverse comment on the sexual 'coarseness' in his novels
that shocked so many critics, nor did she refuse close co-
operation with him on such 'sexy' novels as *The Woodlanders*
and *Tess*.

In regard to many other writers she was equally tolerant.
She could not quite take Zola, but of Rousseau's *Julie* she

merely commented 'queer morals' while not rejecting the book,[3] and Richard Le Gallienne's *Golden Girl* was 'exquisitely poetical at the beginning, crisply amusing in the middle, *though somewhat licentious*, and very pathetic at the end' (my italics).[4]

Her disagreement, and the breach that ruined more than one half of their marriage, centred on one thing – their different attitudes to the meaning of matrimony. Social differences, his lack of consideration, his dancing after new loves and tactless reminders of loves past, even his failure to accept God, could have been overcome. But not his estimate of matrimony. This she saw, as she watched his development as a novelist, increasingly menacing their own marriage. Whether she was right to simplify the issue thus is another question. It also raises the point whether, as a woman of more intelligence than is habitually credited to her, she should have seen or sensed enough of his attitude during their four years of pre-marital friendship to have declined to marry him, even allowing that the alternative would have been to remain an old maid. The answer is partly that in those days his views on marriage had not yet crystallised clearly, partly that the love-at-first-sight of 1870 deepened too quickly into that affection, on both sides, which was never entirely to die, and partly, of course, that she believed him destined for her by God.

In 1913 Florence Hardy told Clodd that according to Hardy's relatives the girl he was mourning had never existed;[5] and J. I. M. Stewart quotes Sir Arthur Quiller-Couch's suspicion that Hardy in his seventies concocted a 'pure fairy-tale' out of his courtship.[6] In the first place the fairy-tale, if it was one, was of Emma's concoction, for it was *Some Recollections* that set Hardy's reminiscences in train; but it is likely that both Quiller-Couch and the Hardy relatives were mistaken. The tenacity of the underlying love between Thomas and Emma in the teeth of all the vicissitudes that beset it and all the misconceptions that for two decades drove it underground does not suggest that it was built on a myth. Furthermore there is confirmation of the genuine happiness of the St Juliot days in a source generally overlooked – the exuberant sketches the pair made of one another. They are not many, but they convey a sense of unmistakable happiness.

What differentiates the Hardys' broken marriage from others was that for two decades they continued to live together though each was convinced that the other's love had perished, and each tried, at intervals, to show that for his or her part this was not true. Both carried the mistaken conviction to the grave. Emma died in the certainty that her efforts to reawaken Thomas's love had failed because it was no longer there. This, rather than a premonition of death, is the likely reason for her saying 'I shall never play again'. Thomas never perceived that *Some Recollections* could have been written only by a woman in whom love still breathed, but regarded it as the re-evocation of emotions long vanished; for after its discovery he continued to regard her as 'the girl who died more than twenty years ago', and none of the subsequent love-poems affords the slightest hint that he revised that belief.

There remain the two questions of her possible insanity, and whether he believed her insane. We may safely discount the silly and often malicious comments of certain Dorchester people that Emma was half-cracked, weak in the upper storey, and so on. Mrs Lorna Heenan, married daughter of Dr Fred Fisher, told James Stevens Cox that in her later years Emma's 'mental condition progressively deteriorated', but she does not say, nor is there other evidence, that her father lent his medical authority to any assertion that his patient was insane.[7] All the serious accusations of insanity come from Florence Hardy, a few in her letters, the majority passed on by Irene Cooper Willis. In his chapter on the Giffords in *The Young Thomas Hardy* Robert Gittings analysed Florence's charges, and demonstrated their invalidity, so thoroughly that in the absence of fresh evidence to contradict him there is little point in going over the same ground here. Florence's motives were twofold: by making Hardy believe that Emma was insane while compiling her black diaries and 'What I Think of My Husband', she hoped to prevent him from believing Emma's charges; and by convincing *herself* that he had been married to a madwoman she could justify her deceit of Emma with the thought that only her own sympathetic association with Hardy had preserved him from despair and collapse.

Hardy fell in readily with Florence's suggestions, for the reasons she intended. Only by assuring himself that Emma had been mad could he discount her terrible accusations and avoid the guilt with which their authenticity would have invested him. That he did not wholly succeed, many of the poems that followed Emma's death show, although it is noticeable how, the farther the death recedes into the past, the more perceptible becomes a note of criticism in the evocation of the loved one. Assuredly Hardy came to believe she had been mad; but that he did so only under Florence's influence is virtually proven by the fact that no reference to insanity occurs in either the letters or the poems written while Emma was alive. It may be objected that this was due to loyalty, especially if we hold that he never lost his underlying love. But the very existence of this latent love should have made it possible, had he thought her not responsible for the things that wounded him, to have responded to her efforts to end their estrangement. Even if we believe that his love did perish during the last years, his whole conduct towards his wife during her lifetime is inconsistent with a belief that she was mad.

Against Florence and Hardy himself, the list of responsible people who were convinced that Emma remained sane, if increasingly eccentric, is formidable; for to those such as Mabel Robinson and Irene Cooper Willis who expressly denied that Emma lost her reason must be added the intimate friends who were never asked to pronounce on the subject but whose attitude towards her was itself a denial, such as Alfred Pretor and Alda Hoare. Even Rebekah Owen never placed it on record that she thought Emma insane, only that others did. Emma's nearest approach to insanity is the possible development, late in life, of a certain degree of persecution mania. There is May O'Rourke's story about Emma reporting to the police that Hardy was trying to poison her,[8] and the occasion when she asked Florence, perhaps but not certainly in macabre jest, whether Hardy was not like Dr Crippen (page 214). These are pointers of doubtful worth; to be considered more seriously is Edward Clodd's diary entry for 25 April 1913: 'Met Hardy. . . . Talked about his wife. She had illusions that she was being followed by some man, that people were conspiring against her: all showing the mad strain in the family blood.' The last phrase is pure Florence. For the rest, one can only comment that, although the illusion of persecution is as a rule speedily made known to the 'victim's' friends, no one in Emma's large circle ever recorded any awareness of it. Even Clodd did not say that his own observation confirmed Hardy's statement.

As the years of their marriage passed, Hardy undoubtedly brought out the worst in Emma, and the worst in Emma brought out the best (as a novelist and poet) in Hardy. When she made her extremely brave decision to advise him to become a novelist instead of an architect she planted the seeds of her own tragedy, for as he travelled to ever greater splendours along the road on which she had set him, and was claimed as its own by a larger and larger part of the world that lined that road, she had neither the degree of sophistication nor the diplomatic finesse to keep up with him and retain her grip. The lameness that dogged her lay not only in the legs. All her pitiful poetising, her silly claims to more than her true share in his work, her waspish denigrations, were frantic attempts to find crutches that would enable her to regain his side and fend off the thieving hordes. But the very actions that prove to us the continuance of her love convinced Hardy that it was dead. Her tactics, by any standards, were of the worst possible sort and had the worst possible results; yet this does not compromise the sincerity of her motives. The tragedy of the Hardys' marriage was due to the commonest of all reasons for human misunderstanding, failure of communication. Emma would have expressed herself if she could, but lacked the power of words. Hardy had the power of words, but was inhibited from using them. So they drifted on, their differences of attitude to religion and marriage never resolved because they were never discussed, until death grew tired of waiting and removed the last chance.

APPENDIX

Florence Hardy and the Giffords

FLORENCE'S TWO-FACED ATTITUDE towards Emma during
Emma's lifetime is clear beyond any dispute from the evidence
of Florence's letters. After Emma's death Florence's attitude
became one of unrelieved hostility. Both phases have had their
apologists: Gittings has excused her behaviour towards the
living Emma by suggesting that the only way in which Florence could extricate herself from the extremely hard circumstances of her youth was by exercising exaggerated sycophancy
towards anyone likely to help her, so that by the time she met
Emma such conduct was natural, even inevitable, towards the
wife of her latest patron. Less tenuous than this exculpation is
the excuse generally advanced to extenuate her campaign of
denigration after Emma's death, namely the complete turn-
about in Hardy's apparent feelings for his first wife – 'apparent', because if the thesis of this book is accepted, that deep
within him his love never died, his reaction to her death was less
a turn-about than an explosion of emotions constricted for
twenty years.

Florence could not have been expected to realise this. Her
eyes beheld only the spectacle of the unhappily married man,
who had seemed to concentrate all his frustrated affection on
her, without warning switching his tenderness to the very
woman who had blighted his life, at the very time when the
removal of the restraints imposed by propriety might have
been expected to redouble his demonstrativeness to Florence.
The shock upset her whole spiritual equilibrium, and that in

237

spite of her dismay she could continue to frequent Max Gate and assume the rôle of Hardy's 'protector' is a measure either of her real love for him or of the strength of her instinct for self-interest – perhaps a blend of both. One or both of these motives was undoubtedly also responsible for the seldom-remarked fact that she appears never to have *spoken* any words defamatory of Emma, except to Irene Cooper Willis in privileged circumstances after Hardy's death. James Stevens Cox, who interviewed some two hundred people while compiling his collection of monographs, the majority people who had known Florence, has stated that not one of the interviewees afforded 'any positive evidence that Florence had any but kindly feelings towards Emma'.

Florence reserved the expression of her true feelings for the letters that, as noted in Chapter 5, she wrote as a means of 'letting off steam' to chosen confidants, principally Edward Clodd and Rebekah Owen. While Hardy engrossed himself in composing his spate of love-poems to his 'late espouséd saint', as the exasperated Florence called her in one letter to Clodd, in arranging visits to Plymouth and St Juliot (to say nothing of the grave at Stinsford), in lauding Emma to embarrassed visitors in front of Florence, and in deriving mournful pleasure from rereading the black diaries and 'What I Think of My Husband', not surprisingly Florence's vilification of Emma extended to the whole Gifford tribe, living and dead. Among the living her main targets, naturally, were the Hardys' *de facto* adopted children, Emma's nephew and niece Gordon and Lilian. Hardy, inevitably, was not disposed to lessen his contacts with these walking memorials to the dear departed. Lilian was at Max Gate, though unsummoned, almost as soon after Emma's death as Florence. For a time the two women competed for the post of mistress of the household – the third potential candidate, the efficient Florence Griffin, was speedily dismissed by her namesake. 'The niece', Florence Dugdale wrote to Clodd in August 1913, 'has just returned. . . . She is still what she was before she went. I am reminded by her, a dozen times a day at least, that "dear Aunt" was a very great lady, and that I am – so she implies – quite a low sort of person. . . . I do not know whether she will stay on after the end of this year – but if she does I don't.'

In other letters to Clodd during 1913 she tells him of the black diaries and of Hardy's explanation of them as the result of hallucination, not wilfulness, on Emma's part, confesses that Emma's virtues are beginning to weigh heavily on her shoulders, mocks at Hardy's references to Emma's '*humanitarianism* (to cats, I suppose he means)', refers to John Gifford's alleged description of Hardy as a 'low-born churl', recalls Thomas's lonely evenings at Max Gate in Emma's day with 'insult and abuse his only enlivenment', reports his allusion to Emma as 'the girl who died twenty years ago', quotes Kate Hardy's remark that an expedition to St Juliot would probably do Hardy no harm 'as long as he doesn't bring back another Gifford', and deplores, apropos of a forthcoming visit by Gordon Gifford, the contented manner in which the Giffords, despite their high birth, seemed determined to live on Hardy's bounty. On 1 January 1914 she repeated her ultimatum of the previous August, telling Clodd she would not 'enter into that compact of which I spoke to you last summer' – in plain English, marry Hardy – 'if Lilian remains'. Adding that Kate and Henry Hardy (but not the gentle Mary?) supported her in this, and that Hardy had told Lilian to return to her mother for a while, she concluded gloomily 'but she will never go, and he is not the man to make her'. (However, she did go.)

In the letters to Rebekah Owen, which begin soon after those to Clodd cease, there is no relaxation of the anti-Gifford campaign. Rebekah is told that the reason why she and her sister were never introduced to Mary, Kate and Henry during Emma's lifetime was Emma's twenty-year ban on the Hardys from entering Max Gate. (Florence appears to have forgotten her own speedy introduction to them elsewhere to avoid this difficulty.) Another letter declares that only Giffords are now allowed by Hardy to stay under his roof; and in October 1915 Florence delivered herself of the venomous caricature of Emma's Plymouth and St Juliot years quoted on page 78. But now her main target is Gordon. In June 1914 he was invited by Hardy to stay at the house. Florence wrote:

He does not appear to be frantically enjoying his visit – but I do my best to be very cordial. He continually impresses upon me the fact that his aunt always promised him that he should inherit Max Gate and all that belonged thereto – but it seems to me that no one – except my husband – had any right to promise such a thing, and moreover, it seems very unpleasant to anticipate my husband's death in such a manner.

In her next letter she explains that she did not tell Hardy of Gordon's pretensions because Hardy might have finally decided to let him have the house. 'It seems so odious to calculate on inheritances and legacies. They *are* a family, the Giffords!'

December of the same year saw Lilian, oblivious to her dismissal less than a year before, again descending on the establishment for Christmas. 'I expect that she will be very rude to me, but I must endure that,' Florence commented; but her anticipation of rudeness did not prevent her from inviting one of her sisters for Christmas as well.

In June 1915 she reported that Gordon was about to marry 'a waitress in a tea shop. I wonder what his aunt would have said. Shade of the late Archdeacon, what do *you* think of your great-nephew?' Hardy was quoted as offering little comment: he might have to support Gordon's wife and any offspring. Florence added that Gordon had refused to make a home for his mother and sister.

Eleven months later, during one of her rare escapes from Dorchester to see a London specialist, she entertained Lilian, 'very resplendent with great feathers in her hat and a pearl necklace and white gloves', to tea at her club, the Lyceum. She found Lilian 'most indignant' because Gordon's wife, Violet, was expecting a baby. He had married in a hurry to avoid conscription, but was no longer exempt. Lilian had told her that when he married it had been 'quite understood' there would be no babies.

By August 1916 two years had elapsed, according to Florence, since Gordon had last communicated with Max Gate, though a surviving letter from Hardy proves that Gordon was in touch at any rate in December 1914. Hardy had now told Florence that he was thinking of taking up the threads once more, and must have proposed an invitation, for Florence wrote to Rebekah that she was determined not to have 'the tea shop girl' and her baby in the house.

These two groups of letters, together with Irene Cooper

Willis's references in her notes accompanying the Hardy letters in the DCM to what Florence had told her, chiefly on the subject of insanity among the Giffords, are virtually the only sources of information drawn upon by Hardy's biographers to deal with the attitude of the second Mrs Hardy towards the family of the first. But there is an important fourth source that throws an entirely different light on the picture, namely the testimony, backed by epistolary and photographic evidence, of Gordon Gifford's daughter Ethel, once the supposed 'tea shop girl's baby' so slightingly referred to by Florence, now Mrs R. G. Skinner.

In the first place, Mrs Skinner testifies that her mother Violet was never a waitress or in any way connected with catering. She was apprenticed to a firm of Court dressmakers, where she eventually became a fitter, responsible for cutting out from her own patterns and fitting all the garments made in the establishment, where she was in charge of the workrooms and staff. After her marriage she opened a small dressmaking and tailoring business of her own in the flat she and Gordon occupied in Hampstead – and one of her customers was Florence Hardy. (The marriage certificate, which might have confirmed her occupation at the time, does not record one.)

Florence's charge that Gordon married in a hurry to avoid conscription – clearly told her by Lilian – is an excessively cruel distortion of the facts as reported by Mrs Skinner. Far from seeking to avoid conscription, within weeks of the outbreak of war the thirty-five-year-old Gordon placed himself and his motor-cycle at the service of the War Office in the capacity of dispatch rider. But during the test of his ability he was so anxious to prove his strength to the army examiners that he broke a blood-vessel in his lung, giving rise to fears of tuberculosis and ruling him out of military service on medical grounds for the duration. Some corroboration of this version of his conduct is afforded by a letter from Hardy, dated 19 August 1914, evidently in answer to one in which Gordon had revealed his intentions. Hardy observes: 'The War Office may not require your services as a dispatch rider yet; but we do not know what may occur, or who may be wanted in the future.'

Against Florence's assertion that while at Max Gate during

June 1914 Gordon constantly repeated that Emma had promised him the house and its contents when Hardy died, the evidence is less certain but not lightly to be dismissed. The immediate reaction of both Mrs Skinner and her husband, who had also known Gordon well, when I told them of Florence's letter, of which they had previously been unaware, was to exclaim that such behaviour on Gordon's part would have been totally against his character. Again, it seems most unlikely that Emma, even at the height of her estrangement, would have considered she had the power to dispose of Max Gate *unless she outlived her husband and had inherited it herself.* One is reminded of Rebekah Owen's remark that there was no reason to suppose Emma would die first. Gordon may well have remarked to Florence that Emma, before she died, had always said that, should she survive Hardy, her nephew should be her heir.

In June 1915, Florence told Rebekah that Gordon had refused to make a home for his mother and sister. Mrs Skinner's version is that Lilian had from the outset been bitterly opposed to the idea of Gordon marrying and had made it 'quite impossible' for him to continue living with their mother and herself, so that he had been obliged to take refuge in a boarding-house. But he continued to contribute to his mother's upkeep as he had done ever since his father, Walter, had died leaving practically nothing. After his marriage his mother readily welcomed Violet into the family, but Lilian always remained hostile – a statement that accords with what Florence said Lilian told her during tea at the Lyceum.

All the evidence points to Lilian, in marked contrast to Gordon, having been as objectionable as Florence makes out. Even her niece can say little in her favour except that she was 'eccentric, but certainly *not* insane' – this in reference to Florence's final observation to Rebekah Owen in July 1920 that 'Lilian is still in the asylum, poor wretch'. Lilian in fact had a nervous breakdown and went into a hospital specialising in such disorders. Thanks to Emma's training in the doctrine that it was not ladylike to work, Lilian spent the latter half of her life eking out an existence on two minute annuities, one, worth £1 10s a week, bought her by Hardy during his lifetime, the other purchased with £250 (less death duties) left her in his will. On this pittance she lived during the winters in seedy boarding-houses in Bournemouth (the Boscombe end), and during the summers, when even these became too expensive, in YWCA or GFS hostels. On her death in 1952 a sale of her effects fetched ninety pounds. Her 'jewellery', which she left to a friend to revert to her niece, consisted of a few Woolworth-type trinkets. Her one possession of any value, a 'large real lace Brussels flounce', she bequeathed to the Church of St John, Boscombe, to be used as an altar-cloth; but today no one connected with the church, even among those whose service covers thirty years, recalls ever seeing the flounce or knowing anything about it.

There is no record of any visit by her to Max Gate after Christmas 1914; apart from that one intrusion, the ban insisted on by Florence remained permanently in force. But with Gordon the story is very different, and very surprising. Mrs Skinner states that from 1924 or 1925 until 1939 she was taken every summer by her parents to Dorchester, during his lifetime to visit Hardy, after his death to visit Florence, and after her death to continue the practice of placing a wreath on Hardy's grave until the war put an end to the journeys. The Giffords did not sleep at Max Gate because initially it was thought that a child about the house for more than a brief time would be too much for Hardy; and following his decease the custom of staying in a hotel continued more or less from force of habit. But the three always went to take tea with him, and on one occasion supper, when he surprised everyone by giving little Ethel a glass of hock. She even achieved the feat of making friends with Florence's notoriously formidable dog Wessex.

During Florence's widowhood the visits were made as near as possible to 2 June, Hardy's birthday. The family was always invited to lunch or tea at Max Gate, and the programme always included an expedition to Talbothays to see Kate Hardy – Henry had died in the same year as Thomas. Once, when she was going away, Florence invited the Giffords to make use of Max Gate for a short holiday. Two letters from her to Gordon remain in Mrs Skinner's possession. The first, dated 8 March 1928, reads:

Dear Gordon – It was very nice of you to write about that small legacy [£250 less death duties]. I did not know the contents of the will, and really thought you would have had ten times that amount. Had another will been made I expect it would have been increased. What Kate and Henry will do with their £30,000 I do not know, living as they do. And also I understood that something was to be settled on Lilian, to revert to your little girl. It is fatal to put off doing things. A codicil named two beds to [be] endowed at the hospital – one in your aunt's name, one in mine. This was not witnessed, and it is therefore void. When I know exactly *how* I stand I must try to rectify matters, if it is possible.

Of course I shall always be very pleased to see you here, with Mrs Gifford and your little girl, either at the end of May or any other time. I am trying to begin work on the biography of my husband, but it is difficult. I have had so many terrible worries too.

With kindest regards and many thanks for the kind way in which you have always treated me, – Yours very sincerely, Florence Hardy.

This year the Giffords placed the first of their wreaths on Hardy's grave before calling at Max Gate, and Florence did not see it until after they had left. Three months passed before she found time to write as follows:

Dear Gordon – I was so pleased to have your letter, but sorry that I had not written before. I can hardly describe to you how touched I was when I went to Stinsford on the evening of June 1, and saw that beautiful wreath that you and your wife had so kindly laid on the tomb. I shall never forget that, and shall hope to show my real gratitude in some practical form one day. . . .

I am sending, with this, the proofs that you wish to read. I can send you others, if they interest you. I know that you will keep them *quite private* and not allow anyone except your wife to read them.

I am exceedingly busy at present, but at the same time *very* sad and lonely. The thought of what will happen to Max Gate when I am gone preys on my mind.

Thank you for your kind offer of help. I shall be glad of copies of the letters. – Yours very sincerely, Florence Hardy.

Here is a very different Florence from Rebekah Owen's acid correspondent, yet even at this point the precise degree of her change of attitude is hard to gauge. In the earlier letter, does her intention to 'rectify matters' refer only to the stillborn codicil, or to Gordon's and possibily Lilian's minute inheritance as well? There was presumably no intentional irony in the juxtaposition of her comments on these pittances and the allusion to Kate's and Henry's £30,000. In the second letter, is the intention to show her 'real gratitude in some practical form' a further indication of resolve to remedy the derisory amount of Gordon's legacy? As Ethel Gifford grew up, the conversation during the annual visits to Max Gate gave her a strong impression that Florence was genuinely concerned to improve Gordon's lot, while her worry over the future of Max Gate took the form of openly expressed speculation on whether to leave it to him, with sufficient income to maintain it, or to the National Trust with the proviso that he should live there as 'custodian'. Yet in the end she did nothing, notwithstanding the evidence of the two letters, the regular welcome at Max Gate, and the photograph of Florence, Violet Gifford, and Ethel standing together in the Max Gate garden, that she had experienced a most extraordinary change of heart, whatever its limitations.

Her thanks to Gordon for 'the way in which you have always treated me' is a strange postscript to her plaints about him to Clodd and Miss Owen, yet it has the air of being genuine. By 1928 she regarded him highly enough to let him (and Violet) read part of the proofs of *The Early Life*. He was also, according to his daughter, one of the very few people in whom Florence confided when she knew she had an incurable cancer. And when Ethel herself left commercial college Florence employed her at her flat in the Adelphi to make copies of Hardy's letters to Florence Henniker, and introduced her to other members of the Dugdale family, with such success that for some years she and one of Florence's sisters, Mrs Richardson, continued to exchange visits.

If the visits to Talbothays took place only after Hardy's death, Kate's softened attitude is easily explained by the removal of her fear that Gordon would inherit all Hardy's money. But what is the explanation of Florence's new demeanour, which must have come about at some time between late 1916 and 1924 or 1925? In part the key is probably to be found with Lilian, whose intense hostility to her brother's marriage is all too likely to have inspired a policy of lies about him the effects of which lasted for years before something or someone opened Florence's eyes to the truth. It is significant that her new friendliness to Gordon and his wife was unmatched by any towards Lilian. Equally significant is a letter Florence wrote to Alda, Lady Hoare, just before Lilian's apparently final visit to Max Gate for Christmas 1914, in which are the words 'I am devoutly hoping, even *praying*, that she won't carry on her old mischief-making tactics'. Yet it would seem she did manage to carry them on, undetected, for a number of years more. Florence may therefore have been moved in part by a desire to make amends for past injustice.

But this cannot be the whole explanation. Lilian was not responsible for Florence's assertion in 1914 that Gordon was constantly reminding her that Emma had promised him Max Gate. Yet fifteen years later Florence was toying with the idea of making him her heir to the place. There is also the question of Hardy's rôle between 1914 and 1924. Presumably he, too, was deceived by Lilian; he seems to have gone along with Florence in both her repudiation and her reacceptance of Emma's relatives.

The biographer of Hardy can only lament that Gordon's rehabilitation did not affect his total exclusion from the *Life*. Even if Hardy decided to leave him in that strange gallery of persons, including Rebekah Owen and Hermann Lea, who found no place in his pages despite the considerable place they had found in his life, Florence might have mentioned him in the final chapters that she wrote herself. But Gordon's belated entry into her good graces did not even deter her from eliminating all the favourable references to his aunt from the book. It needed more than reconciliation with Gordon to reconcile Florence to the memory of Emma.

Notes and Sources

Abbreviations

Bailey J. O. Bailey, *The Poetry of Thomas Hardy:* a *Handbook and Commentary* (Chapel, North Carolina, 1970)

Bristol Gifford family papers, Bristol University Library

Brotherton Brotherton Library, Leeds University

Colby Collection of letters, etc., at Colby College Library, Waterville, Maine

DCM Dorset County Museum, Dorchester

DE *'Dearest Emmie'*, ed. Carl J. Weber (London, 1953). Thomas Hardy's letters to Emma (originals in DCM)

EH Evelyn Hardy, *Thomas Hardy: a Critical Biography* (London, 1954)

ELH Emma Lavinia Hardy

FED Florence Emily Dugdale

FEH Florence Emily Hardy

FH Florence (Mrs Arthur) Henniker

Hawkins Desmond Hawkins, *Thomas Hardy* (Newton Abbot, 1976)

HLMS Carl J. Weber, *Hardy and the Lady from Madison Square* (Waterville, Maine, 1952)

HW Carl J. Weber, *Hardy of Wessex* (New York, 1940; 2nd edn, New York and London, 1965)

247

HWR	Denys Kay-Robinson, *Hardy's Wessex Reappraised* (Newton Abbot, 1972)
ICW	Irene Cooper Willis
Life	Florence Emily Hardy, *The Life of Thomas Hardy, 1840–1928* (London, 1962). One-volume edition of *The Early Life of Thomas Hardy, 1840–1891* (1928) and *The Later Years of Thomas Hardy, 1892–1928* (1930)
Millgate	Michael Millgate, *Thomas Hardy: His Career as a Novelist* (London, 1971)
OH	Robert Gittings, *The Older Hardy* (London, 1978)
ORFW	*One Rare Fair Woman*, ed. Evelyn Hardy and F. B. Pinion (London, 1972). Hardy's letters to Florence Henniker (originals in DCM)
Purdy	Richard L. Purdy, *Thomas Hardy: a Bibliographical Study* (London, 1954; reprinted 1968, 1978)
RO	Miss Rebekah Owen
SR	Emma Lavinia Hardy, *Some Recollections*, ed. Evelyn Hardy and Robert Gittings (London, 1961) (MS in DCM)
Stourhead	Stourhead Collection, Wiltshire County Record Office, Trowbridge
THYB	*The Thomas Hardy Year Books 1–6*, ed. James Stevens Cox (St Peter Port, Guernsey, 1970–)
Toucan	Toucan Press, *Illustrated Monographs on the Life, Times, and Works of Thomas Hardy*, ed. James Stevens Cox (Beaminster and later St Peter Port, Guernsey, various years; collected into two volumes, 1968–73)
YTH	Robert Gittings, *Young Thomas Hardy* (London, 1975)

Title-page: This is the second stanza of a two-stanza poem by an unknown writer found by Mrs Ethel Skinner among her father's (Gordon Gifford's) papers. It is handwritten, possibly but not certainly in Emma's hand, on a small piece of pink notepaper, and bears the title 'To Dear Clarinda'. I feel the lines I have quoted to be appropriate to the theme of the book.

Chapter 1.   *Emma Lavinia Gifford before March 1870*

1   Plymouth did not receive city status until 1928.
2   *SR*, p. 17.
3   Ibid., p. 22.
4   Emma wrote *Some Recollections*, an account of her early life up to the time of her marriage, during 1910, secretly. Hardy discovered the notebook containing the manuscript soon after her death, and reproduced part of it in the *Life*. But the full text was not published until 1961, when it appeared edited by Evelyn Hardy and Robert Gittings. Except where otherwise stated, all the information directly concerning the Giffords in this chapter is drawn from *SR*. The page numbers refer to the 1961 printed edition, but the quotations are from the original manuscript, ignoring the editorial alterations made (not always to advantage) by Hardy.
5   *SR*, p. 15.
6   Ibid., p. 16.
7   *OH*, p. 127.
8   *SR*, pp. 18, 22.
9   Ibid., pp. 18, 19.
10 ELH to Rev. Richard Grosvenor Bartelot, 3 July 1912 (Colby).
11 ELH to RO, May 1900 (Colby).
12 The addresses, in chronological order, are 10 York Street, Courtenay Street (number not known), Buckland Street (number not known), 9 Sussex Street, 9 Bedford Terrace. Only the last-named survives. For details, see *HWR*, p. 240.
13 *SR*, p. 48.
14 Ibid., p. 6.
15 Ronald Pearsall, *Victorian Popular Music* (Newton Abbot, 1973), p. 126.

16 ELH to RO, no date (Colby).
17 *SR*, p. 14.
18 Helen Holder to ELH, 15 Aug 1881 (DCM).
19 *Life*, p. 118.
20 The 'Launceston Giffords' were George Mitchell Gifford, manager of the Tavistock Bank (now Lloyds); his wife Emlin, *née* Rowe; two sons, George William (killed in a riding accident during army service in Corfu, 1864) and Charles Edwin, who served in the Navy; and three daughters, Mary Helen (died of 'consumption', 1861), Kate, and Edith. See Henry Gifford, 'Thomas Hardy and Emma', *Essays and Studies*, new series, vol. XIX (1966), p. 111. Prof. Gifford is the grandson of Charles Edwin Gifford, above.
21 Information from Mrs Pat Munn, Bodmin historian.
22 *SR*, p. 35.
23 Mrs Pat Munn.
24 ELH to RO, 4 April 1901 (Colby).
25 Bertha Newcombe to Mrs Edmund Gosse, 8 March 1900 (Brotherton).
26 Most of her surviving work, if not all, is today in the DCM, where a particularly impressive landscape painting hangs in the entrance-passage.
27 *SR*, p. 43.
28 Information from English China Clays Ltd, St Austell.
29 *SR*, p. 44.
30 Probate of Wills, Somerset House, London.
31 *Complete Parochial History of Cornwall* (Truro and London, 1870), vol. III, p. 18.
32 S. Baring-Gould, 'Cornwall', *Cambridge County Geographies*, ed. F. H. H. Guillemard (Cambridge, 1909–), p. 131.
33 Lanivet Burial Register (Cornwall County Record Office, Truro).
34 *SR*, p. 43.
35 Information from Mr John Holder and Holder genealogical tree in his possession.
36 Ibid.
37 Ibid. There were six children, born between 1860 and 1869. The two eldest both wrote to their father, probably

c.1869 (the letters are undated), while he was away from home, to tell him that because of a severe attack of gout their grandfather (Caddell) had been unable to pay the family an intended visit. Letters in Mr Holder's possession.

38 Quoted by Kenneth Phelps, *The Wormwood Cup* (Padstow, 1975), p. 16.
39 Mr John Holder.
40 *SR*, p. 59.
41 Phelps, *Wormwood Cup*, p. 97.
42 *SR*, p. 47.
43 *HWR*, p. 252, and Denys Kay-Robinson, 'The Face at the Casement', *THYB 5*, p. 34.
44 No connection, as far as I can ascertain, with the Serjeants of St Benet's Abbey.

Chapter 2.   *Thomas Hardy before March 1870*

1 *Life*, p. 8.
2 Although by the boundary changes of 1974 most of north Berkshire, including Wantage ('Alfredston') and the site of the Red House ('Brown House') on the Ridgeway, was transferred to Oxfordshire, Fawley remains just inside Berkshire.
3 *Life*, p. 420.
4 *OH*, pp. 55–8.
5 Information from the late Mrs Moor, of Sutton Poyntz, whose father had been one of the boys concerned.
6 *Life*, p. 50.
7 Gordon Gifford, unpublished lecture on Thomas Hardy delivered at a boys' school in Peckham in 1935 (Mrs Ethel Skinner).
8 DCM.
9 ELH to RO, no date (Colby).
10 ELH to Madeleine Rolland, 13 Feb 1910 and 2 April 1910. I am indebted to Prof. Michael Millgate for access to these letters.
11 *YTH*, pp. 32–5. See also Lady Hester Pinney, *Thomas Hardy and the Birdsmoorgate Murder*, Toucan no. 25.
12 Hardy's father had recalled an episode during his own

lifetime in which four men watching a rick fire for which they were not responsible were arrested and hanged merely for being present (Newman Flower, 'Walks and Talks with Thomas Hardy', *The Countryman*, vol. XXXIV, Winter 1966).

13 *Life*, p. 32.
14 FEH to Dr Marie Stopes, 14 Sept 1923 (British Library, Department of Manuscripts).
15 FEH to Lady (Alda) Hoare, 22 April 1918 (Stourhead).
16 *Life*, p. 116.
17 Ibid., pp. 19–20.
18 Ibid., p. 41.
19 See poem 'At the Word "Farewell"', last two lines.
20 See poem 'Concerning Agnes', second stanza.
21 *The Woodlanders*, ch. XX; *Tess of the d'Urbervilles*, phase I, ch. X.
22 *Life*, p. 31.
23 For the first few months of Hardy's employment they were at 8 St Martin's Place.
24 *Life*, p. 45.
25 William Acton, *Prostitution, Considered in Its Moral, Social, and Sanitary Aspects* (London, 1857; reissued with notes by Peter Fryer, 1968), p. 48 (1968 edn).
26 Ibid., p. 32.
27 Ibid., p. 234.
28 Ibid., pp. 33–6.
29 *Desperate Remedies*, ch. XXI, pt 4.
30 TH to Mary Hardy, 19 Aug 1862. Most of the letter is quoted in the *Life*, p. 28, but the passage containing this information is omitted. See *YTH*, p. 236, n. 51, in which acknowledgement is made to R. L. Purdy.
31 Sparks family letters (Ian Kennedy, Queensland; photocopies at Higher Bockhampton).
32 *YTH*, p. 93.
33 Gregory Stevens Cox, 'Elusive Mr Hardy', *THYB 5*, p. 15.
34 *YTH*, pp. 90 ff.
35 *Life*, p. 50.
36 EH, p. 67.
37 *Life*, p. 53.

38 Puddletown School Log Book, entry for 16 Jan 1868. Mrs Collins, head of the girls' section of the school, wrote that she had had to replace the pupil-teacher for 'neglect of duty', and added 'parents very angry and determine to withdraw her a month hence'. That the 'neglect of duty' was not a moral lapse is implicit in (though not conclusively proved by) the Report of the Commission on Education, 1868–9, which commended the moral tone of the school. Even more cogent evidence against moral delinquency is the failure of the 'withdrawal' to prevent Tryphena from passing the very strict and searching examinations into the past records of all candidates both for entry into the Stockwell Normal College for teacher-training and, subsequently, the post of headmistress at Plymouth Day (Girls) School. Nor must we overlook the strong probability that immediately after leaving the Puddletown school Tryphena was accepted as a teacher in the Nonconformist school at Coryates, where the criteria were hardly likely to be more lax.

39 Sparks family letters (see note 31).
40 *YTH*, pp. 115, 226; Hawkins, p. 31.
41 Coryates had a halt on the Abbotsbury branch-line from the Dorchester–Weymouth main line, the junction being at Upwey.
42 ICW, unpublished article (Mrs Brinley Richards).
43 Bailey, p. 397.
44 *Life*, p. 64.
45 This is the source of Bailey's alternative interpretation of 'At a Seaside Town in 1869'.

Chapter 3. *From St Juliot to St Peter's, Paddington*

1 *SR*, p. 54.
2 *YTH*, p. 144.
3 Julius Mattfield, *'Variety' Music Cavalcade* (Englewood Cliffs, New Jersey, 1969 edn).
4 Phelps, *Wormwood Cup*, p. 21. To catch the first train (8.25 a.m.) from Launceston to Plymouth, Phelps estimates that Hardy must have left St Juliot at 6.15 a.m.

5   TH to FH, 7 Feb 1918 (*ORFW*, no. 137).
6   EH, p. 118.
7   Frances Mabel Robinson to ICW, 17 Dec 1939 (DCM).
8   *Life*, p. 78.
9   Ibid.
10 DCM.
11 *SR*, p. 58.
12 In the letter already cited (n. 7) to Irene Cooper Willis, Frances Mabel Robinson states that during the earliest years of the marriage Emma also kept a notebook in which she recorded phrases heard in conversation that might serve to cheer Hardy when a 'despairing fit' came over him. Miss Robinson, a distinguished translator from the French and a less distinguished novelist, first met the Hardys at the Macmillans' house in Tooting during 1879 or 1880.
13 J. I. M. Stewart, *Thomas Hardy* (London, 1971), p. 26.
14 As he admitted in an interview in 1892 with Edmund Blunden. (See Blunden, *Thomas Hardy* (London, 1942), p. 69.) Emma took the idea from an incident in her own unpublished story 'The Maid on the Shore'.
15 *HLMS*, p. 61.
16 *The Times Literary Supplement*, 1 Jan 1940.
17 ELH to Lady (Alda) Hoare, 24 April 1910 (Stourhead).
18 Quoted by T. P. O'Connor in his obituary on TH, *Sunday Times*, 22 Jan 1928.
19 T. P. O'Connor, article in the *Daily Telegraph*, 13 Jan 1928. Reprinted as Toucan no. 54.
20 Edward Clodd, unpublished diary, entry for 27 April 1913 (Mr Alan Clodd).
21 Rev. Richard Grosvenor Bartelot, unpublished memoirs (Mrs Rosella Voremberg).
22 Albert J. Guérard, *Thomas Hardy, His Novels and Stories* (Oxford, 1949), p. 105.
23 Hawkins, p. 38.
24 *Desperate Remedies*, ch. VI, pt 1.
25 There are also hints of a lesbian relationship between Paula Power and Charlotte de Stancy in *A Laodicean*, notably where Paula, in pink doublet and hose 'like a lovely young youth', dances for Charlotte and Mrs

Woodman in the gymnasium. See Millgate, p. 172.

26   *Desperate Remedies*, ch. I, p. 2.

27   *Life*, p. 83.

28   Ibid., p. 84.

29   *The Yorkshire Post*, 11 Oct 1928, reported a sale of Hardy letters by Puttock & Simpson (London) that included an appeal on these lines by Hardy to the Rev. J. H. Dickenson, then Rector of St Juliot.

30   S. M. Ellis, 'Some Personal Recollections of Thomas Hardy', *Fornightly Review*, new series, CXXIII, March 1928.

31   *Life*, p. 86.

32   Purdy, pp. 11, 331.

33   *SR*, p. 59.

34   Phelps, *Wormwood Cup*, pp. 13–16.

35   Purdy, pp. 6–8.

36   Ibid., p. 11.

37   Vere H. Collins, *Talks with Thomas Hardy at Max Gate 1920–1922* (New York, 1928; reissued by Toucan Press, St Peter Port, Guernsey, 1971), p. 26.

38   To Hermann Lea. See James Stevens Cox, *Through the Camera's Eye*, Toucan no. 22.

39   Phelps, *Wormwood Cup*, p. 38. The post at Treliggon tallied exactly with the description in the poem, but Phelps was unable at the time to photograph it, and when he returned to do so it had been replaced. Today the site is doubly lost beneath the new Bodmin by-pass.

40   *Bodmin Guardian*, 5 July 1934.

41   Dedicated 'To Love, the Queen of Heaven, and to Faith, the Star of the Soul'. London, 1887.

42   Compiled from *Who Was Who 1929–1940*, *Bodmin Guardian* obituary, 20 March 1930, and information supplied by Cornwall County Record Office, Prebendary Gordon Lawes (Rector of Lanivet), Mrs Stickland (Lanivet), Messrs L. E. Long and John Pethybridge (Bodmin).

43   *Bodmin Guardian*, 20 March 1930.

44   *YTH*, p. 165.

45   *A Pair of Blue Eyes*, ch. IV.

46   Information from Mr John Holder.

47   FEH to RO, 24 Oct 1915.

48   Information from Miss Foy Quiller-Couch.

49 *YTH*, p. 174.
50 *Life*, p. 98.
51 *YTH*, p. 192.
52 *Thomas Hardy's Notebooks and Some Letters from Julia Augusta Martin*, ed. Evelyn Hardy (London, 1955), p. 48.
53 *Life*, p. 100.
54 TH to Edmund Gosse, 25 July 1906 (quoted in Purdy, p. 220).

Chapter 4.   St Peter's, Paddington, to Max Gate

1 E. H. Gifford to TH, 4 and 12 Sept 1874 (DCM).
2 TH to Henry Hardy, 18 Sept 1874 (DCM).
3 *Thomas Hardy Society Review*, vol. I, no. 2 (1976), p. 42.
4 Phelps, *Wormwood Cup*, pp. 63–4.
5 FED to Edward Clodd, 7 March 1913 (Brotherton).
6 *Life*, p. 102.
7 Letters of 1881–3 (DCM).
8 For a detailed analysis, see *YTH*, p. 207.
9 Information from A. G. L. Hardy and Geoffrey Worssam (Swanage).
10 Bailey, pp. 544, 550.
11 ELH to Mrs Haweis, 13 Nov [1894] (University of British Columbia).
12 *Life*, p. 111. *OH* (p. 3) suggests that the comment came from Emma's two younger brothers, who according to Florence Hardy were later to comment disparagingly on Thomas and Emma's life at Sturminster Newton; but the phrase accords equally well with the impish style of Kate Hardy.
13 Ibid.
14 DCM.
15 'The Interloper', second stanza.
16 'On Sturminster Foot-bridge', second stanza.
17 Purdy, p. 26.
18 Information from Miss Olive Knott, historian of Sturminster Newton.
19 Note by ICW on p. 157 of Florence Hardy's copy of *The Early Life of Thomas Hardy, 1840–1891* (DCM).
20 *Life*, p. 147.

21 Ibid., p. 121.
22 Ibid., p. 129.
23 Ibid., p. 129.
24 Ibid., p. 135.
25 DCM.
26 Purdy, pp. 35–40.
27 Today Lanherne, 16 Avenue Road.
28 It would have covered the first five novels.
29 *Life*, p. 151.
30 Lady St Helier, *Memories of Fifty Years* (London, 1909), p. 187.
31 *Life*, pp. 155–6.
32 Emma Dashwood to ELH, 1883 (DCM).
33 *OH*, p. 38.
34 Peter Green, *Kenneth Grahame* (1959), p. 220.
35 TH to ELH, 16 April 1891 (*DE*, no. 11).
36 *HW*, p. 143.
37 Mr and Mrs William Jesty.
38 *Life*, p. 261.
39 ELH to RO, 4 April 1901.
40 ELH to Leonie Gifford, 18 Oct [1911] (Bristol).
41 ELH to Lady (Alda) Hoare, 24 Aug 1910 (Stourhead).
42 It is possible to contend that Hardy omitted to mention visits by his relatives because he did not consider the matter important enough for comment. This cannot be ruled out; but one must weigh the probabilities in the context of his general attitude towards his family background. As late as 1913 Edward Clodd, by then a friend of many years' standing, entered in his diary that for the first time he had been allowed to meet Hardy's brother and sisters. Chiefly Clodd blamed Emma's ban on the family from entering Max Gate, but he also rebuked Hardy for allowing his 'half-mad' wife to keep 'these well-bred folk as well as his mother' away. Hardy, however, could easily have arranged for Clodd to meet them in their own home, as he had so promptly done for Florence. The implication is that in Hardy's eyes the 'well-bred folk' were not quite well-bred enough to confront the rather upstage Clodd until it became unavoidable.
43 F. B. Pinion, 'Hardy's House in Dorchester ...', *THYB 3*,

p. 18.
44   *Life*, p. 170.
45   TH to ELH, 13 March 1885 (*DE*, no. 1).
46   *HW*, p. 143.

Chapter 5.   *The Début of Max Gate to the Year of* Tess

1   EH, p. 199.
2   Fanny Stevenson to Robert Louis Stevenson, 10 Sept 1885.
3   *The Diary of Alice James*, ed. I. L. Edel, p. 93.
4   Quoted in Nellie van der Grift Sanchez, *The Life of Mrs Robert Louis Stevenson* (London, 1920), p. 22.
5   Gertrude Atherton, *Adventures of a Novelist* (New York, 1932), p. 263.
6   Ibid., p. 170.
7   *The Later Years of Thomas Hardy, 1892–1928*, typescript, f. 365 (DCM).
8   *HW*, p. 254.
9   Hamlin Garland, *Afternoon Neighbours* (New York, 1934), p. 89.
10 Christine Wood Homer, *Hardy and His Two Wives*, Toucan no. 18, p. 12.
11 Frances Mabel Robinson to ICW, 17 Dec 1939 (DCM).
12 T. P. O'Connor, *Daily Telegraph*, 13 Jan 1928, Toucan no. 54.
13 Jacques-Émile Blanche, *Mes Modèles* (Paris, 1928), p. 84.
14 *HW*, p. 254; also *DE*, p. 23 n.
15 W. R. Rutland, *Thomas Hardy: a Study of His Writings and Their Background* (Oxford, 1938), p. 85.
16 'Clive Holland' (Charles J. Hankinson), *Thomas Hardy's Wessex Scene* (Dorchester, 1948), p. 53.
17 *HW*, p. 215. No source is given, nor does the anecdote appear in MacCarthy's *Memories* or *Portraits*.
18 ELH to RO, 14 Feb 1899 (Colby).
19 *DE*, p. 35 n.
20 'Mr Moule' was Henry Joseph Moule, brother of Horace and sometime Curator of the Dorset County Museum. In an editorial note in *'Dearest Emmie'* Weber explains that

'Emma's general unbearableness' is shown by Hardy's letters to her to have been much greater than a reader of the poems might suppose. He then gives a list of examples that includes 'her aches and pains, her lame knee and sprained ankle, her failing eyesight and her "shingles"'. Hardy was much too humane, as the letters show, to find his wife's physical ailments 'unbearable' – to say nothing of his own frequent minor illnesses through most of which Emma nursed him. He may have been insensitive at times and slow in perception, but where he did perceive he was compassionate and helpful. Weber's obsessive prejudice against Emma does little service here to Hardy and rather less to himself.

21 Isa MacCarthy to ELH, 26 Oct 1902 (DCM).
22 Ibid., 4 Nov 1902 (DCM).
23 Ibid., 4 Jan 1903 (DCM).
24 Ibid., 14 Dec 1903 (DCM).
25 *HLMS*, p. 117.
26 Homer, *Hardy and His Two Wives*, p. 12.
27 *HLMS*, p. 163.
28 Albert Bankes to ELH, 15 Dec 1911 (DCM).
29 *ORFW*, p. xxv.
30 Frances Mabel Robinson to ICW, 17 Dec 1939 (DCM).
31 *DE*, p. 38 n.
32 After Florence Hardy's death Irene Cooper Willis, her executor, found 'hundreds' of letters to Emma from Pretor, and many more from other correspondents, in two ottomans in the 'attics' of Max Gate, where they had apparently been overlooked by both Hardy and Florence (see note by ICW with letters to ELH in DCM). Alas, Miss Willis preserved only a few of Pretor's letters, possibly because of their frequent near-illegibility. Even more sadly, none of Emma's letters to Pretor seems to have survived. He died in 1908, unmarried, and bequeathed his effects to a friend, Alfred Owen Swaffield. Swaffield, who died in 1937, divided his property between his three daughters, all of whom have now died, also unmarried. Their heirs know nothing of Emma's letters.
33 Alfred Pretor to ELH, dated only 1898 (DCM).
34 Dame Rebecca West to Dr Robert Gittings, 3 Jan 1973.

35 *Life*, p. 173.
36 In a lecture on Hardy (see ch. 2, n. 6, above) Gordon Gifford told of a maid at St Juliot Rectory who, while he was staying there once as a boy, woke him with terrible screams occasioned by her seeing the ghost reputed to haunt the house ever since a tragedy involving a Mrs Manning. In Helen Holder's letter to Emma (28 Nov 1882, DCM) announcing Caddell's death she wrote, 'Uncle George and Blenny are mutually delighted with each other', indicating that Gordon was at the Rectory then also. 'Uncle George' was George Mitchell Gifford, the Launceston bank manager; 'Blenny' was Gordon, whose full name before he shortened it by deed poll was Blenheim Lovell Gordon Gifford (birth certificate, General Registry).
37 ELH to RO, 24 April 1899 (Colby).
38 Walter Gifford to ELH, 6 Feb 1899 (DCM).
39 FEH to RO, 1 June 1914.
40 Mr R. G. Skinner and Mrs Ethel Skinner in discussion with me.
41 DCM.
42 Typescript entitled 'Mrs Hardy – Personal Copy [2nd copy]', ff. 254–5 (DCM): not actually crossed out here, but omitted from *Life* as printed, p. 189.
43 *OH*, pp. 45–6.
44 See the poem 'An Old Likeness (Recalling R.T.)'.
45 *OH*, p. 64.
46 Rutland, *Thomas Hardy*, p. 219.
47 Millgate, pp. 263, 281.
48 *HLMS*, p. 238.
49 Sidney Heath, two unpublished articles in DCM.
50 *OH*, p. 66.
51 *Life*, p. 224.
52 Bailey, p. 96.
53 *OH*, p. 67.
54 FED to Edward Clodd, 16 Jan 1913 (Brotherton).
55 Ibid., 30 Jan 1913 (Brotherton).
56 FEH to RO, 3 Dec 1915 (Colby).
57 *OH*, p. 67.
58 Lillie May Farris, *Memoirs of the Hardy and Hand*

Families, Toucan no. 40, p. 65. Other examples: Joyce Scudamore, *Florence and Thomas Hardy*, Toucan no. 19, p. 12: 'Henry ... talked in the Dorset dialect'; Mrs Lorna Heenan in *Hardyana*, Toucan no. 14, p. 17: 'Henry was a very rough diamond. . . . [He] spoke broad Dorset.'

59   *Life*, p. 229.
60   Ibid., p. 231.
61   FEH to RO, 30 Sept 1915 (Colby).
62   *Life*, p. 234.
63   If there is any truth in a story recorded by Clodd in his diary on 13 July 1913, the breach may have been precipitated – and perpetuated – by a quarrel during which Emma accused Kate Hardy of stealing some earrings 'and Hardy looked on while she sent for the police'. That Clodd noted down this necessarily long-past incident only after Florence had taken to vilifying Emma strongly implies that she was the source, unless he had it directly from 'Katie'. What makes the anecdote suspect, as it makes the O'Rourke tale that Emma summoned the police because she thought Hardy was trying to poison her, is the unlikelihood of the police being able to visit – twice – a household about which there was always public curiosity, without the fact becoming common Dorchester scandal; the presence of the servants ensured that the visits could never have been concealed. Either incident would have been first-class fodder for the gossips who wrote, for example, to Rebekah Owen, or for the many former Max Gate employees besides Miss O'Rourke who talked to James Stevens Cox. See Chapter 7, note 90.
64   *Daily Chronicle*, 5 Sept 1891 (cutting in DCM).
65   From 'The Walk'.
66   *Life*, p. 233. But see pp. 256 and 281, and *ORFW*, 16 Sept 1893 (no. 16).
67   *Hardyana*, p. 22.
68   Typescript entitled 'Mrs Hardy – Personal Copy [2nd copy]', f. 332 (DCM). Omitted from the *Life* as printed, p. 240.

Chapter 6.   From Tess *to the Century's End*

1   Mrs Nelis (Beatrix Potter), unpublished note to Carl J. Weber (Colby).
2   FEH to RO, 2 Dec 1915 (Colby).
3   *Jude the Obscure*, pt I, ch. I; *The Well-Beloved*, pt III, ch. I.
4   ELH to RO, no date (Colby).
5   On 22 March 1897, following the publication of Edward Clodd's *Pioneers of Evolution*, Emma wrote to him a long letter (Brotherton) rebuking him for his irreligion and setting out her own beliefs. Apart from its contents, the letter illustrates how, when she thought it worthwhile (as in her correspondence to the press), she could polish up her epistolary style to a degree considerably above her normal untidiness. Some of the more revealing passages (not necessarily consecutive) read:

> The chapters I greatly object to are those with which you seem to have taken so much pains to say, There is no God, There is no Christ. And you also endeavour to take from the latter his best human as well as divine attributes.

> It is to be remembered that whatever conclusions Darwin arrived at, he yet never distinctly denied the existence of a Supreme Thought or Word, which we designate God, although he was much pressed to do so. . . . Of course nothing that a materialist explains to a Christian on this subject alters his opinion in the least. Once his faith is firmly fixed he stands on the safest altitude possible; and scorn cast upon him could be easily repaid by men of the highest intellectual powers. I need not enumerate them who have accepted the doctrines of Christianity. . . .

> It must be the duty of others who are strong in their belief to make a protest against writings which cause incalculable distress and misery. . . . Intellect without religion has done and must always do mischief, and is too often allied to injustice, insincerity, and other baneful qualities.

Despite the theory of evolution, for my part I still believe that man was always man.

I do not see why we should have doubts as to immortality, or that we should not be able to rise in *myriads* invisible to such eyes as ours. In the plan of creation there is no permanence of form, size, time, or quantity: all is limitless.

The last two sentences of the second paragraph unintentionally summarise Emma's attitude to Hardy's work and lack of faith. The final paragraph is especially interesting in its disclosure that the mystical or apocalyptic turn which her own faith was to take so markedly in her final years was already manifest in 1897.

6   *Life*, p. 251.
7   Purdy, p. 89. Millgate (p. 317) doubts that the writing of *Jude* was begun so early; but Hardy's letters to Florence Henniker show that it cannot have been much later.
8   From 'Shut Out That Moon'.
9   Purdy, p. 343.
10 If we are to take the poem 'The Month's Calendar' as a portrayal of fact, Florence Henniker had let Hardy know as early as 31 May that she could never reciprocate his love.
11 *HLMS*, p. 83.
12 ELH to RO, 30 Aug 1893 (Colby).
13 *HLMS*, p. 84.
14 Ibid., pp. 87, 90; ELH to RO, 10 Sept 1893 (Colby).
15 *Life*, p. 260.
16 FED to Edward Clodd, 7 March 1913 (Brotherton).
17 Millgate, p. 317 (see n. 7, above).
18 The dates and information in this paragraph are all taken from Purdy, pp. 89–91.
19 *Thomas Hardy*, p. 265. Evelyn Hardy does sound a faint note of caution.
20 Harold Orel, *The Final Years of Thomas Hardy, 1912–1928* (London, 1976), p. 28.
21 Olive Garnett, unpublished diary (ed. Ann Lee Michell, her niece), f. 435. This is the only mention of the Hardys throughout the diary.

22 Information from Mr Richard Garnett, present owner of the album.

23 Olive Garnett, unpublished diary, f. 6.

24 Ibid., f. 353.

25 Prof. Tom Moser, in a letter to me.

26 *DE*, p. 29 n. Weber quotes Dr Fred Fisher as the recipient of Emma's declaration to this effect.

27 *OH*, pp. 85, 87.

28 Possibly she herself was beginning to feel the physical strain. Writing to RO on 19 Feb 1897, she referred to having 'gout' (arthritis?) in her wrist, and there may have been earlier attacks.

29 TH to Edward Clodd, 10 Nov 1895 (Brotherton).

30 *HWR*, pp. 111–12.

31 Desmond Hawkins, 'Concerning Agnes', *Encounter*, Feb 1977, pp. 45–9.

32 *OH*, p. 82.

33 *Life*, p. 276. Cp. Emma's remark to A. Sutro, page 157 above.

34 Bailey, p. 182.

35 TH to ELH, 27 April 1895 (*DE*, no. 25).

36 TH to FH, 10 Nov 1895 (*ORFW*, no. 30).

37 TH to ELH, 3 Feb 1896 (*DE*, no. 29).

38 TH to FH, [20 June 1893] (*ORFW*, no. 4).

39 TH to ELH, 5 Feb 1896 (*DE*, no. 30).

40 ELH to RO, 16 Sept 1902 (Colby).

41 Douglas Brown, *Thomas Hardy* (London, revised edn, 1961), p. 19.

42 *DE*, p. 29 n.

43 Homer, *Hardy and His Two Wives*, p. 6.

44 *OH*, p. 84.

45 *DE*, p. 29 n.

46 It was first published in *Time's Laughingstocks*, Dec 1909.

47 ELH to RO, 1 May 1901 (Colby).

48 From 'Memory and I', published only four years later in *Poems of the Past and the Present*.

49 *The Well-Beloved*, pt I, ch. VII.

50 *Thomas Hardy Society Review*, no. 2 (1976), pp. 50–9.

51 *Desperate Remedies*, ch. I, pt 2.

52 Alfred Pretor to ELH, dated only 1897 (DCM). Adelina

Patti, the famous singer, had first appeared in London as long ago as 1861, but in 1897 was still a name to conjure with.

53   *Life*, p. 298.

54   Ibid., p. 292.

55   Proof that Emma, who also *read* Ibsen, genuinely liked his work is supplied by her comment to Rebekah Owen: 'I have been reading John Gabriel Borkman. Ibsen has excelled himself in it – pathetic, powerful, and true to the characters in their positions!' ELH to RO, 19 Feb 1897 (Colby).

56   *Life*, p. 292.

57   *Thomas Hardy Society Review*, no. 2 (1976), p. 44.

58   TH to FH, 3 June (in error for July) 1897 (*ORFW*, no. 46).

59   ELH to RO, 27 Dec 1899 (Colby).

60   *OH*, p. 93.

61   Paul Zietlow, *Moments of Vision* (Cambridge, Mass., 1974), p. 36. A curious piece of evidence that Hardy may have thought he had gone too far in *Wessex Poems* lies in his embarking, about a month before the book was published, on the composition of the poem 'Lines to a Movement in Mozart's E-Flat Symphony', each stanza of which evokes some happy aspect of the St Juliot days; in all probability the allusion to the music itself was evocative, if it had been beloved by them at the Rectory. But Hardy abandoned the poem, completing it only after Emma's death. It is supposed that he put the work aside because of the technical difficulties of trying to fit the metre to Mozart's score (minuet and trio movement). But it could have been because he suddenly felt that a new attempt at peacemaking would be fruitless.

62   Two other letters support the inference. On 3 Feb 1908 Emma repeated her wish of nine years earlier to Rebekah Owen: 'TH is selfish about his books. I wish I had a whole library to myself, a big one'; and on 24 April 1910 she wrote to Lady Hoare the letter from which the relevant paragraph is quoted on p. 217. Against these the not always reliable Newman Flower ('Walks and Talks with Thomas Hardy', p. 95) says that she once entered his study just as he had finished his lunch, quarrelled violently with him over the litter, and shortly afterwards had

her final illness, for which Hardy blamed his part in the quarrel.

63 TH to ELH (from the Jeunes' address), 1 April 1894 (*DE*, no. 19).
64 TH to ELH, 13 May 1899 (*DE*, no. 32).
65 Alfred Pretor to ELH, dated only 1899 (DCM).
66 MS Eng. Misc. d.530 f.93–96, Bodleian Library, Oxford.
67 Green, *Kenneth Grahame*, p. 220.
68 *OH*, p. 38.
69 Purdy, pp. 3, 6.
70 ELH to RO, 14 Feb, 24 April, 27 Dec 1899 (Colby).
71 Information from Mrs Ethel Skinner.
72 RO to Catharine Owen, 27 November 1900 (quoted in *HLMS*, p. 136).
73 ELH to RO, 31 Dec 1900 (Colby).
74 Ibid., 24 April 1899 (Colby).
75 Information from Mrs Ethel Skinner.
76 TH to ELH, 12 (?) and 15 March 1900 (*DE*, nos 93, 94).
77 ELH to RO, May 1900 (Colby).
78 *Life*, p. 305.
79 ELH to RO, 27 Dec 1899 (Colby).
80 ELH to RO, 16 Nov 1900 (Colby).
81 RO to Catharine Owen, 27 Nov 1900 (quoted in *HMLS*, p. 136).
82 TH to ELH, 11 Dec 1900 (*DE*, no. 35).
83 *HLMS*, p. 118.
84 Ibid.
85 ELH to RO, 31 Dec 1900 (Colby).
86 Ibid.

Chapter 7.   The Twentieth Century

1 Bertha Newcombe to Mrs Edmund Gosse, 5 March [1900] (Brotherton).
2 ELH to RO, 4 March 1902 (Colby).
3 Or so maintain Bailey and Lois Deacon. But Pinion believes the 'glen' to be the Valency Valley between St Juliot and Boscastle; and this view is certainly consistent with Hardy's approval of the substitution of 'A Spot' for

the Epilogue in Rutland Boughton's musical version of *The Famous Tragedy of the Queen of Cornwall*.

4   F. B. Pinion, *A Commentary on the Poems of Thomas Hardy* (London, 1976), p. 63.

5   e.g. Hawkins (p. 180), who quotes in support the lines from *The Dynasts*, 'O doth a bird deprived of wings/Go earthbound wilfully!'

6   TH to FH, 15 Feb 1901 (*ORFW*, no. 74).

7   ELH to RO, 4 April 1901 (Colby).

8   Ibid., 31 Dec 1900 (Colby).

9   TH to FH, 2 June 1901 (*ORFW*, no. 76).

10 Ford Madox Ford, *Mightier Than the Sword* (London, 1938), ch. VI.

11 *Life*, p. 309.

12 Emily Mary Benita Weber, 'The Social Hardy', *Hardyana*, p. 27.

13 Information from Miss Cecelia Fisher.

14 Newman Flower, *Just As It Happened* (London, 1950), p. 63.

15 Homer, *Hardy and His Two Wives*, p. 10.

16 Benita Weber, 'The Social Hardy', p. 27.

17 Frederick Locker-Lampson, 'Rotten Row'.

18 Painting and photograph in the possession of Mr W. A. Clarence.

19 TH to FH, 17 March 1903 (*ORFW*, no. 110).

20 *Hardyana*, p. 28.

21 TH to ELH, 2 July 1903 (*DE*, no. 43).

22 *Thomas Hardy's Personal Writings*, ed. Harold Orel (Kansas, 1966; London, 1967), p. 71.

23 All in DCM.

24 In the possession of Mr James Gibson.

25 As he told Florence Henniker, 25 Dec 1903 (*ORFW*, no. 85).

26 *OH*, p. 120.

27 Not 'dog', as stated by Gittings. See Pretor to ELH, 1906 (DCM).

28 TH to Edward Clodd, 13 Nov 1904 (Brotherton).

29 FEH to RO, 17 July 1915 (Colby).

30 *Life*, p. 329.

31 Ibid., p. 331, quoting, Hardy says, from Emma's diary –

proving that she still kept up a 'white' diary alongside the 'black'.

32 Blanche, *Mes Modèles*, p. 84.
33 Ibid., p. 83.
34 Ibid., p. 85: 'Tels devaient être l'étiquette, le rythme de la vie domestique dans cette illustre ménage.'
35 Ibid., p. 83.
36 Ibid., p. 84.
37 Unpublished memoirs of the Rev. Richard Grosvenor Bartelot (Mrs Rosella Voremberg).
38 Henry Gifford, 'Thomas Hardy and Emma', p. 110.
39 ELH to Leonie Gifford, 18 Oct [1911] (Bristol).
40 Letter dated only 1902 from London by a resident of Tenantrees, near West Stafford (DCM).
41 ELH to Leonie Gifford, 18 Oct [1911] (Bristol).
42 Mrs Augustus Spencer to ELH, 27 Jan 1906.
43 Flower, *Just As It Happened*, p. 95.
44 Henry Gifford, 'Thomas Hardy and Emma', p. 115.
45 ELH to RO, 26 Dec 1906 (Colby).
46 *Dorset County Chronicle*, 31 Dec 1908. Other papers took pieces on circus tigers, bull-fights, cats ('The Egyptian Pet').
47 See ELH from Josephine McDonald (1911) in DCM.
48 *OH*, p. 152.
49 ELH to RO, 19 Feb 1907 (Colby).
50 Ibid., 26 Dec 1906 (Colby).
51 *Life*, p. 333; Roger Fulford, *Votes for Women* (London, 1957), p. 156.
52 Andrew Rosen, *Rise Up Women!* (London, 1974), p. 104.
53 *OH*, p. 125. I owe to Dr Gittings's and his wife's researches much of the material concerning Florence Dugdale before her introduction to Max Gate.
54 All in DCM.
55 Colby.
56 ELH to Catharine Owen, 26 Aug 1907 (Colby).
57 *HW*, p. 271.
58 *The Nation*, 9 May 1908 (cutting in DCM).
59 DCM.
60 ELH to the Misses Owen, 20 May 1908 (Colby).
61 *Life*, p. 336.

62 ELH to RO, 16 June 1908 (Colby).

63 Ibid.

64 Ibid. Announcing her conversion, Rebekah had written (from Paris): 'I am extremely happy, and my best friends (all Protestants) tell me they love me better than ever. Even I think they ought, for I feel that what was likable in me remains, and what was unlikable grows less.' RO to ELH, 5 June 1908 (DCM). Evidently an increase in modesty was not among the changes.

65 *DE*, p. 49 n.

66 EH, p. 275.

67 Flower, *Just As It Happened*, p. 95.

68 TH to ELH, 9 Oct 1908 (*DE*, no. 63).

69 TH to ELH, 28 June 1908 (*DE*, no. 52).

70 Ibid., 2 July 1908 (*DE*, no. 53).

71 Ibid., 3 July 1908 (*DE*, no. 54).

72 Ibid., 6 July 1908 (*DE*, no. 55).

73 *Life*, p. 342.

74 Ibid.

75 TH to ELH, 19 Sept 1908 (*DE*, no. 59).

76 Ibid., 9 July 1909 (*DE*, no. 66).

77 TH to FH, 19 July 1909 (*ORFW*, no. 106).

78 ICW to EH, 1961. Quoted in *OH*, p. 139.

79 Florence's membership of the Lyceum is evidenced by various allusions in Edward Clodd's diary for 1910, and by the typescript of the *Later Years* (marked 'Mrs Hardy's copy [2nd copy]'), f. 495, in which a deleted line refers to her as 'a literary friend of Mrs Hardy at the Lyceum Club' (DCM). Emma's membership as early as 1903 is to be gathered from a letter dated 17 Jan 1904 in which Constance Smedley writes from the Club to ask whether Emma 'as a member' could perform a certain favour (DCM).

80 On 23 June 1910 Clodd recorded in his diary a meeting with Florence at the Lyceum before she left for Max Gate. On 3 July Florence wrote to Emma thanking her for 'a happy week' there (DCM).

81 In a passage deleted from the typescript (f. 515) of the *Later Years*, which would have followed the allusion to Florence's marriage as in the printed *Life* (p. 363), the

sentence continues: '. . . married the present writer, who had been for several years the friend of the first Mrs Hardy, and had accompanied her on the little excursions she liked to make, when her husband could not go' (DCM).

82 *Life*, p. 353.
83 *OH*, p. 137.
84 FED to ELH, various letters written in 1910 and 1911 (DCM).
85 FED to Edward Clodd, Nov 1910 (Brotherton).
86 As recorded by him in the poem 'To a Lady Playing and Singing in the Morning'.
87 ELH to RO, no date (Colby).
88 e.g., the man bathing from Captain Masters' boat at Swanage ('honeymoon' diary).
89 Flower, *Just As It Happened*, p. 95. Flower, who knew Emma personally, observes that she 'had her humours, conscious or otherwise'.
90 In 1963 May O'Rourke, Hardy's secretary during his later years, informed James Stevens Cox in an interview that Hermann Lea had told her how Emma once went to Granville, Chief Constable of Dorset, to complain that Hardy 'wanted other women' and was trying to poison her. Granville, presumably unacquainted with Emma's reputation for mental eccentricity, if not worse, was sufficiently impressed by her to go to Max Gate, 'dress Hardy down', and caution him. Miss O'Rourke, who died in 1978, refused to allow this story to be published during her lifetime. It should be noted that it was hearsay on her part, and should be weighed accordingly, though Lea impresses one as generally a reliable informant. But see Chapter 5, note 63, above.
91 *OH*, p. 142.
92 Ibid., pp. 128–9.
93 *Life*, p. 354.
94 For example, '[Great Uncle Davie] was a very earnest religious person and would not take the title of baronet because there was no money or land with it and he disliked worldly honours' (p. 26). Or 'My Great Uncle used to preach at home as well as in Church and my Father never

liked him'(p. 26). Or again 'My brother whose voice was rich had also a fine knowledge of music and a special education for a musical profession. He became proficient, but emigrated after leading an irregular life' (p. 15).

95 ICW note accompanying her selection of letters to ELH (DCM).

96 ELH to Lady (Alda) Hoare, 24 April 1910 (Stourhead).

97 Lady (Alda) Hoare to ELH, 27 April 1910 (DCM).

98 TH to FH, 3 May 1911 (*ORFW*, no. 111).

99 *Life*, p. 359.

100 Zietlow (*Moments of Vision*, p. 222) takes 'songs' here as 'clearly . . . . a metaphor for poetry'; but surely this is to overlook, as so many writers do, that Hardy had a real interest in singing and a voice adequate for indulging it.

101 According to the poetic record, only once, as told in 'On the Doorstep' (*Moments of Vision*), was he about to go out when the sound of her singing made him change his mind and stay in. But, although Weber and Bailey both assume the poem to refer to Emma's peace-effort period, there is nothing to indicate that it is not a reminiscence of earlier and more cheerful days; cp. 'To a Lady Playing and Singing in the Morning'. There was no phase of Emma's life in which she did not sing.

102 Albert Bankes to ELH, 15 Dec 1911 (DCM).

103 Bailey (p. 367) believes the poem to be another reference to Emma's piano-playing; but would Hardy have referred to this as 'a little thing'?

104 Carl J. Weber, *Hardy's Love Poems* (London, 1963), p. 48.

105 Yet occasionally Emma must have overcome her inarticulacy and latterday shyness, perhaps in support of some cause about which she felt sufficiently strongly; for in a letter to Edward Clodd dated 3 July 1910 Florence Dugdale writes of typing out 'Emma's Lyceum Club speech'. But it seems that concerning the cause about which Emma felt most strongly of all she remained for ever unable to break silence.

106 K. G. Wilson, 'Thomas Hardy and Florence Henniker', *THYB 6*, pp. 62–6.

107 Zietlow, *Moments of Vision*, p. 217.
108 Unless one excepts the tears the Owens saw in her eyes a few hours before she died.
109 FEH to RO, 13 Dec 1913 (Colby).
110 TH to FH, 17 Dec 1912 (*ORFW*, no. 118).
111 Stewart, *Thomas Hardy*, p. 12.
112 The note is undated, but 'Xmas' is referred to and external evidence points to 1911 (Colby).
113 Alice Harvey ('Dolly' Gale), 'I Was Emma Lavinia's Personal Maid', *THYB4*, pp. 6–9.
114 *Life*, p. 357.
115 Ibid., p. 358.
116 The poem is sometimes said to refer to Cornwall, but see *HWR*, p. 167.
117 *OH*, p. 149.
118 Harvey, 'I Was Emma Lavinia's Personal Maid'.
119 Unpublished article by ICW (Mrs Brinley Richards).
120 Harvey, 'I Was Emma Lavinia's Personal Maid'.
121 *Life*, p. 359.
122 Bartelot, unpublished memoirs.
123 ELH to Mrs R. G. Bartelot, 25 July 1912 (Colby).
124 Emma's planting of the rose-bush 'a month or two before her death' is also attested in a letter by TH to FH, 28 Dec 1918 (*ORFW*, no. 140).
125 *Life*, p. 359.
126 Ibid.
127 *HLMS*, p. 157.
128 *Life*, p. 359.
129 Ibid.
130 Harvey, 'I Was Emma Lavinia's Personal Maid'.
131 TH to FH, 17 Dec 1912 (*ORFW*, no. 118).
132 *HLMS*, p. 163.
133 May O'Rourke, who, as stated in an earlier note, was Hardy's secretary for a considerable period during his last years, became convinced, so she afterwards told James Stevens Cox, that Florence had been determined from the first to marry Hardy 'by fair means or foul'. Miss O'Rourke was informed while at Max Gate that after the marriage Mr Dugdale, Florence's father, had been overheard to say: 'She's pulled it off!' Since neither

of Miss O'Rourke's statements is based on direct observation, obviously they should be treated with reserve.

134   *HLMS*, p. 165.

Chapter 8.   *Assessment*

1   TH to Frederic Harrison, 17 June 1895; *The Letters of Thomas Hardy*, ed. Richard L. Purdy and Michael Millgate, vol. I (Oxford, 1978), p. 134.
2   June S. Lock to ELH, 20 April 1881 (DCM).
3   ELH to RO, 14 Feb 1897 (Colby).
4   Ibid., 19 Feb 1897 (Colby).
5   FED to Edward Clodd, 7 March 1913 (Brotherton).
6   Stewart, *Thomas Hardy*, p. 231.
7   Mrs Lorna Stephanie Heenan (daughter of Dr Fred Fisher), 'Random Memories of Hardy and Dorset Folk', *Hardyana*, p. 18.
8   See Chapter 7, note 90, above.

Index

274